Entering Wonderland

Praise for *Entering Wonderland*

"Harris has identified and mapped out a path through the early months of a pastorate that provide invaluable dialogue and insight into ministry in community. Armed with the guidance of this book, a new pastor should be able to navigate a way through the sometimes daunting and almost always rewarding task of being a Pastor." —**Mike Cole** General Presbyter, Presbytery of New Covenant

"After the Pastor Search Committee is ready to call the new pastor, every other parishioner then is asking, 'Can this person be my pastor?' Harris provides here an essential resource for every new pastor to methodologically discover the undercurrents in a congregation that will make or break a new pastor's ministry. Every pastor starting in a new ministry context will benefit from these insights." —**G. Wilson Gunn**, General Presbyter, National Capital Presbytery

"Harris invites and coaches readers entering new congregations to treat the 'wonderland' of ministry as a place where wondering—sometimes out loud, sometimes not—can lead to good questions and helpful answers. He asks lots of questions and shares some of his own answers, but he mostly presses pastors to '. . . emulate Alice. She was curious—sometimes a little frightened, but she kept asking questions.' I have used his 'Eleven Curious Questions' process in interim pastorates in two very different congregations. It works. Harris is by nature an optimist, but also a realist. In the realities of ministry, including my own, he helps his readers and coaching clients experience the wonder of it."
—**Richard L. Sheffield**

Entering Wonderland

A Toolkit for Pastors New to a Church

Robert A. Harris

An Alban Institute Book

ROWMAN & LITTLEFIELD
Lanham • Boulder • New York • London

Published by Rowman & Littlefield
A wholly owned subsidiary of The Rowman & Littlefield Publishing Group, Inc.
4501 Forbes Boulevard, Suite 200, Lanham, Maryland 20706
www.rowman.com

16 Carlisle Street, London W1D 3BT, United Kingdom

British Library Cataloguing in Publication Information Available

Library of Congress Cataloging-in-Publication Data Available

Harris, Robert A.
Entering wonderland : A toolkit for pastors new to a church / by Robert A. Harris.
p. cm.
Includes bibliographical references and index.
ISBN 978-1-56699-759-1 (cloth : alk. paper) -- ISBN 978-1-56699-717-1 (pbk. : alk. paper) -- ISBN 978-1-56699-718-8 (electronic)

♾ ™ The paper used in this publication meets the minimum requirements of American National Standard for Information Sciences Permanence of Paper for Printed Library Materials, ANSI/NISO Z39.48-1992.

Printed in the United States of America

Contents

Foreword

As a pastor with over forty years of ministry experience, I have observed tremendous joy and absolute desolation in the lives of pastors within the first years of service to a congregation. I recently learned that several of the finest pastors I know have been forced out of congregations they had only served for two to four years. Not one of them had been accused of any impropriety or lack of excellence in their work. Yet, a mismatch between their sense of where the congregation needed to go and that of various persons within the church created tensions they could not overcome.

Before taking the field of a new congregational challenge, a thoughtful day with this book will, on one hand, help any pastor avoid some real pitfalls, and on the other, help him or her join the congregation in a new adventure in ministry together. This book is for pastors who are new to a congregation and not just for pastors who are just starting out and are new to the challenges of pastoral ministry. Whether you are in the beginning of a pastoral career or past the midpoint, you will find Bob's words coaching you into a more fruitful future.

I once attended a workshop on the growing practice of coaching in the life of the church, and Bob Harris was one of the key presenters. When asked about the difference between a consultant and a coach, Bob offered a very useful way to differentiate between them: "A consultant says, 'I have the answers, you have the questions,' whereas a coach says, 'I have the questions, you have the answers.'" The consultant brings expertise. The coach brings curiosity. Bob frames the first months of a new pastorate as the ultimate coaching opportunity.

This is significant because our inclination as pastors is often just the opposite. I recall vividly when I was called as the new pastor of the Pleasant Hills Community Church in Pittsburgh. I was so fired up with new vision and possibilities that I just knew I was to bring the answers to the questions the people were surely asking.

When I accepted the call to Pittsburgh, it meant leaving a fifteen-year pastorate in another congregation. I knew I needed to take a retreat by myself in between the two congregations to just think and pray about two matters. There is always grief in departing a loved congregation and excitement and anticipation for the beginning of a new pastorate. On that retreat, I needed first to acknowledge to my Lord and to myself all of the wonderful moments and the wonderful people I was privileged to have been with during those fifteen years. I also formally needed to let go of the many moments of personal hurt I had experienced in those years. Second, I wanted to prepare myself for my entry into a new place of service, thinking through what I knew of their people, both staff and church members, and of the possibilities and problems I thought I understood about the congregation.

While that retreat proved to be an invaluable preparation for a new ministry, I realized, looking back, that I turned the second half of that retreat into a goal-setting session, figuring out my first steps and the things I wanted to change in the new pastorate. On the one hand, thinking through the issues as you understand them before you begin a new pastorate is wise. Of course there will be things you will want to do. On the other hand, I would have been so much better off if I had had this book in my hands during that retreat, to start with curiosity and not expertise, to come as a coach asking lots of questions of lots of people. Out of such conversations, a new vision, an amalgamation of the dreams of the members of the congregation and of my dreams would have surfaced.

As things turned out in that case, by the literal grace of God, those dear people were patient with me and simply waited until I reached the point of actually listening! Over and over again Bob exhorts the new pastor to be curious and he offers tremendous help in this with his Eleven Curious Questions. After addressing some of the challenges of the first six months in a new place of service, the book goes on to give wise counsel for the rest of the first year and after. The entire book is jammed full of some of the most practical, down-to-earth and doable counsel in one volume on pastoral ministry that I have ever read.

E. Stanley Ott, PhD
    The Vital Churches Institute
    Vienna, Virginia

Preface

"Bob, I'm just hearing too many complaints about you. I'm going to recommend to the board that they grant you a three-month leave of absence to find a new call."

The senior pastor had called me into his office and blindsided me. I suppose I should have seen his verdict coming, but I was young and naive and too full of myself. It was in my second position after seminary, and I didn't have a clue about congregational systems and politics and norms. I had entered that new congregation and hadn't had the sense to be really curious and to get to know the territory before I dispensed all my wisdom and unmatched creativity. So, after just over 18 months, I was out. I hadn't known what I was getting into and what was worse, *I didn't know that I didn't know*.

The Alban Institute and a number of other congregation research organizations have discovered that not only do over 50 percent of pastors leave their congregations in the first five years of their ministry, but many leave the ministry, and many of those leave the church altogether. That is, they lose faith in the church as an institution. Seminaries teach a lot about the Bible and theology, but few prepare their students to lead congregations. A new seminary graduate typically has little insight into congregational systems and the business of running a congregation. Furthermore, it's not just new seminary graduates who run into trouble. Two friends of mine became pastors of prestigious congregations after over 25 years of successful ministry. Yet, when they began working in these new congregations, they ran into buzz saws. They were fired.

Such ruptures of the pastoral relationship are typically very costly to both pastor and congregation. Obviously, the pastor is no longer earning an income and may have to move from congregation-provided housing. A forced termination can end any hopes for future ministry. Pastor and family suffer psychological and spiritual trauma. Ruptures cost a congregation, too. In the Presbyterian Church (U.S.A.), a congregation typically pays several months of severance (assuming that the pastor didn't do something egregious) to pastors who leave without a call to another ministry. Members who were close to the pastor often leave the congregation. Board members are maligned by members, and they sometimes leave. Subsequently when there is a problem, people grumble, "Oh, here we go again. This is just like what happened when we had to fire Pastor Joe."

What goes wrong? And what might be done to help pastors who are just beginning ministry in a new congregation? What steps might be taken to help pastors and congregations develop a mutually enriching relationship so that both grow in wisdom and stature and in favor with God and people?

YOU'RE IN *WONDERLAND*, NOT IOWA

For a pastor, entering a new congregation is like Alice falling down that rabbit hole into *Wonderland*. Some members of the new congregation seem to have an uncanny resemblance to those whom Alice encountered.

- The Queen of Hearts: the matriarch who wants to run everything (I heard of one congregation where the matriarch gave all four committee reports at the board meeting) and cries, "Off with their heads"—or alternately, "You might try another congregation"—if someone crosses her. (Obviously, congregations might have a patriarch who runs everything, too.)
- The Cheshire Cat: the member who is always smiling and agreeing with you but never seems to show up.
- The White Rabbit: the member who is always behind, somewhat bemused and confused.

You might read *Alice in Wonderland* and *Through the Looking Glass* and see other familiar characters, such as the Mad Hatter and Tweedledum and Tweedledee. [1]

The musical *The Music Man* begins with a train car full of salesmen singing about how "Ya gotta know the territory" (in that case, Iowa). Too many pastors enter a new congregation thinking that they already know the territory, and almost certainly, they don't. How can you get to know the territory and faithfully lead this new congregation?

For starters, we can emulate Alice. She was curious—sometimes a little frightened, but she kept asking questions. What is going on? Who are these characters, and why do they behave this way? Why do I sometimes feel so big and sometimes so small? What's behind that door?

In the Presbyterian Church (U.S.A.), those ordained to the ministry or as elders or deacons are asked, "Will you seek to serve the people with energy, intelligence, imagination, and love?" I would respectfully urge that "curiosity" be added to this list (though imagination might encompass curiosity). I think it's critical for a new pastor to be very, very curious. So here's my question to you, the new pastor: "Will you seek to serve the people with energy, intelligence, imagination, and love—and *lots of curiosity*?"

WHAT I OFFER IN THIS BOOK

I am not writing as a consultant, counselor, or spiritual director. Neither is this book a psychological self-help book, instruction manual, or cookbook. I don't have a prescribed process for getting you into that new congregation. I write to you as an experienced pastor (ordained in 1968) and leadership coach. What I offer here is an array of tools and tips that I and others have found helpful. Just as my home workbench has a variety of items—hammer, tape measure, paint can opener, drill, electric saws—I offer you a variety of tools; some especially important to use when you first come to the congregation, some to be used only when necessary, some to keep handy all the time, and some, you may never use.

Each chapter begins with stories and reflections on situations I have experienced or have observed (as a coach, consultant, or friend). I then offer a model or models and some theory and theology about how one might deal with the challenge. Then I offer some specific tools and tips for being more effective as a pastor and leader. You will be challenged by coaching assignments that lead you to reflect on the material and decide what specific actions you will take to meet the challenges you face. Each chapter concludes with a "so what?" section in which I will sum up the chapter and challenge you a bit more. You will discover that I not only draw from resources on leadership in congregations, but also in the private and public sectors. I list these and others in an annotated bibliography. You will also find lists of the tips, tools, and assignments in the appendixes.

Now you may be wondering what I mean by "coaching tools." Think about tools for a moment. Some tools are simple. I use a hammer to drive a nail. A doctor uses a scalpel to make an incision. I will offer some tools to help you carry out specific tasks. For example, you will find several exercises that will help build trust among leaders and members.

Other tools are analytical. A builder calculates the maximum likely load of snow on a roof before final design and construction of a structure. A surgeon uses various scans to determine the type and extent of a tumor before operating. Some of my tools will help you analyze the congregational system and also take a hard look at yourself.

Questions are analytical tools. I ask my coaching clients lots of questions, pressing them to think more deeply, to observe more carefully, noting both details and the big picture. You will see such questions sprinkled throughout the book. Here are some questions that I frequently use as I coach:

- What did you learn from this experience?
- What might you have done differently?
- What are you curious about?
- How might you reframe the situation?
- What results are you seeking?
- Why are these results important?
- What will that result look like, feel like? What will you hear?
- What specific commitments will you make and by when do you expect to fulfill them?

What are tips? Most of them are bits of wisdom that I picked up through my ministry. Many of them are in the category of "why didn't someone tell me this before I made that mistake?" Here's the first tip:

Tip 1: You don't know the situation, so keep asking questions. Be curious.

Because I am offering you a kit of tools and tips, I don't want you to *read* this book. This isn't just another book on church renewal. I want you to *use* it as if I were coaching you. Please take time to determine which tools will be useful in your situation and to reflect on the coaching questions. Make commitments to yourself to take specific actions. Take time to observe and reflect. Let this book help you *read yourself and your congregation.*

Following is a collection of coaching tools and tips that I am confident will help you as you enter a new congregation. Enjoy your trip into Wonderland!

Acknowledgments

All of us stand on the shoulders of those who have gone before. I have been very fortunate to study under, be friends with, and learn from terrific people, and so I must acknowledge at least some of them. I can't begin to list all the teachers and mentors who have helped me grow through my four decades of ministry: Presbytery staff, professors, counselors, colleagues, workshop leaders, and the Alban Institute and its former stable of consultants and teachers (of whom Ed White is a special mentor). Members of congregations I have served have pushed me and encouraged me to grow. Faculty and colleagues from the Georgetown University Leadership Coaching Certificate program introduced me to the science and art of coaching. My mentor coach, Val Hastings, guided me through the certification process. My clients have taught me many lessons about coaching as I assisted them. Beth Gaede, the editor Alban assigned to me, has patiently challenged and encouraged me; you benefit greatly from her work! Kathleen Dullea, a longtime friend with a keen eye, caught numerous grammatical errors and omissions in the semifinal draft.

My wife, Mary Helen, and my sons and their wives—Doug and Karen, Ben and Jenny—have kept me grounded and pressed me to persevere in this quest to help pastors grow. Our grandchildren, Marney, Luci, Julia, and Kevin are gifts of wonderment and joy.

The spirit of the living God has opened doors when I've been in transition or confusion and led me into amazing opportunities and new connections.

So I am very grateful. I owe so much to these and others. And now I'm glad to pass this on.

Here's to getting off to a great start in your new congregation!

Part I

Entering *Wonderland*: The First Six Months

As I entered each new congregation I served through my ministry (five called positions and four interims), I was flooded with a swirl of emotions. Chances are you have had similar experiences, such as

- Excitement about the possibilities
- Confusion and amusement about why some people seem to think you're their savior
- Anxiety about whether you are up to the new challenge
- Sadness as you reflect on friends and colleagues you left behind
- Curiosity as you wonder who these people really are
- Enthusiasm as you contemplate initiatives you might take

I'm sure that I had many assumptions about the new congregation, and members and leaders in the congregation had many assumptions about me and hopes for me (some warranted, some not).

I think that in the first six months a new pastor should focus on getting to know people and assessing the congregational system. It is also critical to have a conversation as soon as possible with the governing board regarding mutual expectations concerning how you focus your time. In addition to getting to know people, I think you need to plan and lead an excellent worship service and provide high-quality pastoral care.

The first six chapters will help you get to know the members of the congregation (and help them know you). I am confident that if you follow this general process, you will, by six months in or so, have learned what memories they treasure, who the real leaders are, and how well the leadership team functions, and that you will have assessed the organizational structure and mission. You will also have identified key norms of the congregation and also the minefields you had best avoid (at least initially).

You are in the honeymoon period, a time of mutual delusion, and that's ok. Enjoy it! A good marriage often has more than a bit of mutual delusion! However, begin planning for the real relationship to begin, for the time when you know them beyond their bright smiles and great hopes and they realize that you aren't the new messiah.

Chapter One

What Do You See?

Taking a Close Look

Two weeks before I moved to Columbus, Ohio, to begin my ministry in a new congregation, a large chunk of plaster fell from the sanctuary ceiling during worship, nearly hitting the organist. When I arrived, a large net had been suspended from the sanctuary ceiling to catch any more falling debris. On my first Sunday, six teens and I were on the rather new elevator and suddenly it got stuck—just before worship. Fortunately, the door opened and I was able to jump the three feet to the floor.

Welcome to Indianola. This congregation had a great tradition of fine music, social action, good education, and ministry in the community. But they hadn't taken care of their lovely old building. One contractor noted regarding the roof, "You have 100-year slate and 10-year nails."

I hadn't noticed anything too bad around the building a few weeks before when I met with the search committee. I had been quite taken with the members of the committee, the congregation's story, and the exciting possibilities for mission. Now, however, the leaders and I faced a whole array of challenges. In addition to ten-year nails and a scary elevator, we needed to deal with inadequate lighting and dismal restrooms.

WHAT DO YOU SEE? WHAT MIGHT YOU LOOK FOR?

"Our pastor has both feet planted firmly in the clouds!" observed one lay leader to me. That leader could be describing me as I entered each called pastorate. I focused on the people and didn't notice important things about the building. I didn't realize that observing the building more closely would have told me a lot about the members.

For example, one congregation I worked with had a grand piano front and center—in front of the pulpit. I didn't recognize until later that the musician needed to be the center of attention. In another congregation, the organ console was centered at the rear of the chancel because it was a tracker organ (that is, there was a direct mechanical connection between the keys and the pipes), so the organist/choir director was also quite visible to the congregation. I didn't realize that this visibility led to some congregants criticizing the organist/choir director for showing off.

In the one manse in which we lived, the storm door off the driveway needed to be replaced. The congregation's building manager came with a new one that he bought on a close out. Why did he get such a good deal? Because it didn't have safety glass, which had recently been mandated by a new state law. My wife and I had two preschool boys and weren't at all happy with this indifference to our children's safety.

I know of one congregation that—because the previous pastor had bought a house in the suburbs—let its manse deteriorate. When the new pastor chose to live in the manse and discovered serious problems, he was labeled as a complainer. Dramatically better was the experience of another pastor friend whose congregation, during the interim period, totally remodeled the manse. The congregation transformed it from a pretty dull 1960s-style decor to an inviting, sparkling home with new bathrooms and kitchen, and fresh paint.

TOOL 1: CHECKLIST FOR A FACILITIES SCAN

Following is a series of questions you might ask as you walk around the building and grounds. You may have noticed all these things when you first interviewed, but perhaps not. I encourage you to record your observations in a journal, computer, notebook, or some system that works for you.

Office/Study

- Your workspace, including desk, chair, bookcases, and filing cabinets: Are they up to date?
- Other furniture: Are there comfortable chairs and a coffee table for counseling or small meetings?
- Condition of paint and décor.
- Proximity of the pastor's study to other office space: For example, is the administrative assistant's office (or the main office) contiguous to the pastor's study or some distance away? What do you prefer? Does it matter

if the assistant knows who you're meeting with? Do you want the assistant to screen anyone who drops by?

- Does the door to the pastor's study have a window? A window indicates that the church is aware of recommendations regarding clergy sexual misconduct. Can the furniture be arranged or is there a curtain to provide some degree of privacy for parishioners who don't want people to know they are counseling with you?

Technology

- Computers: How adequate are the congregation's computers? What type of computer is in the pastor's study? Are you expected to provide your own? Do you want to? To what extent is the congregation wired for the internet? How fast is the connection?
- Church wi-fi system: Are the various computer components networked? Can the pastor print directly from the study to the office photocopier?
- Website: Is the website up to date? Most newcomers check websites before visiting a congregation. I've seen websites that feature programs that happened two years ago. Is it attractive and easy to navigate? Is it informative? Does it include links to sermons, both written and aural (podcasts)? Are there links to videos of special programs? Is the webmaster competent and committed? Volunteer or paid?
- Audio-video systems in the sanctuary and elsewhere: Is there an up-to-date audio system? How accessible is it during worship? Are there wireless microphones? Is there a video projector and screen? Does the system include recording capability? Are there persons who are trained in how to use this equipment?

Sanctuary

- Is it clean? Attractive?
- Lighting: Is it adequate and easily controlled? Some sanctuaries are incredibly drab and gloomy.
- General layout and design: Does it work for you or against you? Does it point to God, the choir, or the preacher? What does the architecture say?

Church School, Nursery, and Other Areas for Children

- How is the preschool area? (Nobody is quite as fussy as new parents.)
- Are these areas well maintained, attractive, and up to date?
- What indicates that children are loved and treasured (or not)?
- Do you smell any odors, especially in the restrooms?

- Are furnishings comfortable and up to date?
- What do the books, decor, charts or maps, art, and so forth tell you about the style and quality of church education?
- Is there a library, and if so, how up to date and well kept is it?

General Maintenance of the Building

- How well has the building been maintained? What are problem areas? What have leaders told you about issues? What are mutual expectations about the pastor's role in dealing with the problems?
- How are the restrooms? (You might compare them with a good-quality chain restaurant.)
- Generally, how attractive is the building to newcomers, especially young families? Especially take notice of entry areas, hallways, bulletin boards, signs to various rooms, and outdoor signage. What do they say? What will a newcomer learn about the congregation from a casual glance?
- What is the condition of the HVAC system?
- Any problems with flooding? One pastor's study flooded the day after his books arrived and many were damaged before the staff could rescue them from the water.
- What impact will building renovation costs (if needed) have on the congregation's budget?

Clergy Housing (If Provided)

A good benchmark for assessing its condition might be that of a high-quality rental unit.

- State of repair, cleanliness.
- Are the colors acceptable? Will the property folks consult with you before painting?
- Appliances: How new are they? Have the furnace, air conditioner, water heater, kitchen appliances, and washer and dryer been serviced?
- Safety issues: Are there any dangerous windows, signs of defective wiring, mold, defective plumbing, or debris? Any sign of vermin, insects, or other pests?
- Ongoing maintenance: Who is responsible? What authority does the pastor have to call a plumber or other service technician if there is an immediate problem?
- Furniture (if any): State of repair? Who chooses it? What does the pastor bring?
- Window and floor coverings: How do they look? What is expected from the new pastor? What do you (and your family) expect?

TOOL 2: A SAMPLE OF PERCEPTIONS AND PERSPECTIVES OF PEOPLE OUTSIDE THE CONGREGATION

Now that you have made some initial observations, identify whom you might talk with about the congregation and community. Who might give you perspective and history about your congregation? Judicatory executives? (Might there be a file on your congregation in the denominational office?) The interim pastor? The former pastor? Other pastors in the community?

Who might you talk with about the community? A leader of the chamber of commerce? Someone with the school system or city government? A realtor?

Some Questions to Ask

- What do you know and need to know about the community?
- What do they know about the congregation? How well is it known in the community and for what?
- Are there negative stories about the congregation you need to know about? Any scandals, betrayals, or fights?
- How easily are newcomers assimilated into both congregation and community?

There's a big difference between a transient metropolitan area and a very settled small town or medium-sized city. I have a friend who discovered that 80 percent of the people in his new congregation had grown up in the area (with around a population of 300,000) and known each other for years. A couple who had lived there for over 30 years were still considered newcomers.

COACHING ASSIGNMENT 1: WHAT HAVE YOU LEARNED SO FAR?

You have been at this congregation a month or so and have some initial impressions. You are beginning to have a real sense of the emotional and spiritual climate in the congregation. You can find your way around the community and perhaps have selected a place to live for now.

I encourage you to take some quiet time and listen to your intuitions—your gut hunches—and reflect on your observations. However, don't jump to any fixed conclusions, and don't start demanding changes unilaterally. Getting to know the people and the community and leading worship and providing pastoral care will keep you busy.

Here are some questions to help you think.

Building, Grounds, Equipment, and the Like

- What do the facilities tell you about the congregation—its norms, self-image, hope, pessimism, theology, and so forth?
- How well prepared were the pastor's study, the manse (if any)?

Congregational Members

- How were you welcomed? Was there a welcome reception your first Sunday?
- Did someone provide maps and helpful material about the community?
- What does your welcome tell you about the congregation and the status of a pastor?
- Are there any people who seem to run the whole show?
- Who wants a lot of your time initially?
- Who badmouths the previous pastor? What do you hear about the previous pastor? What does that tell you about the status of a pastor in this congregation?
- Do leaders seem to be life-giving people or life-draining people? (If you were not a pastor, do you think you'd want to be part of this congregation?)
- How does what they need in a new pastor compare with what you offer?

For a married pastor:

- What impact will your becoming pastor of this congregation have on your family?
- What support will your spouse need? What expectations have been expressed concerning your spouse?

For a single paster:

- Has the church had an unmarried pastor before, or are you the first?
- What impact will your becoming pastor of this congregation have on your social life?
- Who will be in your support system?
- Are there fellow pastors with whom you can be friends?

If you have children:

- What do you know about possible schools for your children?
- How do these schools compare with those in your previous community?

Community

- How does this community compare with where you've been? Think about weather, cultural, and recreational opportunities, commute times, job opportunities, and so forth.

As you envision serving this new congregation, what makes your heart sing? What weighs you down?

Generate more questions. What else do you need to think about?

NOW WHAT?

At this early stage of your ministry in this congregation, you should have way more questions than answers. Perhaps you are a bit frustrated and confused. You have some preliminary notions of what is going on here, but I encourage you to hold those notions lightly. Use them as operating hypotheses but be ready to change and adapt them as new data emerges.

Now it's time to be much more intentional about getting to know them.

Chapter Two

How Can I Really Get to Know Them?

You Can't Guess

In the preface, I briefly mentioned that I was fired from a congregation I served. Here's what happened in somewhat more detail. I was called to be the assistant pastor in a 1,200-member congregation in 1971; it was my second call out of seminary. I was young, naive, and certainly too full of myself, and I absolutely did not understand who the real leaders were, what experience they had with previous pastors, how they resolved conflict, and the character of the senior pastor.

Though the Vietnam War was starting to wind down, there was still a lot of dissension over the war as well as over other social issues. I was assigned to work with the youth and a group of married couples. The latter group opposed the war and was fairly liberal, theologically; I fit right in. We discussed peace and justice issues, advocating an end to the war. Further, since I was assigned to lead an occasional innovative worship service, I was encouraged by them to be really creative.

Here's where I ran into difficulty: The young leaders and I implicitly and explicitly criticized the way things were being done, especially the style of worship. I even suggested in a sermon that I didn't sense the Holy Spirit moving in worship! This was especially naïve of me since I failed to recognize that a number of conservative business executives were leaders in the congregation and that a previous assistant pastor had been pressured to leave because he was too liberal.

To compound my difficulties, I confronted the senior pastor about his using a moving sermon illustration as if it were his experience, when in fact he had lifted it from a sermon preached by a nationally known pastor. His response was simply, "Well, preachers do that all the time." I retorted that I thought it was plagiarism.

After blundering into these minefields, I was given a three-month leave of absence to find a new call.

I made no attempt to get to know how things really worked in that congregation. Further, I didn't realize I was being pushed out by a pastor who was probably afraid of being exposed as a plagiarist. I didn't know how to handle his behavior, so I meekly accepted what they offered. There was so much that I didn't know. I paid the price.

I've heard of pastors who have been told by search committees that the congregation wanted to start using contemporary worship forms. They tried some liturgies, music, and other forms that worked well in their previous congregations. After two months, there was the inevitable uproar. "What's going on?" the pastor would exclaim. "I'm doing what the congregation wants me to do, aren't I?"

I know pastors who encountered boards who couldn't make a decision about anything. Board members seemed to be filled with suspicion and anxiety. Before they could make a decision, some board members seemed to need permission from a powerful person who was not on the board. The pastor was mystified by their inability to decide.

Has something like this happened to you or a friend? From conversations with the search committee, you thought that you had a really good understanding of the congregation. You had great ideas for fulfilling their dreams. But things fell apart. Did the committee lie or intentionally misrepresent the situation?

Many pastors have found themselves in all kinds of difficulty because they didn't take time to understand the inner dynamics—that is, the system— of their new congregation. They didn't know who the real leaders were, what competing agendas were in play, which practices or rooms or furniture were untouchable, and what landmines to avoid. Predictably, they soon had to seek a new call.

"Whew!" you may be thinking before asking, "I don't think I'm quite so obtuse as you were, but how do I avoid making mistakes like this myself? What might help me find my way around in this Wonderland?"

DON'T GUESS: BE CURIOUS

I believe that one of the most important gifts you can give to the congregation in your first year—and beyond—is to be clear about *not knowing*. Be open and curious. Lead with questions.

For example, if a couple who normally attends worship stops coming, it's important to wonder what's going on. Are they on vacation? Are they having marriage problems? Are they upset with something or someone in the congregation? Is someone ill? How can you find out? Who will check on them? You? Another leader? Does your system work so that people don't go AWOL?

I often tell my clients to play the dumb card as long as you can. You may prefer to call this tip "the curious card" if "the dumb card" makes you uncomfortable. (One capable client—a blonde woman—did not like the "dumb" word. She was not and did not want to be considered a "dumb blonde.") The key is to ask questions. You don't know. Learn as much as you can.

For example, you can make observations and ask questions:

- I noticed there is plastic taped over a hole in the stained glass window. Is anyone taking care of that?
- I noticed that Jimmy, who appears to have an intellectual disability, almost always helps hand out bulletins. You seem to have found a terrific way to get him involved. Tell me about how that happened.
- It appears that the median age of the women's group is around 70. How do younger women get involved in the congregation?
- I'm impressed by the number of people who are involved in hands-on mission activities. How long has that been the case?
- The organist plays hymns much slower (or faster) than in most congregations I've been in. Has it always been that way? What is your assessment of the pace of the music?
- The teens seem to really have a wonderful sense of community and purpose. Tell me about them and their leaders.
- It appears to me that Joe and Susan don't seem to speak to one another either at the board meetings or on Sunday mornings. What's going on?

I encourage you to be curious, intentionally "not knowing." The idea is to be fully present to members of your new congregation, being open to possibility and new understanding.

Here are two specific suggestions: one fairly simple, the other more complex. First, I think it is vital that you try to get to know your congregants by name and help them get to know you. Jesus teaches us to love our neighbors as ourselves. In his letters, Paul describes us as being one body and declares that agape is the greatest gift. Loving involves our getting to know each other. Relationships are key.

How do you get to know their names and help them get to know you?

"Good morning, Bob. I'm Charles Jones." A pleasant older gentleman introduced himself to me as he left worship on my first Sunday in my first congregation after seminary. He repeated his name the next Sunday—and the next and the next—until the day came when I warmly said, "Good morning,

Charles. How are you this morning?" That was the summer of 1968, and I can still remember him. He knew that this young associate pastor needed all the help he could get.

Most members of that congregation introduced themselves only once, and probably most didn't expect me to remember their names. It was a big church, and I had primary responsibility for youth and their families, and I did learn their names quickly, although it took longer to learn others. But Charles taught me that everyone likes to be known by name.

Drawing from what I learned from Charles, I made a request many times during the first couple of months in subsequent congregations: "Tell me your name seven times." Typically people joke around, some saying their name seven times the first Sunday I suggest this, but they get the point. They know I want to learn their names and that I need their help.

At this point you may be saying, "But my congregation has several hundred (or more) in worship. This is impossible!" The congregation I initially cited had 3,000 members. The senior pastor in that congregation didn't begin to know all the names, but for many years he had an associate pastor who could remember not only everybody's name but also details about them! Unless you have a remarkable memory, you won't remember all—or even most—of the names in a very large congregation, but you will learn many. And no matter how big the congregation, it's essential to try.

Beyond knowing their names, it's even more important to know who various persons are within the congregational system. Who are the real leaders? About what are people anxious? How do they deal with differences? Are there cliques—for example, of liberals and conservatives, or founding members of the congregation and newcomers?

How do you discover how the congregational system works? You can do it intuitively, simply doing your job and paying attention. However, that takes a while and increases the odds that you will accidentally insult someone, bring up a very volatile unresolved issue or violate an important congregational norm.

Another method is to interview the congregational leaders and others who wish to be interviewed. I have used a fairly simple interview process—Tool 3—that has really helped me understand a new congregation. Several of my clients have also found it helpful as they entered a new congregation. One of my clients in a program-size congregation (averaging around 150 in worship) noted that after he had interviewed some 40 leaders in his first six months, he had learned most of what he needed to know to do well in this new congregation.

Interview a broad representation of leaders using these questions. Note that I say *interview* them. Don't just send out a questionnaire. Use these questions as a springboard for conversation. There is nothing like a face-to-face conversation to get to know people and help them get to know you. You will see their body language and sense the emotions behind their responses. They will see that you are really interested in their perception of their congregation and their suggestions for you. Furthermore, if you are using these questions in an interview, you can quickly adapt them, either asking good follow-up questions or skipping questions that the person has already answered.

I have found that people like being interviewed. Most people like to give the new pastor their take on things. Interviews demonstrate that you are genuinely curious about this congregation and its people. You want to get to know them and what makes them tick. You aren't someone who has dropped in with a pat formula to improve them. You're not punching a time clock.

What's a broad representation of leaders? In a family-size congregation, it might be 10 people, but in a pastoral size or larger, I encourage you to interview at least 25 to 35 leaders.

Introduce the interview process to your governing board and start by interviewing them. After you have begun interviewing the board, tell the congregation that you can be most effective as their pastor when you get to know them in greater depth. Explain that a particularly helpful method you have found (or have read about) is to interview members of the congregation, beginning with formal leaders. Invite people to ask you to interview them. Take notes while you're listening; it affirms to your interviewees that you're really paying attention.

I have typically interviewed people one at a time, but have sometimes interviewed couples, and in a few instances, I have met with adult education classes and existing small groups. Stress to individuals and couples that their answers will be confidential. (However, you can't really promise confidentiality in a group since you can't control what group members will say later.) Remember, your primary purpose is to get to know them. However, explain to them that their responses will possibly be compiled with the response of others in a report or series of reports to the board and congregation. (At this point you won't know whether you're going to prepare a formal report.)

As you are reading this, you may be exclaiming, "I am so busy writing a weekly sermon, making pastoral calls, planning for weddings or funerals, planning the board's agenda, and dealing with complaints about the music or youth group! And you are telling me that I need to find another 25 hours to interview people one on one? I don't have time to do that!"

To this concern I offer two questions: Would you rather have people warn you now about potential minefields or loose cannons or would you prefer to stumble unknowingly into them later? Are you genuinely interested in getting to know the leaders of the congregation and the way its system works and do you want them to get to know you as one who is there for them?

Trust me. Doing these interviews really works.

In the following analytical tool (Tool 3: Eleven Curious Questions), you will find eleven basic questions with some possible follow-up questions in each cluster. The questions within each cluster are arranged in order of importance, with the primary question first, followed by samples of questions you might ask to go deeper.

The key in using this is to be relaxed and curious. You are using this to get to know each person and the congregational system, so follow through with questions that occur to you. You aren't an employee of some sociological research firm required to ask standardized questions. Trust your instincts, relax, and enjoy the conversation!

TIPS AND TOOLS FOR GETTING TO KNOW PEOPLE

Tip 2: Be very intentional in not knowing. Ask lots of questions to clarify what is going on both with individuals and with the congregational system.

Tip 3: Invite members of the congregation to tell you their name on seven different occasions.

TOOL 3: ELEVEN CURIOUS QUESTIONS

Date:

Person (s) (or group and its members):

1. Tell me about a time when you felt especially proud of some members or leaders of your congregation, when you felt they were really following Christ. What makes this incident stand out in your mind?
2. Who do you especially respect as leaders? Why do you hold them in high regard?
3. Tell me why you're glad you are a member of this congregation. Why did you join this congregation instead of another one? (Did you try other congregations?) How have fellow members been especially helpful to you? How would you assess the friendliness of this congregation? How easily do people here welcome newcomers? Quickly? Or do people have to be members for several years before they really feel part?
4. How has being part of this congregation helped you and members of your family grow in faith? Please give me some examples of experiences or classes that made a difference. How did you change?

5. Tell me a story about when congregation members resolved a conflict or difference effectively. What do you think the congregation learned from this experience? How effectively do leaders and members handle differences now?
6. What have you especially valued about your pastors and other congregational staff? (Be specific.) Do any sermons, initiatives, or attributes of your previous pastor come to mind?
7. Tell me about a time when you were disappointed with members or leaders. What happened? (Seek the cause of the disappointment—for example, a betrayal, someone simply not working hard enough, or having unrealistic expectations.)
8. Complete this sentence: "God is calling this congregation to be . . . "
9. What do you think God wants your congregation to emphasize in the next three to five years?
10. What else do I need to know in order to thrive in this congregation and community?
11. Do you have any other concerns or suggestions? What chronic frustrations or differences do you hope I can help the congregation deal with?

Tip 4: Describe reality as you see it, and start a conversation.

Tip 4 is inspired by Max De Pree, former CEO of Herman Miller Furniture Co., who asserted, "The first responsibility of a leader is to define reality. The last is to say thank you. In between, the leader is a servant and a debtor."[1]

I tweak this notion a bit. As a new pastor, you can't define reality. You don't know members' reality. But you can describe reality as you see it and then start a conversation about it with both individuals and groups in the congregation, especially leaders and members of committees.

It's important to recognize that the reality you see will almost certainly not be the reality others see. But you're simply describing reality as you see it, and exploring their perceptions (as they have reported them to you in the interviews) will start and inform great conversation.

Take care not to *blast* them with your perceptions of reality by making statements such as, "I observe that you are a crowd of dolts stuck in the 1950s!" That might lead to World War III or at least to your early departure! I usually say something like, "As I have talked with you and others in the congregation, I have heard a lot of people saying that they are having trouble hearing clearly in worship. Is that your experience? If so, have you explored what might be done to improve the acoustics?" The idea is to explore questions, misunderstandings, and confusions. Be very clear that you are seeking to understand them. Chances are newer members on the board have some of the same questions but have never asked them.

Describing your reality and starting a conversation also helps them to know themselves better. One of my clients serving a congregation with a history of conflict told the board, "What you have told me in so many words is that you habitually form circular firing squads here! There's a lot of pain and hurt feelings!" Members of the board nodded sheepishly in agreement. He got them started on a more positive trajectory.

COACHING ASSIGNMENT 2: LEARN MEMBERS' NAMES

Invite members and friends of the congregation to tell you their names at least seven times. Then, using whatever method works for you, try to remember as many as possible. For example, if the congregation has a pictorial directory, you might work through it. Repetition is what works with me; that's why I ask them to tell me their names seven times! Start with leaders, but expand the circle quickly. Set a realistic goal for yourself, such as, "By six weeks from now I will know the names of 30 percent of the worshiping congregation." How will you hold yourself accountable for achieving this goal?

COACHING ASSIGNMENT 3:
INTERVIEW MEMBERS OF THE CONGREGATION

- Set up interviews, publicizing them as you deem best.
- Set a goal such as, "By three months from now, I will have interviewed all the members of the board and at least half of those identified as respected leaders in the congregation. "Decide how you will hold yourself accountable."

COACHING ASSIGNMENT 4:
ANALYZE WHAT YOU HEARD IN THE INTERVIEWS

You will have learned a great deal about the congregation by doing these interviews. Now I urge you to systematically analyze your conversations. What stories have you heard? What emotions were expressed?

At this point, I want you only to reflect on what you have heard. Unless some major concern surfaced, you don't need to take any action. Your main objective in interviewing people was to help you get to know them and they you. Having said that, some intensive reflection will help you identify the real leaders, competing agendas, areas of anxiety, potential hazards, and so forth. Here are some lenses that might help you see the situation more clearly.

CHALLENGES, TRIUMPHS, AND KEY LEADERS

What did you hear about challenges met (and not met)? What stories do you hear repeated over and over? What leaders were especially important? What were ramifications of actions and decisions? How can you draw on these stories? Keep in mind that as leaders in your congregation work to discern God's leading they might be inspired and guided by their stories.

I know of a congregation struggling with cultural and demographic changes. As its leaders wrestled with a vision, two archetypal stories came to mind. Some years ago, its choir was languishing with perhaps ten singers a Sunday. A board member who was a professional musician stepped up and said, "I'll take over the choir, but I need to limit the number to 25." People chuckled. Yet a year later, he was adjusting his upper limit to 35. The board empowered that leader to use his gifts. In that same congregation, a member of the board identified a great need for clothing for needy children. Under his leadership the congregation started a clothing bank that now serves hundreds of people every year.

As interviewees talked about previous pastors, was there a "King David"—that is, a pastor against whom all other pastors are measured? Be especially alert to stories about your predecessor's style. What did you learn about that pastor's competence, integrity, strengths, and weaknesses?

SENSE OF PURPOSE

As you asked the questions about who God is calling the congregation to be and what members feel called to emphasize, how clear were the responses? To what extent was there a sense of unity of purpose? Are there signs of strongly competing agendas?

Some years ago I was one of the finalists in a church in which a few people wanted the congregation to adopt a charismatic worship style. I raised some questions about this desire and wasn't selected as their new pastor. The man who was selected didn't spot this minority view and subsequently ran into serious difficulty.

Optimally, the leaders have a clear sense of where God is leading this congregation, and they selected you as the best person to take them forward. However, sometimes that isn't at all the case! A colleague came to a new congregation thinking he understood clearly what the church wanted and needed but discovered that there were at least two competing agendas among board members and that the selection committee had still another agenda!

Furthermore, these leaders hadn't taken time to try to discern God's yearning.

Responses to this question will help you clarify (1) the extent to which they have even thought about God's hope for the congregation, and (2) whether there are competing agendas for the congregation (one of which might be to do church the way they did it 25 years ago). If you hear of many competing agendas for the congregation, you would be wise to put the brakes on an initiative pushed by a few but opposed by many.

OTHER CHARACTERS IN THIS CONGREGATION

What leaders do people most respect? (Consider both informal and formal leaders.) Some of these people will be mentioned in some of the big stories. Others won't, but are still highly respected. Especially note any younger members who are well respected. You can help them grow as leaders and also take precautions to help them avoid burning out.

Also identify those who assert themselves as leaders but are not respected. Are there any people who are labeled as bullies or troublemakers? Is there a Queen of Hearts who wants to control everything? (Remember, you're not taking action at this point; you're just trying to get the lay of the land.)

One of my teachers noted that "a system sends its sickest to you first." Be aware of who comes to see you in the first month and pay attention to your gut reaction. What is your response? Be very cautious if they tell you how awful your predecessor was and how wonderful you are. My experience, and that of friends, is that in a year or so, these folks will be just as critical of you as they now are of your predecessor.

Are there any people around whom you need to be cautious? With whom do you especially connect? Who might be good sounding boards as you try to understand the congregation?

TRUST AND COMMUNITY

To what extent do interviewees feel like they know one another and have a significant number of friends in the congregation? Do they tell stories of mutual support in times of illness, death, or other difficulty?

To what extent do their responses indicate a spirit of welcome and hospitality? Do old-timers speak dismissively of the newcomers?

What is the trust level? Was their previous pastor trustworthy? If the previous pastor betrayed them with misconduct, laziness, or generally poor leadership, you will often be confronted by both unrealistic optimism about what you will bring (you're the new messiah!) *and* deep pessimism at the same time (pastors can't really be trusted). Members will behave like people whose spouses left them for another person. They have been burned and are understandably cautious, and yet they are usually hoping to find Mr. or Ms. Right. If your predecessor was not trustworthy, then you have to work extra hard to demonstrate your trustworthiness.

What stories of trust and mistrust did you hear? What implications do those stories have as you contemplate sermons, classes, and how your leaders will work together? I'll say more about building trust in chapters 3 and 5.

THE IMPORTANCE OF WORSHIP AND SPIRITUAL GROWTH

To what extent did the interviewees value growing spiritually and in community? Did they tell stories of Bible study groups, of retreats, of inspiring worship? What impact did these experiences have on their growth in faith?

Did any interviewees make a distinction between being disciples of Christ and simply being members? What is the level of commitment to following Christ? To what extent was there a real sense that they were living in the way of Christ?

Research shows clearly that intentional spiritual growth is an important component of vital congregations. I'll say more about this in chapter 8.

AREAS OF ANXIETY AND HOW THEY DEAL WITH ANXIETY

About what are people anxious? Does the anxiety come from within or from outside? In many congregations, the neighborhood has been changing dramatically over the past 25 to 50 years, and people don't know what to do with the change. The community might be morphing from a sleepy rural town to a burgeoning exurb or perhaps from a solid middle-class community to one of struggling immigrants sharing overcrowded housing.

On one hand, anxiety might stem from having a deteriorating building and not enough people to maintain it, and on the other hand, it could be from having a building that's too small for a growing congregation.

Are a number of people anxious about death and suffering because several beloved members have died in the past year?

Many congregations experience anxiety over varying expectations about music choice. What kind of music will best enable current members to worship? What kind of music will also draw in young adults who might prefer a different style of music? Did interviewees tell you about tensions concerning music and worship style?

What answers did you hear regarding how they have dealt with differences? In one congregation where I asked this question, I heard lots of examples of when they *didn't* handle conflict effectively. *Nobody* came up with a positive experience. As people talked about handling differences, did you hear of any conflict between staff members or leaders? Any big church fights? I'll focus intensively on this subject in chapter 5.

People facing difficult personal issues are often very anxious. Be aware of any members who are obviously troubled, especially if they are in leadership positions. How might you respond to them? With solid pastoral care? By encouraging and guiding friends to be more supportive and helpful? By limiting the influence they have as leaders?

As people talked about what makes for anxiety, did any identify holy objects, such as a piece of art painted by a son or daughter of the congregation? Perhaps someone mentioned that antique mirror in the ladies parlor that was donated by the dominant family in the congregation and that must not be touched. Maybe someone commissioned a stained glass window in memory of the first pastor?

What are minefields that are best to avoid for a while? Have any issues, staff members, or holy objects been mentioned with such anxiety that you decide they might be best handled later? Or has something come to your attention that you realize must be dealt with promptly?

I stress again that I simply encourage you to be aware of such things. You won't be acting on most of these insights right away. But they will guide you as you work with leaders and interact with various groups and individuals.

Tip 5: Ask, What is obvious?

When our elder son was studying high school physics one evening, my wife, Mary Helen, groaned, "Physics—ugh! I would have never made it through physics in college if your dad hadn't helped me." Doug looked at her with complete incomprehension and responded, "But Mom, it's so obvious!"

What was quite clear to Doug most assuredly was *not* obvious to Mary Helen.

That flipped on the proverbial light bulb for me. What is obvious to one person isn't necessarily obvious to another. I recalled times when I was met with blank stares after I had asked questions about some biblical passage. I thought that my questions were preliminary to the deeper inquiry I planned, since the answers were obvious. Yet the answers weren't obvious at all to the class members. Conversely, I thought of times when Mary Helen noted something like, "Sally looked kind of down yesterday, didn't she?" And I hadn't noticed anything unusual.

As a leader, you need to be aware of what is obvious to you and what isn't. What do you see or hear that others don't seem to catch? And what do you miss?

Are you able to see ahead, thinking strategically, without much effort, noting the ways in which different factors interact and anticipate potential possibilities? Most people aren't.

Do you love to see numbers fall into place, finding it easy to set up budgets and keep track of cash flow? I am (and probably most pastors are) bored stiff by such details and so make mistakes.

Is it obvious to you why the bush in the front yard is dying or why water is seeping through the foundation? Many people don't notice things like this.

As you reflect on what people told you in the interviews and on what you have observed, please be curious about what is obvious to you and not to others. Conversely, be curious about what is obvious to others and not to you. What have people called to your attention that surprised you? What more do you need to learn?

NORMS

Those behaviors that jumped out at you—both expected and unexpected, stated and unstated—are often expressions of the norms of the congregation. Every organization or system has norms, beliefs, standards, and expectations that are sometimes explicitly stated but often not written anywhere. You often find out about norms when you accidentally break one.

Families have norms. My parents raised me to hold doors open for women or those older than me (although people who were born after 1980 might find that norm rather quaint). Family holiday celebrations are fraught with opportunities for a newcomer to accidentally break a cherished norm. ("Did you notice that he started eating before Daddy?")

Sometimes norms are constructive, sometimes not. "In this family we put a high priority on studying and getting good grades!" is an example of a generally constructive norm. The belief that white people were inherently superior to African Americans was a destructive norm that still haunts our society.

I suspect you can list norms that govern your family. Now I would like you to consider what the norms of your congregation are. Examples of congregational norms that I have seen or heard of include the following:

- If you have a problem in this congregation, there's no point in going to the pastor or board. They aren't going to listen to you anyway. You need to start stomping and screaming right away!
- We take care of each other when someone is really sick or hurt, but good luck if you have a minor condition. You're on your own.
- The pastor/finance chair/Mrs. Jones (who gives lots of money) controls everything.

- We don't like change.
- We handle change well if we have a chance to really talk about it.
- We are friendly to each other but not so much to newcomers. People have to be members for ten years to really become part of this congregation.
- The pastor is an employee, almost a flunky.
- The pastor is our spiritual leader.
- This congregation calls strong pastors and then fights with them!
- Our congregation sings the best classical music in the area.
- We are on the cutting edge of new worship forms.
- We have a dynamite youth program, and everything else is subordinate.
- We are a congregation of small groups, not a congregation with small groups.
- We are a poor congregation, so we don't take care of either our building or pastor.

Based on your overall observations and your interviews, try writing the key norms of the congregation in simple declarative sentences. I have found that taking time to write out norms helps me see the congregation much more clearly.

NOW WHAT?

Why take all the time to analyze the interviews and write down names, norms, challenges and other responses? Because it helps to understand the inhabitants of this Wonderland into which you have come. Chances are you have had some significant surprises as you've interviewed people and reflected on what you've found. I suspect that you have also been affirmed in much of what you thought you knew when you came to the congregation. You are clearer about who the real pillars of the congregation are. You have heard of challenges and triumphs, about their sense of how the Lord is leading them. You are getting a much clearer picture of this congregation, including what members are not at all clear about! As you gain a sense of what their reality is, you can have really important conversations with leaders about issues, hopes, and dreams.

Using the interview tool and analyzing the responses will be time well spent. Gathering this information will help you avoid landmines and guide initial decisions. Listening to leaders' responses will help you assess the strength of the board and other leadership teams in the congregation. I'll say more about building a strong leadership team in chapter 5.

Make getting to know the congregation a top priority! Describe what you see and then be curious. Invite people to explain things to you.

Ask what is obvious to you and not to others. Be aware of what you are oblivious to.

What is going on in people's lives? Be a detective! Now you're getting to know the territory!

Chapter Three

How Solid Is the Foundation?

Assessing the Trust Level

As Alice ventured deeper into Wonderland, she found herself at a tea party where the conversation was quite unintelligible, and then she stumbled into a croquet game played using hedgehogs as balls and flamingoes as mallets. The Queen of Hearts continued to demand execution of any who thwarted or otherwise annoyed her. Alice was very puzzled.

You are getting a handle on who makes up this new church. By now you know who the most respected leaders are. Perhaps you have identified the Queen of Hearts, the Cheshire Cat, and any number of other characters. And you have probably been caught up in some strange tea parties and other games that this congregation likes to play.

Perhaps you have seen small groups of board members talking with one another after worship and noticed that they quickly stop talking when certain other members approach them. You sense something is wrong but can't figure out what is going on. Or maybe you have heard some of the longtime members recalling how a group of newcomers tried to make radical changes in worship and now they are asking if two newer members are really qualified to be on the board. "Will they try to put something over on us?" you have heard them wondering. Or the pastor selection committee had promised that they would have the pastor's study completely remodeled before you arrived. "It will have fresh paint and carpet, a new desk and chair, more comfortable chairs to sit in for counseling." Nothing has been done, however, and when you ask about it, the property committee chair arches an eyebrow and remarks that he didn't know anything about what those people promised. You sense a lack of trust and aren't sure what to do.

Or, conversely, you have been pleased with the openness and spontaneity of the board. Members seem very comfortable with each and carry no hidden agendas. Decisions can be made quickly. You see newcomers drawn into the life of the congregation. When people disagree with one another, they can laugh about their differences and show respect for one another. There is an atmosphere of trust.

Or perhaps your new congregation is somewhere in between, sometimes trusting, sometimes not. What is the trust level in your congregation? And how important is trust, anyway?

TRUST: THE FOUNDATION FOR COMMUNITY

"Trust" is generally defined as a firm reliance on the integrity, ability, truth, or character of a person or thing. It often has connotations of hope: if I trust in someone, I can hope that they will behave with the integrity and ability that I expect.

As I have coached and consulted with pastors, I have heard horror stories about how destructive persons (sometimes the previous pastor) have gained and abused their power and totally destroyed trust in their congregations. Newspapers regularly carry stories about pastors who have engaged in sexual misconduct. They have breached the trust that members of their congregations placed in them and often have irreparably damaged their congregations.

Just as trust in other institutions and professionals has dropped, Gallup polling data indicate a significant drop in confidence in organized religion over the past 30 years. In 1973, 65 percent of those polled replied that they had either quite a lot or a great deal of confidence in organized religious institutions. In June 2012, only 44 percent had the same level of confidence. [1] Similarly, the percentage of people who rate the honesty or ethics of clergy as high or very high dropped from 61 percent in 1977 to 50 percent in 2009. [2] You simply can't assume that members of your congregation have a high level of trust in pastors and even their own congregation. Our society is damaged by mistrust. I hope that you are not in a congregation that has been traumatized by an egregious breach of trust. If you are, it's critical to bring in someone who has specialized training in handling these situations. The last portion of this chapter deals with more serious breaches of trust.

Assuming that your congregation is fairly normal, there will almost certainly have been some breaches of trust. Whether intentional or unintentional, it's part of our nature to let others down. A top priority for you as a new pastor is to validate and build trust in you as the new pastor and also to assess the trust level of the congregation and its leadership, and to build and keep building trust.

Consider for a moment how so much of what we do is predicated on trust. I take an elevator from our 20th floor condo and trust it to function properly, then get into my car and trust that it will work, trust most drivers to follow traffic laws, trust the supermarket to keep food clean and stored properly. I trust my family to love, respect, and rein me in when necessary. I trust neighbors to be honorable people, even giving some the keys to our condo when we leave on vacation.

At the same time I need to have appropriate caution and mistrust. Though most banks and investment advisors are trustworthy, I think of Bernie Madoff. While our air traffic system is generally trustworthy, I was on a plane recently when the pilot announced just prior to takeoff that a tire had a nail in it and had to be replaced. Maintenance workers had not noticed it; I was grateful that someone saw the problem *before* takeoff!

I did an online search for "trust" using the Oremus Bible Browser and found 242 citations for trust. The vast majority of the citations urged followers to trust in the Lord. A significant number cautioned readers against trust in royalty, wealth, or their own power. Jesus predicted that Judas would betray him, the disciples desert him, and Peter deny him. And yet, he trusted the disciples before and after his death and resurrection to carry his gospel of love and life.

In his letter to the Corinthians, St. Paul extols agape (love) as the greatest gift. Wouldn't you like to be part of a congregation whose primary norm is the agape Paul describes in I Corinthians 13? How do you lead your congregation toward that ideal? I think that a foundation for reaching that agape is to build trust. If members of your congregation are mired in suspicion and internal political games, then there isn't much chance you can lead them to experience the life of the new reign of God. If members of your congregation don't trust each other or you, then you can't begin to build a community that is characterized by the agape of Christ.

Assessing and Building Trustworthiness

My wife and I trust each other to be faithful and to seek each other's well-being. I have been fortunate that most leaders in every congregation in which I have served have been trustworthy. Yet I know that in every one of those congregations, there were some who were not trustworthy. At best they were unreliable. At worst, they undercut the congregation's ministry. How do you know whom to trust? How do you show yourself as trustworthy? As you assess trust, it's important to take human nature seriously: each person is capable of great good and great evil. Recognizing that real trust is neither blind nor gullible, how do you assess the trust level in your new congregation?

Stephen M. R. Covey, cofounder and CEO of CoveyLink Worldwide and an expert on leadership development, speaks to audiences around the world. Covey offers a detailed analysis of trust in his excellent book *The Speed of Trust: The One Thing That Changes Everything*. Covey asserts that trust has two dimensions: character and competence,[3] which help us assess whether someone is trustworthy.

Character

When I consider people's character I reflect on their integrity, asking if their words and deeds are consistent. Do they practice what they preach? Most of us can spot phonies fairly quickly; we'll be fooled only once. Think of persons you have initially trusted but who, after you got to know them, didn't ring true. Perhaps you caught them in a lie. Perhaps something just didn't feel right. Whatever the cause, you wondered about their integrity, and so you didn't trust them.

Humility is another sign of character. Think of the leaders whom you most respect. Chances are they convey a sense of humility. People who claim to have all the answers make me nervous, especially those who claim to know the mind of God! I know I don't have all the answers! Demonstrating that you know the limits of your ability and knowledge helps people see you as a person of integrity.

Similar to humility is vulnerability. Patrick Lencioni, a leading consultant for business and government, asserts that those working together on a team need to take risks and be vulnerable with each other.

> This is what happens when members get to a point where they are completely comfortable being transparent, honest, and naked with one another, where they say and genuinely mean things like "I screwed up," "I need help," "Your idea is better than mine," "I wish I could learn to do that as well as you do," and even, "I'm sorry."[4]

Lencioni is writing for a business audience. How much more does his advice apply to congregations and especially their leaders?

Being vulnerable is very difficult for some pastors. Sometimes members of our congregations have the very unrealistic expectation that we pastors never harbor doubts about our faith, are never angry with God or our spouses, and are always faithful in our prayer and Bible study. Sometimes parishioners expect us to be able to answer questions that are beyond any human knowledge. I have found that sharing the struggles in my own spiritual journey is a great help to those who are also seeking to see God more clearly. Being both humble and vulnerable helps members see my personal strength and enhances my trustworthiness.

Courage is another indication of character. Sometimes I am not sure what the right decision is. Yet I decide and act based on prayer and understanding of what God yearns for. I imagine that most of us are courageous at least some of the time, taking a stand for what we believe to be right. Yet at other times, neither you nor I have acted or spoken for what we know is right. Perhaps we haven't shown courage. Our courage is a clue to our character.

Reliability is another dimension of integrity. If someone is going to be in the hospital, I don't promise to visit unless the situation is fairly serious. However, if someone is critically ill, I will visit frequently, sometimes sitting with a patient's family during surgery. Don't make commitments lightly. Consider whether you will comply with a request before saying "yes."

Another part of a new pastor's demonstrating reliability is simply showing up when it is important to be present. In his third month in a new parish, a friend of mine who is an interim pastor attended his second meeting of the men's group, and one member noted, "Well, you've already met more with us than the previous pastor did in his seven years here."

While the importance of showing up may seem obvious, I have heard of pastors who are very hard to find. They are either preparing their sermon, in a clergy support group, serving on a denominational committee, or simply not available when a parishioner attempts to get in contact. One secretary told me that she would not know where the congregation's pastor was for days at a time.

I think that being reliable means that you show up early for worship and visit with people before and after worship. Similarly you are early for meetings and available for visits afterward. Members can count on your being easily available. Of course, the degree of availability varies from congregation to congregation. The larger the congregation, the less time the pastor will have for socializing. But be clear about what you can and will do. I urge you to err on the side of being available.

Intent is still another dimension of character. *Why* do people do what they do? If I were exploring your intent as pastor of your congregation, I might ask why you are there. Did you go there because you were desperate for a new call and a call committee wanted you? Did a bishop or district superintendent send you there? Do you have a sense of God's calling you to this ministry position, that you have something unique to offer to the members of the congregation? I think most pastors have some sense of call to their congregation. They enter with good intent.

However, I think that some pastors see one congregation as a stepping stone to another congregation, perhaps one that is larger or in a preferred location. Their attitude is this: "If by my preaching and evangelism, I increase the attendance, number of members, and income, then I'll get a call to a congregation three times this big!" Serving their congregation and community well isn't so much their intent as advancing their career.

Most members of your congregation will be asking themselves if you, their new pastor, really care about them. Are you there for *them,* or do you have another motive for coming to their congregation? Whatever your other agendas, it's important to communicate through your words and actions that you care for them. Showing you care builds their trust in you.

Now consider the intent of members of the congregation. Why do various members join a particular congregation? Perhaps they become members so they can grow spiritually. Maybe they hope they can be part of a community of people who love each other. Maybe they want to be part of a mission-minded congregation that is making a difference in the community. Or perhaps they see this congregation as a great venue in which to sell insurance or gain new clients for their law practice. Are people part of the congregation because of their commitment to Christ and serving as Christ's disciple, or are they there so they can get needs met for power or security or lots of attention? As you listen to people talking and observe their behavior, what do you surmise about their motives? Are they coming from a caring intent? Or from some other intention? What can you conclude about people's intent as you observe and listen?

Building a foundation of trust begins with character. Members of your congregation need to see you as a person of strong character. As you assess formal and informal leaders, reflect on their character.

Competence

Having good character doesn't guarantee trustworthiness, of course. For members of your new congregation to trust you, they also have to believe that you are competent enough to meet or exceed their expectation. My friends and colleagues consider me a person of high character but they shouldn't (nor would they) trust me to be their accountant, plumber, or surgeon, because I am not at all competent to perform any of these jobs!

Steven Covey asserts that competence has dimensions of both capability and results. Football coaches must understand the game, be able to teach players, and develop strategy for each game. They must be capable. But they must do more than be capable. They have to motivate their players and win games. To be seen as competent, the coach must be both capable and deliver results. Similarly, members of your congregation will be asking if you are competent enough to be their pastor; they will assess your capability and the results you deliver.

Congregations vary widely in the competence they expect from their pastor and their views about how you will meet their expectations. Consequently, I think it is essential to clarify what leaders expect of you and develop mutual expectations of what constitutes your being competent. Notice that I say "mutual expectations." Some possible expectations might include the following:

- You preach a sermon on a par with what they are used to (or better).
- Your sermons are so fantastic that the congregation will double in size in two years!
- You demonstrate that you understand scripture and theology and are also able to preach and teach about your common faith in ways that they can apply in their own lives.
- You need to be able to both explain and also demonstrate the grace of the Lord. You can preach in lofty phrases about God's justice and help members understand how that justice applies to their buying coffee.
- You will be a key leader of leaders, drawing members of the board together into a team of spiritual leaders.
- You won't meddle with the leaders who really run the congregation.
- You are an effective counselor or are able to refer them to the appropriate counselor.
- You understand the basics of the business aspects of the congregation and can work effectively with those who handle property and finance.
- You will be especially attentive to wealthier members of the congregation and ensure that they both give generously to the congregation and make it a beneficiary in their wills.
- You will be the key leader in the community for myriad causes that individual members hold dear (e.g., protecting feral cats, establishing low-income housing, stopping gun violence, ensuring Second Amendment rights to gun ownership).

What results count in your new congregation? You can be sure that there will be some in your congregation who will have what you think are outrageous expectations. If you and leaders aren't clear about mutual expectations, then some members almost certainly will decide you are not competent because you haven't met their unfair and unrealistic expectations. They won't trust you and so won't follow you. So it is important to have a mutual agreement with leaders about what you think the Lord yearns for you and the congregation to achieve. What constitutes competence on your part? What results count? I provide a tool later in the chapter for clarifying expectations.

Similarly, you need to assess the trustworthiness of leaders in the congregation. Does someone promise to develop a new congregational website and months later nothing is happening? Does the musician consistently lead the choir in performing spiritually uplifting special music, or do the choir's offerings make you wince? On whom can you count to make sure the various HVAC components are functioning properly? Which members lead the exciting youth program or teach popular adult Bible studies? What leaders are competent? In the next two chapters I will provide you some tools to assess the gifts and competence of both formal and informal leaders. You need to know who are trustworthy and who aren't.

Trust is one of the most important foundation stones for any organization, especially a congregation. High trust in a congregation enables decisions to be made smoothly and effectively. People give you the benefit of the doubt when you forget an appointment or don't make a pastoral call or make a misstatement in a sermon. Without trust you will be mired in suspicion, indecision, and sabotage. If members of your congregation don't trust you, then they will second-guess your decisions, challenge your authority, discount your teaching, and perhaps even ignore you.

Taking time to build trust between yourself and the congregation and to assess and build trust among members is absolutely essential in the first six months or so of a new ministry. You simply can't assume that people are going to trust you or that they already trust each other. If trust in your congregation is a little shaky, I urge you to use some of the following tools and tips. Even if the trust level is high, use some that seem appropriate, because these exercises will help members trust you and each other even more.

COACHING ASSIGNMENT 5: ASSESS THE LEVEL OF TRUST AMONG MEMBERS, ESPECIALLY THE LEADERS

Please reflect on what you see members doing and what you hear them saying. Keep a journal to help you collect your observations and insights. Here are some questions to help you observe.

During meetings, how do members interact with one another? Do particular members seem to distrust one another? Are there alliances (e.g., of old-timers vs. newcomers)? What signs of respect or disrespect do you observe and hear? Is there easy laughter, or are there tense interchanges?

When the board or a committee votes or prepares to vote, do members vote readily and with considerable consensus, or are there motions to delay action on proposals?

What issues seem to make people anxious? What do you suppose is behind the anxiety? How might you find out what is creating the anxiety? With whom might you talk?

Ask similar questions as you observe the interactions of staff members. What is the emotional temperature of the office? Warm? Icy? Frightened? Try writing a metaphor or two describing what you experience. "Entering that office was like going to a wake. It seemed like some were on the verge of tears. There was no energy." Or, "I felt like I was walking into a war zone. You never knew where a sniper was hiding until you or someone else was zinged. The musician was a Humvee. He rolled over everyone." From a positive perspective you might write, "Our staff meetings are like a really creative workshops! We bounce ideas off one another and come up with wonderful plans for worship."

Reflect on the character and competence of leaders. As you concluded the Eleven Curious Questions interview process, who were identified as respected leaders? Which leaders have you observed are especially trustworthy, and which are not? Have you heard of some members who are deliberately subversive or who have some agenda that overrides the health of the congregation?

Don't take any action on your assessments at this point. You are still trying to understand this territory.

COACHING ASSIGNMENT 6: ASSESS THE LEVEL OF TRUST TOWARD THE OFFICE OF PASTOR

Because the overall trust of pastors has declined in recent decades, it's important to assess how people think about the very office of pastor. Again, I would like you to observe and keep notes in a journal, and reflect on clues that indicate the extent to which members trust you and have trusted previous pastors. Here are questions for consideration.

To what extent do members extend trust toward you? Are they open and easy to talk with, or are they guarded? Do you have any sense that previous pastors betrayed them? As you interviewed leaders using the Eleven Curious Questions, did you pick up any indications that a lot of members simply don't trust pastors?

When you made some kind of mistake, were there some members who (in your opinion) overreacted to that mistake? What might have been behind that overreaction?

If you pick up some signs of longstanding mistrust toward the pastor (not just you—any pastor), talk with a judicatory official or someone you trust about what you have observed. Be curious about the origins of such mistrust.

Tip 6: Step up during a crisis.

An interim pastor friend was stopped as he entered the sanctuary on his first Sunday with the congregation. "Pastor Joe, Mary died last night." Mary was a very beloved, long-time member. He was immediately thrust into getting to know her family and organizing and leading a funeral service. By leading a moving, sensitive service that praised God and honored and celebrated Mary's life, he immediately established himself as a strong, caring pastor. In the congregation where plaster had fallen, I helped coordinate a response to the sadly neglected building. I gained trust as an organized, practical pastor.

What would it have been like to be a very new pastor on September 11, 2001? On that traumatic day I was interim pastor of a congregation with a significant percentage of persons connected with the armed forces. Other leaders and I knew that this attack would have far-reaching implications for their families and friends. We immediately planned and held services for several evenings, using scriptures ranging from psalms of lament to Gospel proclamations of hope. We gave participants a chance to talk. The services drew people together. If you helped lead during the aftermath of the 9/11 attacks, what did you learn from what happened? How might you apply that learning to future crises?

While a crisis interrupts your plans for getting to know people, it nonetheless gives you a wonderful opportunity to lead. You can demonstrate your depth of faith and show your compassion and care. You will show them who you really are.

Tip 7: Catch them in the act of doing something well!

Many years ago I took a nifty course in teacher education. It offered an instrument for assessing teacher effectiveness. The idea was that I would observe a teacher and then offer my perceptions. Following its approach, I observed a husband-wife team who were excellent teachers. Reviewing my notes, I laid out to them what I observed and paused for their response.

"Shall we write out a formal letter resigning as teachers?" they asked.

Dumbfounded, I asked, "What do you mean? You're great teachers!"

All they heard (and perhaps most of what I reported) was criticism! I didn't affirm them! They perceived that I thought they were terrible teachers!

Telling members that you appreciate their efforts when they do something helpful or well demonstrates that you notice them and care about what they do. This builds trust. Keep track of the times you say, "I affirm you, I appreciate you" in a week. Be sure you catch people in the act of doing something well!

A caution—don't negate the affirmation with kind suggestions as to how they might improve what they are doing. "Oh, I really liked the introduction you wrote for the scripture you read this morning. But here's how it might have been even better!" Making those "helpful suggestions" can dramatically reduce a person's motivation.

First Steps to Building Trust

What are some things you might do to build trust quickly? How do you help members get to know you, to be confident that you are trustworthy, a person of character and competence. You have begun the process by interviewing leaders using the Eleven Curious Questions, thus demonstrating that you care for them and are interested in their perspective. Here are some additional steps that will help build trust.

TOOL 4: MEET MEMBERS IN SMALL GROUPS

I encourage you to find a variety of ways in which you can meet with people in small groups. Start with existing groups—the board, committees, small study or support groups, choir, and so forth. Depending on the time you have available, you might ask a team to organize some home get-togethers with groups of about six to eight people. Try to get face-to-face with as many people as possible in the first six months or so.

What do you do in these get-togethers? You have two primary objectives: to get to know them and help them know who you really are. Building trust involves listening and sharing so it's important to listen closely and also by telling them about what makes you tick.

In these conversations I encourage *you to share first.* By opening the conversation you model the length and depth of the response they might offer to your question. By going first you also demonstrate both courage and vulnerability. You demonstrate to the members of the group that you are authentic and secure within yourself.

However, be sure you don't yammer on and on! This isn't your opportunity to spend an hour talking about yourself! The appropriate length of a response depends on the question. For example, in response to a question about my family, I might talk for three minutes or so about my wife, sons, their wives, and children (trying not to brag about my grandchildren!). For deeper questions, I normally talk for five to seven minutes and encourage participants to do the same. For example, when I tell about two scripture passages that have been important in my spiritual growth, I often talk about how in my sophomore year of college, a study of Amos 5 awakened me to the biblical mandate for justice and how that ultimately was a key factor in my deciding God wanted me to enter the ministry. Depending on the setting, participants might take more time.

Here are some conversation starters you might use in such a get-together. Choose which would be appropriate for the particular group. For example, if you are meeting with a committee you'll be attending regularly, you may use one at each of several meetings. Don't even think about using them all at the same gathering! Alternately, if it is a group with which you'll rarely meet, such as a women's circle, you would use just one. You will note that some of these are similar to the Eleven Curious Questions.

- Please tell me your name, where you grew up, and what led you to this congregation.
- Please tell me something about your family.
- Please tell us more about yourself—your job, hobbies, community work, and so forth.
- What one or two scripture passages or Bible stories have been important to you in your spiritual growth?
- What are one or two important challenges that you have dealt with? How did your faith help you deal with these challenges?

You might adapt some of the questions you used in interviewing leaders. The important thing is to demonstrate that you want to get to know members of your new congregation and that you want them to know you.

TOOL 5: CLARIFYING EXPECTATIONS AND TOP PRIORITIES

I think it's very important to develop mutual expectations about what your top priorities are for the first year or so. To do that you need to try to figure out what congregational members expect, but most important, what board members expect of you and each other. How varied are the expectations? And how realistic? Are there common wishes, hopes, and needs?

I have found that many pastors get into difficulty because they don't take time to have a good conversation with leaders about mutual expectations and top priorities. Pastors blissfully follow their particular interests, ignoring what key leaders think is really important. If you don't take time to clarify expectations, then you are bound to disappoint a number of key members. They will then lose trust in you as their pastor.

Conversely, when the board and pastor are clear on priorities and communicate the priorities to the congregation and the pastor spends time and energy in accordance with them, then trust will build. You will be seen as a leader who both has strong character and is competent. So, how do you clarify expectations?

Here is an approach to clarifying priorities I have used for clients and for myself. It is best done in a half-day retreat or meeting involving both board members and members of the pastor selection committee. You might invite a coach or consultant or judicatory staff member to lead the retreat.

1. Open with prayer and a trust-building exercise. (15 minutes)
2. Ask participants to individually list what they expect you to do and to note roughly how many hours/week they expect you to spend on each task. You might give them the job description that was developed in

the pastor search process or a denominational list of pastoral responsibilities. (5 minutes)

3. Quickly compile the results and estimate the total number of hours per week their expectations would require you to work. (5 minutes)

4. Discuss what you see in their list and then invite them to describe what they see. Note similarities and variations in their expectations. (10 minutes)

5. List 10 to 15 responsibilities, each on a separate sheet of 11" x 17" paper, and tape these on a wall. I suggest that you prepare around 8 to 12 sheets in advance identifying typical expectations (for example, sermon and worship preparation and leadership, teaching an adult Bible class, evangelism). Also add expectations that were on the congregational profile that was prepared for the pastor search process and any you heard as you interviewed leaders using the Eleven Curious Questions. Invite the leaders to add other expectations to the sheets on the wall. Post them too. Invite participants to reflect on the array of expectations before them. Invite questions for clarification about the meaning of specific expectations. I encourage you to limit the sheets on the wall to no more than 15. Be sure to summarize and combine expectations that are similar. It's better to post one sheet saying "sermon and worship preparation" than two sheets with "sermon preparation" on one and "worship planning and preparation" on the other. (20 minutes)

6. Instruct the participants to each indicate what they think the top six priorities should be for you in your first year by writing their name on six of these sheets. I suggest that you tell them that after they make their selections, they may take a 10-minute break.

7. In the total group, review the voting and identify the top four to six priorities and have a conversation about why these are most important. If the congregation did a mission/vision study during its search process or has done one recently, reflect on how study findings correlate with the priorities the board just identified. Discuss what these top priorities likely mean you will and won't do in your first year (recognizing that surprises always happen). Invite conversation about how board members will respond when members complain about something they think you should be doing. For example, Mr. Jones may have expected you to visit his homebound wife monthly, but the board and you agree that quarterly visits are sufficient since other members are visiting her. Instead of visiting homebound persons so frequently, you and the board have agreed that, in an effort to welcome newcomers, you will visit every newcomer to worship. Or perhaps you and the board determine that you should spend eight hours a week with musicians and a contemporary worship planning team to begin a new ser-

vice or strengthen an existing one. Most important, you and board members agree that if members complain that you haven't met their expectations *and in fact* you have been meeting these mutually agreed expectations, the board supports your focus and use of time. (30 minutes)

8. Discuss how your focusing on these priorities directly affects how you will work with leaders and various committees. For example, previous pastors may have been expected to attend every committee meeting. These priorities might mean that you won't normally attend the property committee meeting but that the chair of the committee will talk with you about plans and any issues they are dealing with. Perhaps you and they will explore having an all committee evening at which you will attend portions of the meetings as necessary. If there has been staff dissension and the board wants you to spend significant time strengthening staff relationships, then you might not have time to teach an adult class, and so the education committee will have to arrange for someone else to teach that class. Take time to be clear about what you expect of each other. (20 minutes)

9. Clarify how achieving these top priorities will be measured. For example, board members and you might agree that the most important thing is for you to talk with most of the church members as soon as possible. Together you might set a goal that by the end of your first year, you will have had conversations with 75 percent of the active members. (20 minutes)

10. Request that the board passes a motion naming these priorities and that the appropriate lay leaders communicate these priorities to the congregation through varied media (e.g., newsletter, email, oral announcement). Also request that the personnel committee adapt its appraisal instrument to reflect these priorities. (See chapter 10 for a detailed description of this process.) (10 minutes)

If you take time to develop mutual expectations with the board and communicate these priorities clearly, then members know what to expect, thus building trust as you meet the expectations.

Tip 8: Plan your sermons a season ahead.

Another way to build trust in you is through your sermons. Your sermons are critical vehicles to help the members of the congregation know who you are. In your sermons, you can tell stories about your challenges and hopes, and about how your faith has helped you grow. You can show them that you can laugh at yourself and thus demonstrate that you are approachable. Your sermons are great vehicles to show that you have listened to members and know something of their concerns and hopes and the congregation's important stories. You demonstrate your character through your sermons. Sermons also show that you have biblical and theological knowledge appropriate for this congregation, thus giving evidence of your competence.

Planning your sermons several weeks ahead establishes you as a reliable pastor and helps build trust, especially if your predecessor was not very reliable. To the extent that you have significant preaching experience, I think it's good to rework old sermons if possible during the first year or so. That will give you more time to meet and get to know people. However, be sure to review these old sermons to make sure they are timely and relevant to current issues and that they show you are beginning to know members of this new congregation. You can't just dust off a sermon you preached six years ago and use it unchanged.

I found that musicians and education leaders especially liked my planning sermon and worship texts and themes several weeks in advance. They could then plan music or special educational events to complement what I was planning. Since I typically based my sermons on lectionary texts, they could use some of the many resources based on the lectionary.

Further, I have often been amazed by how a reading in the week's lectionary is precisely the right passage to reflect on when something big is happening. One vivid memory is when Ezra's sermon at the Water Gate popped up during the Watergate hearings in 1973. Another was that week when my first-grade son was bumped by a car but not hurt *and* my wife was unhurt in a collision with a dump truck. The lectionary Gospel reading was from the Sermon on the Mount: "Don't be anxious—the Lord counts the hairs on your head!" "OK, Lord, that's enough examples for this week," I protested.

A more recent example was when I was invited to preach at a congregation torn by conflict. The text for the day was Jesus' parable of the prodigal son. I noted that it might better be called the parable of the prodigal father and called on members to emulate the father's radical forgiveness of both sons. Planning ahead doesn't prevent your responding to current issues.

Though I like the lectionary, I have known some very effective preachers who use other approaches to plan several weeks in advance. Sermon series might be developed on the Lord's Prayer, the Sermon on the Mount, a major theme from scripture such as liberation and salvation, or by working through a Bible book for several Sundays. The possibilities are limited only by your imagination.

I encourage you to see your sermons as being more than the vehicle for proclaiming good news, but also as media for building trust in you as a person of character and competence.

COACHING ASSIGNMENT 7: DECIDE WHAT STEPS YOU WILL TAKE TO BUILD TRUST

You have now been in this congregation for two or three months, maybe more. You have kept a journal in which you have noted your assessments of the trust level. You have probably found some minor breakdowns of trust. And you are only too aware of the mistrust that abounds in our culture. What will you do to build trust? Please consider what I have written, what you already know about building trust, and develop a plan to systematically build trust in this new congregation. Start with the leaders and work through the rest of the congregation.

Dealing with Significant Breaches of Trust

There are times when a pastor enters a congregation where there have been major conflicts and breaches of trust. Perhaps the previous pastor engaged in sexual misconduct, embezzled funds, slandered a member, or did something equally egregious. In such cases the very office of pastor is suspect. Sometimes a current or former lay leader engaged in some kind of major betrayal.

Optimally you, the new pastor, know of the situation. If you are part of a denomination that exercises oversight over its pastors and congregations, then it is likely that a denominational leader (perhaps a bishop or executive) will have taken action to address the situation. Appropriate legal action will have been taken when laws have been broken.

But sometimes many members of the congregation are not aware of what happened. Perhaps congregational leaders or judicatory officials kept the betrayal a secret. Perhaps they kept the secret to avoid making a public stink or they thought that such information would split the congregation. Sometime the malefactor simply leaves the church and moves elsewhere, leaving silent victims behind. Nobody in leadership knows what has happened and neither do you, the new pastor! Pastors entering such congregations encounter a great deal of mistrust and cannot figure out what is going on. Such mistrust shows up in many ways. Sometimes members second-guess any recommendation a pastor makes. Sometimes an atmosphere of suspicion permeates the congregation. One colleague discovered that some women would not step into the pastor's study because the previous pastor had engaged in sexual misconduct. Congregational leaders might attempt to micromanage the pastor in an effort to control his or her behavior.

Whatever the case, once there is evidence that a major violation of trust has happened, outside help is needed. There are a number of people who have special training in helping congregations recover after a major trauma. See, for example, *When a Congregation Is Betrayed: Responding to Clergy Misconduct*, which was written by a team of experts who help "afterpastors," that is, those pastors who come into a congregation where there has been such a major violation. The editor's preface notes that the contributors

> write not only for people who are professionally interested in the betrayed congregations, but for those who must deal day to day with the aftermath of clergy misconduct. They give readers tools to engage congregation members in the issues surrounding clergy misconduct, so real healing can occur; provide resources to help congregations understand the victim's/survivor's experience, and offer strategies to help afterpastors and other leaders survive personally, thrive, and serve well, and manage situations that might never be good.[5]

Another excellent book for afterpastors dealing with sexual misconduct is *Restoring the Soul of a Church: Healing Congregations Wounded by Clergy Sexual Misconduct.*[6]

While an in-depth analysis of how to deal with such major breaches of trust is beyond the scope of this book, practically every new pastor encounters lesser breaches of trust that still have an impact on congregational life. Given that reality, what might help?

For over twenty years, Michelle and Dennis Reina, founders of the Reina Trust Building Institute, have researched and written about the behaviors that build and break trust. The Reinas use a strong word, *betrayal,* to denote an action that breaks trust. They assert that

> Betrayal is an intentional or unintentional breach of trust or the perception of a breach of trust. An intentional betrayal is a self-serving action done with the purpose of hurting, damaging, or harming another person. An unintentional betrayal is the by-product of another person's self-serving or careless action that has the same result.[7]

You may have heard about problems before you began serving this congregation or discovered some afterward. You may have been brought in as a trained afterpastor to deal with the chaos. Whatever the case, it's critical that you have help dealing with major betrayals, so don't try to handle them all by yourself. However betrayals were handled, they still foster suspicion and get in the way of making good decisions, so they should not be ignored. The following framework will help you think about rebuilding trust, whatever the level of betrayal.

Seven Steps to Rebuilding Trust

In their books, the Reinas describe a trust-building process they have used with considerable success. Here are the steps with some comments based on my experience. As you read these steps about rebuilding trust, recognize that they won't necessarily proceed in a strictly predictable manner, but odds are good that you will cover them, some formally and some informally. The

Reinas work in the business world, but their ideas can easily be translated for congregations.[8]

Step 1—Observe and Acknowledge What Has Happened

Different observers see different things. It's important to be as objective as possible in describing what actually happened. Listen carefully to understand the impact on the one who was betrayed as well as the betrayer—and yourself as the new pastor. The Eleven Curious Questions interview process I introduced will likely encourage members to tell you about their feelings of having been betrayed.

To the extent possible, I think it is important to discuss what happened with leaders. So, for example, if a treasurer embezzled funds, it is critical for leaders to know what happened. Otherwise they might be confused about policies that were set up to prevent any recurrence of financial malfeasance or they won't continue those policies. Then, as possible, tell the congregation what happened. Open up opportunities for people to have a conversation, optimally in groups of 6–10.

Step 2—Allow Feelings to Surface

I have worked with congregations in which there is an incredible amount of pain, especially if the pastor betrayed them. Listen carefully for the feelings. If a person expresses anger, dig deeper to find what is behind the anger. I think that anger is a secondary emotion; there are always other feelings behind the anger, such as fear or frustration or embarrassment. Be prepared for strong feelings to surface, and acknowledge them. Do plenty of active listening and if it is helpful, take notes (although if you take notes, assure the person that confidentiality will be respected).

Step 3—Give Employees Support

Take advantage of opportunities for people to describe the incident(s) and express their feelings about what happened. If a new pastor doesn't pay attention to old feelings of betrayal, those betrayed feel undervalued and often nurse old grievances. Those opportunities may have already emerged as you interviewed people. Perhaps a member stopped by and asked, "Could we talk a little bit?" and proceeds to offer a litany of grievances.

The Reinas note that often people are reluctant to talk about their feelings of betrayal. Be alert to any sign of reluctance and show them you are interested in what they have to tell you. Be sure to listen empathically, helping them confront any fear or feelings of helplessness or guilt. Explore with them what some options are for dealing with the breach of trust.

Again, if some egregious behavior surfaces, you need to bring in an outside expert. But even if the betrayal wasn't bad enough to warrant outside help, you still need to listen carefully and encourage members to describe what happened and express their feelings however strong they may be.

Step 4—Reframe the Experience

Reframing is an important tool that coaches use. I try to help clients see issues they face in a broader context.

- What was going on that led to this incident? What other issues in the congregation were occupying the person who broke trust?
- What outside pressures might have been at play and influenced their behavior? Might there have been some emotional or physical illness that led to this behavior?
- How might have leaders more positively handled the incident?

I often encouraged parishioners and now urge my clients to make a distinction between what they experienced and their interpretation of that event. For example, someone might still be upset with the previous pastor because the pastor didn't call on her dying father and concluded that the pastor didn't care about her or her father. While that might be true, I ask if there might have been something else going on in the pastor's life that precluded her from making a call at that moment.

At one congregation where I was an interim pastor, some members were angry with lay leaders for "kicking the previous pastor out." I developed a process by which lay leaders helped those who were upset with the pastor's leaving to understand the circumstances that led to his departure, factors the upset members had not been aware of. We reframed the experience, and most understood and agreed with the action the leaders had taken.

A caution—don't attempt to reframe an incident before adequately hearing complaints and concerns of those who feel betrayed. Otherwise they may feel revictimized. An example of terrible reframing would be to tell a woman who was a victim of a male pastor's sexual misconduct that he and his wife had been having problems and that he was lonely, so she shouldn't be so angry with him and should just get over it! Reframing doesn't excuse the behavior. Rather, it helps all involved to see the incident in a larger framework.

Step 5—Encourage Members to Take Appropriate Responsibility

As the new pastor, you almost certainly have no responsibility for the major breach of trust. In this step you gently encourage members to take appropriate responsibility for whatever happened. I recognize that this may be difficult since one person may be the primary offender and others victims and so believe they bear no responsibility. But it's important to lead them to assess what even minor contribution they made to the situation.

Think of circumstances that lead to a marriage dissolving. Whenever I counseled couples seeking to be married a second time, I always asked, "How did you contribute to the demise of your first marriage?" Each partner has some role in the breakup, even when one is more at fault. It's vital that individuals take responsibility for what they did or did not do before they enter a new marriage.

If the treasurer embezzled funds, then fellow leaders need to acknowledge that they allowed a system to develop in which there weren't proper checks and balances. If the pastor habitually was late and lazy, leaders need to acknowledge that they didn't make their expectations clear and hold the pastor accountable. Even in cases of sexual misconduct, those who suspected something but kept quiet need to recognize their complicity.

Anxiety and fear often contribute to breaches of trust. Leaders in one congregation I served were anxious about some reactive members who got upset over almost any decision. Some key leaders had been approached by a developer about selling some property the congregation owned, and because of their anxiety, they discussed the possibility in a secret meeting. Word leaked out that this was being considered and, sure enough, the reactive members were outraged, with one explosive man alleging that the treasurer was being paid off by the real estate developer! I worked with the leaders to help them take their responsibility for not handling this potential action transparently.

Even when one person is more at fault in breaching trust, virtually everyone contributes to the problem. Encourage those involved to ask what they contributed to the problem and what they might do to prevent any future problems. For what might they take appropriate responsibility?

Notice that I use the modifier "appropriate." If there has been egregious behavior by anyone, that must not be excused. However, to the extent that leaders didn't take appropriate safeguards, then they need to own some of the responsibility. Be alert for opportunities to encourage both leaders and members to take appropriate responsibility for breaches of trust.

Step 6 — Show Members How to Forgive

As the new pastor you have now helped them describe what happened, express their feelings, see what happened from a larger perspective, and recognize their part in the difficult situation. It is at this point that the Reinas suggest that people work on forgiveness. Notice how far down the list is the admonition to forgive! It simply is not easy to forgive someone who has hurt you deeply, and it is even harder to reconcile with that person. You have to hear people's pain before encouraging them to move on.

Having said that, nursing a grudge is self-destructive. Lewis Smedes, long time professor at Fuller Theological Seminary, declares, "If you cannot free people from their wrongs and see them as the needy people they are, you enslave yourself to the past, you let your hate become your future."[9] For several years I carried a grudge against that senior pastor who fired me but over time grew enough to forgive him and even be grateful for what the experience taught me. I had to let go of my bitterness and forgive before I could grow to be a better person.

As you help people wrestle with the possibility of forgiving those who broke their trust, it is important to distinguish between forgiveness and reconciliation. Reconciliation requires that each person admit their part in the division and seek forgiveness. If there are members of your congregation who feel betrayed by and are angry with one another, I hope that working through the steps will help them forgive and reconcile. However, I recognize that is often not possible. If some members feel let down by the previous pastor or some leader who violated trust, they still need to—and can—forgive that person, whether or not the person is aware of having been forgiven.

Forgiveness is a gift that God gives to help us let go and be restored to wholeness. One of your roles as the new pastor is to help people forgive. This will help build trust.

Step 7—Encourage Members to Let Go and Move On

As you have led members through this process, you may well have felt just as betrayed as they have, especially if you didn't realize the extent to which there had been a betrayal. One colleague expressed his frustration about a pastor who had engaged in sexual misconduct well over two decades previously. "I still hear stories about this guy! It's like his ghost is hanging around!" Both he and members of the congregation need to move on. What has happened has happened. Encourage congregational leaders to let go of their anger and suspicion and move on. Point out what the consequences were for the betrayer (if any were exacted).

One way you can help members move on from experiences of betrayal is to help them learn from the experience. For example, when there has been financial mismanagement, you might lead those in charge of finances to have better controls, including regular audits. You can later affirm how they have learned to conduct business and make decisions that affect the whole congregation in a much more open manner.

When there have been cases of sexual misconduct, you can bring in someone who can help assess the building and the organizational structure to minimize the possibility of further occurrences. For example, many congregations have put windows in office doors, done background checks on those working with children, and insisted that professional staff take training in maintaining healthy boundaries.

Another way of helping them move on is to point to a higher vision of what this congregation might be. Urge them to catch a glimpse of God's vision for them. Help them to see the good that is happening now!

So, that's it. Easy, right? Not! None of these steps can be done easily and quickly. A betrayal that seems minor to most people may be very significant to a few. The key is that you recognize that trust has been broken and that you must continually build and reinforce trust.

COACHING ASSIGNMENT 8: DEAL WITH MAJOR BREACHES OF TRUST

When there has been a fairly serious breach of trust but not something so egregious that denominational support is required, I recommend that you

- Systematically document what you know, noting what you have heard happened and the interpretations of whatever happened. Identify ways in which this breach of trust is currently affecting the congregation. Who mistrusts whom? Is the office of pastor compromised?
- Identify what you are curious about. What inconsistencies are you aware of? What are important gaps in your knowledge?
- Determine whom you will talk with about what has happened (e.g., a denominational official or coach or counselor). Clarify whether or not to bring in a consultant or other expert to help.
- Assuming that you don't need an outside expert, develop a process for building trust. Might you use the Seven Steps? In what venues will you encourage members to talk about their experience of betrayal (e.g., board meetings, one-on-one conversations, small groups)? How will you help reframe what happened and get members to recognize and take responsibility for their part in misunderstanding and betrayal?
- Consider from what scripture passages might you preach about injury, pain, anger, and forgiveness. Remember Jesus' prayer: "Forgive us our sins as we forgive those who have sinned against us." Jesus told Peter to forgive 77 times (Matthew 18). Many Psalms seek God's forgiveness. Jeremiah saw a day when the Lord would forgive the iniquity of the people (Jeremiah 31). Jonah is a great parable of God's grace. Paul urges the Ephesians to "be kind to one another, tender-hearted, forgiving one another, as God in Christ has forgiven you." Some other passages that I have used are the story of Absalom's rebellion against David and Jesus'

parable about the unforgiving servant. Might there be some recognition of betrayal and a commitment to forgiveness in the liturgy?

• Help members clarify what "moving on" might look like. How would the congregation and its leaders be different?

FINAL WORDS ON TRUST

Almost more than any organization, a congregation needs to be built on trust. After all, we pastors urge members of our congregations to trust in the maker of heaven and earth. We proclaim that in the Lord, we have our hope. We sing "Amazing Grace," celebrating God's grace for us.

Be clear—you will encounter some degree of mistrust simply because we live in an era of mistrust, and so you will have to prove yourself worthy of trust. You must assess the level of trust among members in your new congregation. And you must continually work to strengthen trust in yourself and between members.

If we break trust or allow leaders to break trust with members of the congregation and each other, then we undermine our basic proclamation. Those who are searching for faith watch to see if we are trustworthy before placing their trust in the Lord! But if we work hard to build trust, then decisions can be made effectively and transparently. You and members of your congregation can work together to do the work of the Lord.

In chapter 5 I will say more about building trust in your leadership team. I urge you to review the elements of trust and tips and tools in this chapter and do all you can to build trust in every part of your congregation.

Chapter Four

Who's Leading around Here?

Assessing Individual Leaders

As I worked with one congregation, I found myself asking, "Who's leading around here?" The congregation had a relatively inexperienced pastor who was strong in pastoral care but not administration, a dysfunctional board system, and several spiritually immature lay leaders who insisted on their own way. Some of my clients serve congregations whose leaders describe themselves as "old and tired." Some serve congregations whose members have little leadership experience or time to spend in leadership positions. In several cases, these congregations have a substantial number of members who are recent immigrants and have to work 80 hours a week just to survive.

Other clients serve congregations that have declined dramatically in membership over the past twenty years and are now averaging 100 or fewer in worship. Yet they have three boards—a governing board, a board of deacons (pastoral caregivers in Presbyterian parlance), and a board of trustees, each with 10 to 15 members. Further, they have six to eight committees. As you can imagine, the leaders often run from one meeting to another. Those congregations have been so constrained by their organizational structure that they desperately filled officer positions with whomever would say yes, regardless of their qualifications.

As a new pastor, you may find yourself asking, "Who's leading around here?" You know who the board members are and realize that some are not really respected as leaders. You may see the same few people doing everything while many others are passive consumers. Or you may find that one person or family (the Queen of Hearts and her minions) dominates the congregation. You are also beginning to identify those respected leaders who don't currently have an official position. How might you assess the formal leaders of the congregation and then identify and strengthen other leaders?

A first step in assessing leaders is to reflect on their spiritual commitment and maturity. They may be effective leaders in other aspects of their lives, but that does not mean they are emotionally or spiritually mature enough to lead a congregation. What is their motivation? In a world of competing commitments, to what extent are they committed to following Christ and then leading others to be disciples of Christ, and leading them in this congregation?

"Wow!" you may be thinking. "How do I assess these commitments?"

Here are some suggestions. Try to assess *why* they are leading. Do you observe leaders pointing to serving Christ or pointing to themselves? Why does Jim want to be chair of the Worship Committee? To lead people into joyful praise of the Lord, or to get up in front of the congregation and perform? Why is Sue the perpetual treasurer of the congregation? To use the congregation's resources to further the reign of God, or to exert power over others that she no longer has since she retired from her supervisory position?

I have observed that there are people in every congregation who want to be leaders in order to satisfy their desire for status, affection, or power. Their primary motivation isn't to serve Christ. Noting how destructive such persons are, Karen Vanoy and John Flowers, United Methodist pastors and consultants, have written a provocative and helpful book. In their preface, they observe that

> The church may be the only organization that doesn't exist for the sake of its members. Although individuals in every congregation have needs, the church as body of Christ is in need of no one and nothing except Christ alone. He is our "raison d'être." Through his power, we are equipped to do every good work in the world, and it is for the salvation of the world that we exist. [1]

Jesus didn't tell his followers to organize into clubs that would provide them a platform to show off, boss others around, denigrate those with whom they disagree, or to control hired servants such as pastors or musicians.

Assessing leaders' spiritual commitment would mean that you might be curious about such behaviors as these:

- frequency of worship attendance
- how they demonstrate love toward others
- leadership of and participation in various groups (e.g. small groups, adult education classes, teaching children, singing in the choir)
- how they welcome and encourage newcomers to the congregation to get involved
- their knowledge of scripture and theology

- their comfort with public prayer and talking about their faith
- their humility and courage in discussing various issues
- if they have a very narrow partisan agenda
- their ability to envision and implement new forms of ministry

So, difficult as it might be, try to assess the spiritual commitment and maturity of leaders.

Next you need to assess how capable leaders are. Are they skilled enough that members respect them and follow their leadership? I graduated from seminary in 1968. While it was a tumultuous time, most congregations had solid lay leaders who had been longtime members and understood how the congregation should work. Concerned that too many pastors were trying to be corporate CEOs and confident that the lay leaders were capable of running their congregations, congregational leadership experts and seminary professors urged pastors to be "enablers," that is, to enable lay leaders to take real leadership. Pastors didn't need to lead. I bought into that idea—and suspect that many other new pastors became "enablers," expecting capable lay leaders to do the real leading while they studied and did pastoral care.

While this hands-off leadership approach might have worked at some point, it certainly doesn't now. Think of the dizzying changes that have swept our culture. Families no longer put practicing their faith on Sunday morning ahead of soccer or swimming or other sports. Going camping or white water rafting trumps being in worship. Many teens and twenty-somethings are very leery of religion in general. They are turned off by the atrocities fanatics commit in the name of religion, and most mainline worship doesn't move them as much as the concert they heard the previous week. Among the many opportunities competing for their attention, organized religion simply isn't important to the majority of young adults.

Most congregations with which I have worked include a mix of leaders. Some are very competent. They understand the denominational and congregational systems. Others have been part of the congregation but don't know how to lead in a congregation. Further, congregations have often embraced middle-aged newcomers. Some of these are new to faith; others dropped out of organized religion as teens and young adults, and now, finding new meaning in faith, enthusiastically embrace their new congregation. Responding to the newcomers' enthusiasm, current leaders invite them to become leaders. However, these new leaders often have little idea how congregations function effectively, nor do they know anything about denominational beliefs'and polity.

An interim pastor told me about one such new member, a sales executive who was chairing the mission study in her congregation. The executive focused on doing market research to determine how best to reach the demographic segment in the neighborhood. "How do we get more people in the pews?" was the question. She had no knowledge of or interest in the Great Commandment or Great Commission. The interim pastor had to press the committee to consider these biblical and theological principles so that the pastor search committee would find a pastor whose theology fit the congregation.

Without proper education as to what competencies are needed to lead a congregation, these newcomers and many long-time members expect the skills that serve them well as leaders in other dimensions of their lives to serve well in leading a congregation. How well do those weekday skills work? Sometimes they work well. An elementary school teacher leads the children's education program. A banker steps right into a financial management position. However, sometimes the transferred skills don't work so well. One friend of mine who served a congregation with a number of leaders who were lobbyists observed, "Skills that serve well on K Street in Washington don't work very well in leading a congregation!"

Effective congregational leaders need to be competent and spiritually committed. Even when leaders are deeply committed to Christ, if they aren't competent, the congregation is in trouble. Sometimes they are competent but don't have the commitment to lead. How might you assess leaders' competence and commitment? In what areas are they competent? Your challenge as a new pastor is to assess both the motivation and skills of leaders. What gifts do they bring to their leadership? How can you help them work together? Just as an orchestral conductor draws out this violinist or that horn player as necessary, an effective pastor leads the congregation—and especially top leaders—in a kind of symphony that brings out their best gifts and skills in different situations. Your challenge is to get all the musicians playing together!

Members of the board of the condominium in which I live are all highly competent and committed in areas of property management and finances. What a gift they are to us residents! That they aren't particularly interested in forming a sense of community among residents (or competent to do so) isn't terribly important. Congregations require competencies different from those of a condo board. Competencies in a congregation might include managing property and finances, designing opportunities for education and spiritual growth, building community building and offering hospitality, planning music and worship, and responding to people in the community who are hurting in both body and spirit.

What range of competencies have you already identified? What seems to be missing? In one small congregation with which I am familiar, nobody was able to oversee the maintenance of a fairly large building. Leaders were pressed into doing jobs for which they had neither interest nor competence.

TOOL 6: THE COMPETENCE-COMMITMENT GRID

A simple tool for assessing leadership is the competence-commitment grid (see table 4.1). Competence increases from left to right; commitment from bottom to top. You might think about members of your board and, noting their areas of competence, place them on the grid, in the spot that indicates their degree of commitment and competence.[2]

Optimally, every leader will be highly competent and highly committed. Such a leader simply needs the pastor to be a cheerleader and occasional consultant. Each facet of the congregation will have formal and informal leaders who are both competent and committed. However, in most congregations leaders exhibit a range of competence and commitment. After you have assessed leaders' competencies and commitments, then you will have some idea of whom you can count on to be effective leaders and what leader education is needed to raise competence levels of those who aren't so competent.

I think it is important for a pastor to actively seek to get the most competent and committed leaders to serve on the governing board. How you accomplish that depends on your congregational/denominational system, but a board made up of highly competent and committed leaders dramatically strengthens a congregation. Does your congregation have a congregational officer nominating committee? If so, what is the pastor's role? Presbyterian pastors are automatically ex-officio members of the nominating committee. While I normally didn't press for certain people to be nominated to the board, I suggested promising younger members and also discouraged the committee from nominating any who were caught up in personal turmoil and who wouldn't be able to serve at this time or who simply could not play well in the sandbox with others. Regardless, I always encouraged nominating committees to seek those who were spiritually and emotionally mature. And I also helped the nominating committee review the competencies of those remaining on the board and to identify new board members who had gifts and skills to complement those of the ongoing members. For example, if a board member who knew everything about the building was retiring, we would make sure to nominate a new member with similar knowledge or at least the potential of gaining it.

If the officer nominating committee couldn't fill all the positions that the structure expected because qualified people declined to be nominated, then I

Table 4.1

Low competence—High commitment	High competence—High commitment
Low competence—Low commitment	High competence—Low commitment

would tell the committee that they should report this to the board and suggest that perhaps the board needed to examine the congregation's structure. Perhaps the congregation didn't really need all those officers, and they needed to change their structure. I will discuss issues of structure in chapters 8 and 9.

As you think about current leaders' competence and commitment, what do you conclude? Are there leaders who are both competent and committed to oversee the various ministries of the congregation—education, financial and property management, evangelism, and so forth? In what areas are there weaknesses?

TOOL 7: THE MYERS-BRIGGS TYPE INDICATOR

Though I have not had significant training in its use, another helpful tool to assess the leadership is the Myers-Briggs Type Indicator (MBTI), one of the most widely used temperament/personality instruments. Based on the work of Karl Jung, Katherine Cook Briggs and her daughter, Isabel Briggs Myers, developed this fairly simple instrument in the 1940s. It gives important clues about how you think and behave and what you are inclined to do well. If you haven't taken this inventory, I strongly encourage you to do it. Most metropolitan areas have persons certified as MBTI administrators. You can also find assessments online.

The instrument identifies four polarities.

Attitudes: Extraversion or Introversion

This polarity has to do with one's orientation to the world and others. One who is more extraverted (E) draws energy from interacting with others. An introverted type (I) is drained by being with people and needs time to think and reflect. As a pretty strong E, I get a little stir crazy when I'm stuck in the house for several days. I need to get together with friends and colleagues.

Functions: Sensing/iNtuition and Thinking/Feeling

Sensing/iNtuition

This scale assesses how people gather information. S (sensing) types notice details without trying. They prefer information they can see, touch, hear and otherwise gather themselves. N (iNtuitive) types see the big picture, looking for patterns, trying to understand the underlying theory, and combining ideas to create new possibilities. I joke that my wife, Mary Helen, and I can walk through a room and Mary Helen (a strong S), without consciously trying, notices the temperature of the room, both thermal and emotional, the expression on people's faces, what they are wearing, and so on. On the other hand, I (a strong N) focus on whatever lofty thoughts are occupying me and don't notice anything (unless I decide to focus on specific things in the room)!

Thinking/Feeling

This function indicates how people make decisions once they have gathered information. Do you decide with your head (thinking [T]) or with your heart (feeling [F])? Does logic guide your decision-making process, or do your relationships and the impact of your decision on particular people guide your decisions? I tend to be in the center of this continuum. I value research and data, but my feelings often have the upper hand. My preference depends on the issue.

Orientation to the Outer World Judging/Perceiving

This polarity has to do with whether you prefer making decisions about information (judging) or leaving decisions open to more information (perceiving). J (judging) types (of which I am one) don't like loose ends flapping in the breeze. We like things well structured and organized. P (perceiving) types tend to sit loose in the saddle. Keep gathering and processing information and don't close any doors prematurely. Keep your options open in order to make the best decision. Note that "judging" doesn't mean "judgmental." Nor does "perceiving" mean "more perceptive than most." The poles describe how we prefer to represent ourselves to others. I may be very J on the outside, but inside be very flexible. Or I may appear to be very flexible and open, while having a very firm agenda.

Most people are close to the middle of each polarity continuum, but some are very inclined to one pole. For example, I am inclined to the E side of the E-I polarity, but my T and F are very near the middle. Regardless of what your preference indicate, it is very important to recognize that one pole is not better than the other. These are simply ways of describing how people see the world and interact with others.

These four polarities can be put together into 16 temperaments that help people understand themselves and others. I have learned that as an ENTJ, I have to take care to keep my mouth shut, not interrupt, and listen carefully when a more introverted person presents a carefully crafted thought and explains it or struggles to put a not so clear thought into words. I have to be patient when one who prefers to gather information (a P) takes longer than I would to make a decision. I have learned to value those strong S types who attend to details and ask the hard questions about how to get from A to Z in my grand plan. They anchor me to reality. On the other hand, I help lift their eyes from the immediate to what might be. They need me! I have found this tool immensely helpful in building understanding among leaders. They suddenly realize that other people aren't trying to drive them crazy! They're just being who they are!

One caveat regarding the MBTI: I have known people who, after they see their results, declare that this is who they are and that nothing can change it. "Well, I'm a strong introvert, so nobody should expect me to go out and visit people. It's just not who I am!" "I'm an N," so I can't attend to details; don't expect me to be able to read a budget."

As I have matured, I am much more comfortable being by myself, even learning to meditate and journal. I have learned to keep track of financial details. And I'm sitting looser in the saddle, telling myself that "all will become clear." I encourage you to learn your Myers-Briggs temperament and then seek to grow your shadow, less dominant side.

How does this help you assess yourself and leaders? With the caution that we should not rigidly apply these categories, your knowing that a leader is a more introverted, intuitive, feeling-oriented person might mean you can depend on that person to be more empathic. One who is more sensing/thinking/judging might be especially helpful in handling finances. If the vast majority of members of the board are introverts, they may have difficulty leading a newcomer outreach program.

Knowing your own type and that of the board members will help you assess the leadership gifts already in members of the board. You can then help them use those gifts and find others not on the board who complement the gifts of the board members.

TOOL 8: THE GALLUP STRENGTHSFINDER

Another helpful tool for assessing leadership strengths comes from the Gallup organization. Gallup researchers define a strength as a combination of talent, knowledge, and skill.[3] All are necessary for something to be considered a real strength. I think of athletes who show amazing raw talent in high school or college but don't work hard enough to grow in their knowledge or skill to really develop this talent into a strength. Top athletes who keep working with a coach to develop improve their play. Odds are that you have seen pastors who are gifted but don't keep growing. I have known pastors who have a remarkable gift for public speaking but who don't work to develop sermons that are biblically and theologically solid. Rather, they weave together moving stories and poetry into a nice speech. They say *nothing* beautifully.

Gallup researchers identify 34 key strengths of leadership and group them into four domains of dominant strengths. Some of the strengths are commonly used attributes, such as responsibility and self-assurance; others are unique to the Gallup model. Unfortunately, I cannot reproduce them in this book, but you can easily find the model on the internet by searching for "strengths based leadership." Key insights are that people should develop their top strengths and manage their weaknesses, and that the most successful leadership teams have a good blend of strengths.

I encourage you to get the book *Strengths-Based Leadership*.[4] When you buy it, you will receive a code that enables you to go online and take a StrengthsFinder weighted-pair inventory, which will then identify your top five strengths. The three-page report I received was quite fascinating. I found myself saying, "What's this? Why that one and not the other?" The report gave me lots to think about.

One of my clients who took the StrengthsFinder found that he had virtually no strengths in an area having to do with strategic planning. This insight was especially important, since the governing board of his congregation was pressing him to develop such a plan for the congregation. He just couldn't seem to get started. When I asked him if there were any leaders in his congregation who obviously had these gifts, he replied, "Sure, I can think of several." The next time we talked, he told me that he had recruited two leaders to organize a strategic planning process and had said, "You guys plan it and I'll sell it." He had considerable strengths in relationship building and communication. He was a salesman!

The Gallup researchers declare that you should work to grow your top strengths rather than wasting time growing in an area where you simply have little or no talent. (Consequently, I call a plumber rather than doing it myself.)

IMPLICATIONS FOR A MULTIPLE STAFF CONGREGATION

If you are a new pastor of a multiple staff congregation, I encourage you and your staff members to do both the MBTI and StrengthsFinder and discuss your insights. As a staff, reflect on how your strengths mesh with each other and those of other leaders in the congregation. Then make sure that there are leaders whose strengths complement yours. If you're a bit disorganized, then it's important to employ someone, such as an administrative assistant (AA), who will help keep you organized. If you're seen as cold and analytical, then you need an AA who is warm and welcoming. If you tend to be more introspective, sometimes taking too much time to make a decision, then an associate pastor who will help you realize that you have enough data to make a good decision is invaluable. In chapter 2, I mentioned an associate pastor in a 3,000-member congregation who knew everyone's name; what a help he was to the head of staff.

Assessing both your strengths and those of other staff members will help you work with the board more effectively. For example, if most of the members of the board are not too organized, then you may need either to draw on your own or a staff member's organizational strengths or find some informal leaders who will get things better organized. Conversely, if the board is largely made up of business leaders who are very results oriented, then you may need to draw on your gifts to connect and encourage.

COACHING ASSIGNMENT 9: USING THE COMPETENCE-COMMITMENT GRID

Draw a simple Competence-Commitment Grid.

1. Based on your experience of the leaders so far (both staff and lay leaders), where would you place them on this grid?
2. What more might you need to know about their competence and commitment, especially regarding their spiritual maturity and commitment. You might review the list of behaviors that indicate spiritual maturity and commitment earlier in this chapter and adapt it your situation. Then listen and observe. Be curious.
3. Clarify the areas in what they are especially competent and committed.
4. Assess their emotional and spiritual maturity.
5. Consider the tasks that need doing to keep the congregation functioning well, and determine if there any significant vacuums in leadership. Decide how you will address these.
6. Decide what leader education opportunities you will either design or organize to both strengthen competence and commitment. Who might help you lead this training?
7. Decide how you will address any concerns about those who are neither motivated nor competent—elected perhaps because nobody else would say "yes." How can you minimize their negative impact while leading them to deeper commitment?

COACHING ASSIGNMENT 10: USING THE MYERS-BRIGGS TYPE INDICATOR

- Using one of the online instruments or meeting with a trained Myers-Briggs facilitator, learn your Myers-Briggs temperament, but don't hold it too tightly. Outline some of its implications for your leadership
- If congregational leaders are amenable, have them do the MBTI. (Many have probably already done it.)

- Have a conversation with leaders about their insights, both about them-selves and each other. How does the MBTI help them understand you and each other better? I suggest that you have a half-day retreat led by a facilitator to discuss these insights.
- Encourage leaders to reflect on how their spiritual gifts are manifested in their type. For example, an ESFJ might have the gift of caring, or an INTJ might have a real gift for managing finances to do the work of Christ.

COACHING ASSIGNMENT 11: USING THE GALLUP STRENGTHSFINDER

Take the Gallup StrengthsFinder by buying *Strengths-Based Leadership*, ob-taining your unique password, and then taking the online weighted-pair ques-tionnaire, which will give you your top five strengths.

- Reflect on your top five strengths. Notice how these strengths are mani-fested in your work already. For example, if you have a number of strengths in the relationship domain, then you are probably empathic and enjoy working with people. Perhaps others turn to you to strengthen exist-ing relationships and build new ones. What strengths surprised you?
- Consider the other strengths and guess what your next five strengths might be.
- How might you be more intentional in using your leadership strengths? Be aware of strengths that you have taken for granted (e.g., strategic planning or influencing) that others don't seem to have. How might you use these strengths to build up the congregation?
- Identify what strengths you need to grow. What steps will you take to bring about that necessary growth? By when will you take these steps?

Now try guessing what strengths staff members and key leaders have. To what extent do members of the congregation's staff and lay leaders comple-ment each other and you? To what extent are leaders too much alike? What areas of expertise are underrepresented? How might you compensate for strengths that are not present but needed?

PRELIMINARY ASSESSMENTS ABOUT LEADERS

Interviews have given you important information about the leaders, both staff members and lay leaders, in this new congregation. You are working regular-ly with staff members. You have observed leaders in worship and various activities such as board and other meetings. You have a sense of which leaders are especially trustworthy and which aren't. You also have indications of the emotional and spiritual commitment and maturity of the formal leaders.

By using the tools in this chapter to assess their strengths and commitment, especially as they complement your and each others' strengths, you are getting a better sense of how to best relate to various leaders.

Chances are you have learned something about yourself too. I hope that you aren't in despair, thinking that you are a terrible fit for this congregation. Rather, I suspect that the Holy Spirit has moved and led you and this congregation together—you with your strengths and weaknesses and the congregation with its array of people with all their wonderful gifts and maddening idiosyncrasies!

With a clearer understanding of the individual strengths of leaders, now I want you to work on how you and the leaders work together as a team and lead this community of saints. How will you direct this orchestra to praise and serve God? With all this in mind, let's now move to another helpful tool for assessing the leadership of the congregation.

Chapter Five

Assessing the Leadership

The Five Dysfunctions of a Team

I live in Falls Church, Virginia, a suburb of Washington, D.C. The once mighty Washington Redskins had for several years been a pathetic shadow of their former selves. Week after week, fans were subjected to the spectacle of a quarterback desperately trying to escape charging defensive players, over-paid linemen whining about having to work too hard, and a dysfunctional relationship between the team's owner, team management, and coach. In short, they didn't play as a real team.

How well do your leaders function as a team?

In a small, solo-pastor congregation, the primary leadership team may be the pastor and the board. A larger, multiple-staff congregation has several interlocking teams—the pastoral and professional staff; the broader staff, including support personnel; and then the board and various committees. Regardless of size, it's important that leaders work together as a team. That's easy to say but harder to realize!

There's the board where one person dominates, or the board where two people hate each other. I moderated a board meeting in a very conflicted congregation where one person told me before the meeting that she was probably leaving the congregation because some members of the board had treated the pastor so badly. At the end of the meeting some members came up to me and started ranting about how awful the pastor had been and how he needed to be held accountable and shouldn't even be a minister anymore. I think of congregations where the director of music won't speak to the organ-ist or the preschool director refuses to come to staff meetings. I think of pastors and associate pastors who have no respect for each other or where one feels threatened by the other. So as you assess the leadership of your new congregation you need not only to assess their individual competence and commitment, but how they work together. To what extent is your governing board or staff really a leadership *team*?

THE FIVE DYSFUNCTIONS OF A TEAM

Patrick Lencioni, in his book, *The Five Dysfunctions of a Team*, identifies characteristics of dysfunctional teams:

- lack of trust
- fear of conflict
- lack of commitment
- avoidance of accountability
- inattention to results [1]

Lencioni arranges these issues in a pyramid, with "lack of trust" at the bottom, because it is the foundation for the others, and "inattention to results" at the top.

Do you ever describe your board or staff using phrases like these? I outlined these dysfunctions for the board of one congregation soon after I started working with them. They laughed and said, "That's exactly the way we were operating!" They had just gone through a process to remove a pastor who was behaving very erratically and were only too aware that they hadn't been working well together. They and I understood that they needed to change their behavior.

DYSFUNCTION 1—LACK OF TRUST

I addressed the importance of trust in chapter 3. While it is vital in the congregation at large, it is absolutely critical among leaders. What are your initial readings of the trust level among leaders? Are they open and spontaneous or guarded? Is there easy humor and laughter (an indicator of trust) or heaviness and sarcasm?

Do members of the board deal openly with differences, or do they avoid them and have parking lot sub-meetings after the meeting? Are there signs that people have emailed or talked over the phone with one another, forming alliances against others?

To what extent do some leaders use the board's rules (bylaws, constitution, and the like) to get their way, perhaps to overrule or simply disregard what others think?

How nervous are leaders about introducing change? As I noted in chapter 3, secrets or betrayals in a congregation typically lead to great resistance to change. Another clue that there is a whole lot more to some story is that people are unwilling to talk about it.

By now you may think I'm a trust nut. If you do, you are most correct! I am a trust nut because I've seen erosion of trust cause terrible problems in quite a number of congregations. I have seen pastors forced out of their parishes and congregations split. Such ruptures are terribly expensive—emotionally, financially, and especially spiritually. When church leaders are not trustworthy, we undermine trust in the Lord.

When staff members trust one another and they and the board form a trusting team, then that trust spreads to the congregation. Conversely, trust also spreads *up* to the leadership. I think of one congregation that formed a strong network of small groups. Group participants "checked-in" with each other at each meeting, briefly sharing what was happening in their lives outside of congregational activities. Because several members of the board had experienced how this built trust in the small groups, they began to "check-in" with each other at board meetings. They learned how important it was to really get to know one another and pray for one another. This awareness changed the atmosphere of the board meetings from one of simply doing business to really being brothers and sisters in faith.

One colleague told me that when he came to his congregation, the board meetings lasted for three hours. He told them he wanted to introduce a time of singing and prayer to begin their meetings and was initially met with resistance, but when the board began their meetings this way, they found that the meeting duration actually decreased! They had built more trust based on deeper common faith and consequently were able to conduct their meetings more efficiently.

Particularly if there has been some conflict in the congregation, you need to begin building trust among leaders is in their meetings. Here are some exercises and practices I have found effective when working with a board that can be adapted for staff and other situations.

TOOL 9: SHARING BIBLE STUDY

Often called *Lectio Divina or African Bible Study*, a short, small-group Bible study at the beginning of a meeting builds trust, encourages participants to wrestle with how God is speaking to them individually and as leaders, and also quickly involves those who arrive early or on time. They don't have to make small talk while waiting for a few late arrivers.

Select a fairly short scripture passage (five to eight verses) that you think would be helpful to board members and print three translations of it on a sheet of paper. Add the following instructions and then, as people enter the meeting room, put them in groups of three to four and hand them the following instructions. Plan to take about 20 minutes for this as an opening activity. It is important to limit the size of the group to no more than four so that everyone can have an opportunity to speak and pray and be prayed for.

Each small group follows this process:

1. Someone reads the passage aloud. All reflect silently on it for 2 minutes.
2. Share with one another a word or phrase that strikes you. No discussion. (1 minute)
3. Someone else reads the passage aloud, using another translation. All reflect again for about 2 minutes.
4. Each person shares a word or phrase that touches your life and briefly explains its meaning to you. (1 to 2 minutes each)
5. Someone else reads the passage aloud using another translation.
6. Reflect individually on how, through this scripture, God seems to be leading you or your congregation. (1 to 2 minutes each)
7. Take turns praying for each other, using insights and commitments that emerged in the conversation as a basis for your prayer. (3 minutes)

A similar tool is E. Stanley Ott's *Word/Share/Prayer* exercise. A copy of that and a link to 80 *Word/Share/Prayer* sheets is in Appendix E. This tool is designed to take 21 minutes.

TOOL 10: SHARING FORMATIVE SCRIPTURE PASSAGES

Ask each board member to identify two scripture passages that have been important to them, perhaps one that has strengthened and comforted them, challenged them, or has become a foundation stone of their faith. Over the course of as many meetings as necessary, ask board members to take turns sharing the scripture and telling why they are important. It is important that you, the new pastor, go first in order to model both the depth and the length of this sharing. Suggest that they take five to seven minutes each. If you have several staff members, do this exercise in staff meetings or on a staff retreat to strengthen your staff team.

I have found that this very simple exercise is especially helpful in bridging gaps between liberals and conservatives. I first used it in a group of pastors, both liberal and conservative, who (myself included) were being somewhat snarky in presbytery meetings. The six of us took turns sharing passages over three lunch meetings. (Being preachers, we took closer to 20 minutes each). As we got to know one another better, the conservatives realized that we who are more liberal had a deep relationship with God, and those of us who were liberal recognized that the conservatives weren't un-thinking literalists. Further, we came to realize that the very terms "liberal" and "conservative" were pretty meaningless. For example, I take the Bible very seriously and find God speaking through it. I've been married to the same woman for fifty years and am pretty fiscally frugal (some would call me cheap!). Does that make me a conservative? On the other hand, I think it is very important to interpret scripture in light of new understanding of what the biblical authors were saying, juxtaposing those insights with current events and my own experience. I have been a peacenik and civil rights advocate. I think it's critical to control gun violence. So am I a liberal? Most of us embody a mixture of different ideas and opinions.

When board members share their formative scriptures verses, they will often make themselves remarkably vulnerable. I recall one leader who cited Psalm 23, noting how much it helped when her husband died. Another de-scribed how Jesus telling disciples to love their enemies helped him deal with difficult people at his job. He was startled when, after listening to and pray-ing for those who were difficult, he understood them better and found them not so difficult!

TOOL 11: SHARING A LIFE CHALLENGE

Over several meetings or perhaps on a retreat, invite members to tell their colleagues about some challenge they have faced and how they dealt with it, either positively or negatively, and, if appropriate, how their faith helped them deal with it.

Since everyone has had to deal with challenges this exercise is especially helpful if the group is quite diverse in educational or socioeconomic level. When I helped organize a 50th reunion for the class of 1959 at Mt. Vernon High School (in Missouri), we planners realized that some of us had ad-vanced education and had traveled widely while others had no post–high school education, choosing to stay on the farm on which they grew up. So we invited members of the class to share challenges. One classmate told of having to deal with a fire that ultimately sank a minesweeper on which he was the officer on duty; he was afraid he'd be court-martialed. A woman who had married a classmate and stayed on the family farm said, "Being married to Ray for 50 years was my greatest challenge, and I dealt with it through cussedness and determination!"

In an urban congregation leaders may include long-time members and immigrants, those with advanced degrees and some with little education, some who are quite wealthy financially and others who are struggling. This exercise builds trust across many divisions.

TOOL 12: SHARING SOMETHING ABOUT YOUR CHILDHOOD AND YOUNG ADULTHOOD

Share with others what work your parents did, about your first elementary school, about your first car, your first job as a young person, and so forth.

TOOL 13: LARGE FLOOR EXERCISES

A large floor exercise is an activity in which people use their bodies to show what they think or how they feel about something. I like doing large floor exercises with leaders on retreats to get them to talk about how they perceive their strength as a team. Here's how it works with the issue of trust.

After introducing the "five dysfunctions" pyramid, ask the leaders to array themselves in a rough line across the room. Point to one wall and say something like, "I want you to stand over there if you think members of our board feel the highest degree of trust possible toward one another." Then point to the opposite wall and say, "And if you think members of the board do not trust one another at all, stand over there. Or you may stand somewhere along the continuum. Stand roughly where you think the level of trust is."

After they array themselves (and you place yourself somewhere on the line), ask them to discuss what they see. For example, participants might observe that they are pretty trusting or untrusting or that there is a bit of divide between old timers and newcomers.

- Invite those who are at one end to engage in conversation with those at the other end.
- You might say "I see Jim over here. Your sense is that board members really trust one another. And Mary is over there. Mary, you apparently have serious reservations about the trust level among members of the board. Would you two please have a conversation describing how you observe trust or lack of trust as we operate as a board?" As they have a conversation, encourage them and then other board members to be curious about why people have different perspectives.
- As members converse, encourage them to explore the reasons that board members either trust or mistrust one another. Ask what barriers they see to building trust and what can be done to eliminate those barriers.
- Ask, "How does trust or mistrust among board or staff members reflect trust or mistrust in the congregation?"
- Some of my clients describe boards in which a few members see themselves as representatives of the more traditional members of the congregation, and others identify themselves as the progressive caucus. Another division I have seen is between long-time Caucasian members and new

immigrants. Board members who see themselves as representatives of a particularly constituency often find it necessary to check with constituents before voting on an issue. Sometimes trust issues center around the previous pastor. If that pastor played politics and didn't build trust, then there is often a norm that "we line up our votes before the board meeting and make sure we get what we want." Try to be as descriptive as possible. Get members to describe what signs of trust or mistrust that they have seen and heard.

• Ask, "Why is building trust important?" five to seven times, each time building on the previous answer and digging deeper. Your objective is to lead them to understand the necessity of building trust.

I suggest you repeat the process with the other dysfunctions and explore why resolving differences, building ownership and mutual accountability, and clarifying desired results are important.

I have used large floor exercises with any number of issues for which there aren't clear solutions. For example, you might invite people to indicate whether they prefer more formal or less formal worship, or whether they think God is calling the board to engage in more social-justice advocacy or hands-on service.

In most cases, I suggest that you lead this exercise as I have described it. I assume people trust you as the new pastor. However, if the previous pastor fostered divisions and mistrust or if you have already done things to destroy trust, then you should have an outside facilitator.

TOOL 14: LEAD A STAFF AND/OR BOARD RETREAT

Retreats, especially overnight, are great venues for building trust. They help people really get to know one another. I recommend off-site retreats, even if in another congregation's building. It is easy to get distracted on your home turf. I suggest that you have one within your first six months. Three of the exercises above, Sharing Formative Scripture Passages, Sharing a Life Challenge, and Large Floor Exercises, are well suited for retreats.

On your retreat, take significant time for members to tell about their spiritual journeys. I have done this in several ways. For example, on one board retreat, I simply invited people to tell the others about their spiritual journeys. We began this exercise at about 7:30 p.m. on a Friday evening at a conference center. Though we had planned for this to end around 10:00 p.m., people got into it so deeply that we went until midnight. There was a lot of laughter, some tears, some very profound conversation.

You can imagine that when a woman tells about her tumultuous adolescence and young adulthood, fellow members will understand how she is so effective in working with teens. When a man describes his climbing back after bankruptcy, members get new insight into his frugality, which previously had seemed excessive.

On some retreats I have provided lists of significant scripture passages and suggested that people select three to five from the list that represented important events in their lives. So, for example, one person might choose the story of Abram and Sarai leaving Ur, saying that the story reminded them of leaving home and family and moving to this new city. Another person might use that same story to talk about changing careers, feeling that God was leading in a new direction. If your congregation has a stack of pictures illustrating Bible stories, you might spread those over several tables and invite people to select three to five pictures that reflect their faith journey.

Tip 9: Ask "Why is this important?"

As you reflect with leaders on their trust level, ask the question, "Why is building trust important?" five to seven times, each time building on the previous answer and digging deeper. For example, the first time you ask, someone might say, "So I won't have to watch my back." Follow up with "And why is that important?" Someone else responds, "So we are safe and can work through problems together." Follow up with "Why is it important that we work through problems?" "So we can accomplish something and not be like Congress!" "And why shouldn't we be like Congress?" "So we can be the church—a little like the people Jesus wants us to be!"

Asking "Why is that important?" leads to a much deeper understanding of the deep reasons for being in community and the core values of the participants. This process builds energy and clarity.

COACHING ASSIGNMENT 12: BUILDING TRUST

Assess the trust level in your staff or leadership team beginning with yourself. Then choose and implement some steps for building trust.

- Work through the "Why is this important?" exercise for yourself. Why is having a high trust level in the board important to you?
- Commit yourself to being vulnerable in the leadership team. Your being open, acknowledging that you don't have all the answers, and being able to laugh about yourself and speak movingly about how your faith has helped you through some tough times will help others open up and be more trusting.
- Decide what exercise(s) you will use to help build trust among staff or board members. One of the tools I described above? Something else? How

will you introduce this idea to the group? How will you describe its importance—especially to that board member who simply wants to gets the business done and go home? Make sure there are ongoing practices that build trust.

DYSFUNCTION 2—FEAR OF CONFLICT

When members of the board are afraid of conflict, there is a very high probability that bad decisions will be made that may well sabotage any progress. If members of a leadership team are afraid to disagree with one or two strong leaders, then they may withhold important information, resulting in bad decisions being made. A relatively new administrative assistant in a congregation in which I was a new interim pastor gave a strong-willed member permission to schedule his daughter's wedding for a Saturday on which the social hall and parking lot was going to be occupied by nearly a hundred square dancers! She was afraid to tell the member that the building was not available. I didn't catch the schedule conflict until two weeks before the big day. This sent us all scrambling! We then set up procedures to make sure that unpleasant truths were voiced.

I think of a fight-phobic congregation that was given a large bequest to buy a new pipe organ. Led by the musician (who was primarily an organist), they bought an organ that was much too large for the sanctuary. He had a wonderful instrument on which to practice his craft, but its sheer physical presence dominated the chancel, obscured a lovely stained glass window, and prevented easy use of videos.

A group in another congregation mounted a campaign to construct a building that would rival the megachurch across town. It featured an auditorium with expensive audio-visual equipment, projection screens, and so forth. They could have rousing contemporary worship (as they defined "contemporary"). However, some long-time members hated the idea and vigorously resisted the proposal. Because leaders didn't work out differences effectively, the pastor and most of those who wanted this new kind of worship and worship space were driven out of the congregation by the old-timers.

One colleague told me of a congregation in which members of an extended family controlled things so tightly in his small town that those new to both town and congregation were afraid to voice their concerns. These fearful members made comments such as, "It could cost me my job," "My son wouldn't make the high school team," and "They could put me out of business."

Members of the congregation will face competing commitments. Leaders might be wrestling with whether to pay for a youth worker or to employ someone to build a praise music group. Perhaps the roof needs fixing, so leaders wonder if mission giving should be cut to pay for the repairs. Leaders (including you) are pulled first one way and then another.

Members and leaders of congregations might be divided over hot social issues (especially in diverse mainline congregations). The style of worship and music generates friction between generations. You might want to introduce livelier music and some older members deem it too frivolous and younger members think of that same music as their parents' music and not like it! Whenever there are plans that affect the building, there are differences, especially if you are planning a major addition, but even changing the color of the sanctuary walls or carpet can create angst. People disagree about how the new pastor should allocate time and priorities. The annual budget is often the venue in which various competing commitments play out.

When leadership teams are afraid of conflict and cannot deal effectively with differences, leaders and members engage in backstabbing, e-mail barrages, parking lot gossip sessions, manipulative politics, turf battles, and the like. Such behavior is extremely demoralizing, exhausting, and disillusioning. I recall one earnest leader who, under attack, remarked, "I shouldn't have to watch my back in church like I do at work! I can't stay in this place any longer!"

Sometimes a kind of phony niceness paralyzes a board. Members think that Christians should never disagree or that they should never say anything that might upset someone else, so they keep quiet when they disagree with a proposed decision. Be clear—I am not saying that being kind and generous is bad, but fake niceness undermines effectiveness. "Pastor, that was such an interesting sermon" (while thinking, "I've never heard anything so outlandish"). "Mrs. Jones, I really appreciate your suggesting that we set aside a Sunday to recognize the Daughters of the American Revolution. I'll ask the worship committee to explore the idea" (while thinking, "Over my dead body will we do that!"). A Cheshire Cat smile and an over-the-top need to be nice indicates fear of conflict.

When members of a board know how to have good fights, they recognize that they will have differences and address those differences straight-forwardly. They respect each others' points of view, listening respectfully to what the other is saying. They seek the best solution for the congregation and to further the mission of Christ. More than disagreeing without being disagreeable (not a bad start!), they come up with mutually satisfactory solutions. Recall Paul telling his readers, "Speak the truth in love, to be angry but not sin, to not let the sun set on their anger" (Eph. 4:15). Paul certainly dealt with differences in the first congregations!

Do members of the board and staff know how to have good fights, or do they have only bad fights? Once trust is built (or at least begun to build), then leaders need to and can learn how to fight effectively. I encourage you to assess whether members of your board are fight phobic or are able to deal effectively with their differences.

Tip 10: Be aware of your internal reactions and your external responses to stress.

A key to dealing with differences effectively is that leaders (especially you, the pastor) know how to handle their own anxiety. To the extent that you become anxious and reactive, you feed the group's anxiety and conflict will build. Conversely, even though you are anxious inside, when you portray a nonanxious presence and lead with curiosity and imagination, then the group's anxiety and conflict will begin to subside. What are your emotional default reactions? With whom might you discuss your own anxiety before you start dealing with that of others? What are possible ways of handling both your internal stress and the external stressor? (I discuss handling anxiety further in chapter 7.)

Peter Steinke, following the lead of his mentor, Rabbi Edwin Friedman, deals masterfully with the role of anxiety in boards. He suggests that anxiety is like a virus. When leaders come under stress and don't handle their anxiety, the vibrations go everywhere in the board. Their survival instincts kick in and members are convulsed in a fight or flight crisis. Conversely, when leaders are mature and recognize that stress and anxiety are normal, then they can calm people down and engage their best selves. I encourage you to read one (or more) of Steinke's books. (See the bibliography for specific resources.[2])

I typically encourage clients to be aware of their internal reactions to stress and their external response and then carefully manage their own anxiety. With that start, they can help people fight effectively and fairly.

TOOL 15: GROUNDING YOURSELF

How might leaders deal with anxiety? First, ground yourself spiritually so that you quiet your own anxiety. I find that the Taizé chant, "Come and Fill Our Hearts with Your Peace," helps me ground myself in God's peace when I am in an anxious situation or a simple prayer for myself and those with whom I differ will often suffice.[3]

TOOL 16: EXPLORING STRESS COMMUNICATION STYLES

How do you communicate when you are under stress, especially if you feel threatened? I have observed that some people shut down, others start talking more loudly, and still others change the subject. It's really hard to deal with differences and solve problems when we're in these reactive modes. Virginia Satir, a pioneer family therapist, asserts that virtually everyone has default stress communication styles that get in the way of open communication. Our words and bodies don't fit with one another. Without thinking, we go automatically to one or two of four modes. By knowing our default style, we are then more able to be aware that we are lapsing into automatic reaction and not thinking clearly. Here are Satir's four default stress communication styles:

• Blamer—blames everyone else for the problem
• Placater—takes everything on as if it were his or her fault
• Computer—shuts down emotionally and is coldly logical, not recognizing emotions
• Distracter—changes the subject ("Oh, look, what a lovely butterfly!")

Rather than lapsing into one of these default reactive modes, it is best to engage in "leveling or flowing" behavior. Satir writes, "In this response all parts of the message are going in the same direction—the voice says words that match the facial expression, the body position, and the voice tone. Relationships are easy, free and honest, and there are few threats to self-esteem."[4]

Here is a learning activity to help people understand their communication styles under stress.

Pass out a sheet describing the four default stress communication styles, explain them quickly, and show rough poses for each style (two minutes): (1) blamer—posture: scowl and point your finger at an offender; (2) placater—posture: get down on one knee, hold hands up in supplication, emoting "It's all my fault!"; (3) computer—posture: cross arms on chest with no facial expression; (4) distracter—posture: dance about, pointing here and there, exclaiming "Oh, look!"

Then divide the group into small groups of four. Tell them that they are four siblings. Their widowed mother, still living in the family home, is showing signs of dementia. They need to decide where she should live and with what level of support. Explain that groups will role-play this scenario four times, and group members will trade roles, so everyone will eventually play all four. Ask each person to adopt one of the four default styles to begin. (About 5 minutes)

Give participants five minutes to role-play a family meeting using the first role. Do three more rounds, so each person tries each default style. (Five minutes for each role configuration, 20 minutes total)

Ask each small group to discuss what happened in the role-plays. What did they learn about themselves? What are their default stress styles? (5 minutes)

Then gather the total group and share insights. Discuss what having straightforward, respectful, candid communication in such a family situation would look and feel like. Invite participants to identify times when they were aware they (themselves—not someone else) moved into a default stress communication style and how that impeded good communication. (20 minutes)

This exercise is often hysterically funny and can reveal a lot to people about themselves.

Tip 11: Learn how to have a good fight.

When I engaged in premarriage counseling, I always asked the couple "Have you learned how to fight?" I stressed how important it is for couples to develop effective ways to handle differences. The issue wasn't whether there were or would be differences. It was how they would deal with the differences. Methods and attitudes that work in a marriage also works with members of a leadership team. Here are some elements of good fights.

- Practicing respect, respect, respect. Look for any signs of disrespect and address them in the meeting or privately, as appropriate. Be curious: what is behind the disrespect? How might mutual respect be developed?
- Listening carefully to each other and making sure that each demonstrates an understanding of the other's position before responding. You might say something like, "Let's see if I understand you correctly, Jim. You are convinced that we need to fix the roof before we make a donation to the local food pantry. Right?" Model this type of response and encourage others to follow it.
- Figuring out what is behind any anger. Most psychologists and others trained in human relations declare that anger is a secondary emotion. People get angry when they are frustrated, put-down, sad, let down, frightened, and so forth. It is important to draw out that person who is upset (though perhaps not in the meeting itself).
- Being candid about personal motives for advocating a position. What is important and why? What in their experience generates their strong opinion?
- Avoiding name-calling, labeling, or psychoanalyzing.
- Generating and then improving alternatives, and then finding a mutually satisfactory solution to the issue.

Clarifying Mission and Vision

Clarifying God's yearning for this congregation call is also a critical part of dealing with differences and building a team. If your leaders don't have a sense of who God is calling them to be and what the priorities are, then they individually will pursue whatever they think is most important. One person might believe that the congregation exists to take care of her. Others might want the congregation to care for the poor or have the best teen program in town. Still another wants the congregation to be the base for his political aspirations. Lack of common purpose is a recipe for anxiety and frustration!

Writing for a business audience, Patrick Lencioni asserts that leaders must be absolutely clear about their organization's purpose, more specifically making the world a better place.

> In order to successfully identify their organization's purpose, leaders must accept the notion that all organizations exist to make people's lives better. . . . Nonetheless, every organization must contribute in some way to a better world for some group of people, because if it doesn't, it will, and should, go out of business.[5]

He makes this assertion about businesses! How much more his words apply to congregations!

If leaders aren't clear about what God's wish is for the congregation, then they cannot make effective decisions. At this point in your new ministry, I encourage you to assess how clear leaders are about the congregation's mission and vision. I'll deal more with assessing the congregation's mission and vision in chapter 8.

Tip 12: Develop ground rules with the board.

Work with board members to develop explicit ground rules and to discuss what behavior they expect of one another on this board. A helpful resource is "Guidelines for Presbyterians in Times of Disagreement."[6] If you don't set mutual expectations and hold people responsible for their actions, then you are setting yourself up for being bullied by the least emotionally mature people in the congregation (who sometimes get themselves elected to the board). A sample Covenant of Behavior is provided in appendix F. See chapter 10 for more thoughts on difficult people.

Be curious about seriously disrespectful or disruptive behavior. Initially you might explore the behavior with emotionally mature, respected leaders, saying something like, "I was surprised and dismayed by what happened in the meeting, where Jim was screaming at Mary. Nobody said anything or tried to calm him down. Has this behavior happened before? How might we do better?" Explore with mature leaders how best to handle those who disregard any behavioral covenant.

Tip 13: Don't take yourself too seriously.

Do you ever take yourself too seriously? I do. In the Washington, D.C., area, we see lots of politicians taking themselves too seriously. You see it wherever you live: corporate leaders, local politicians, doctors, helicopter parents, and wild drivers. Many congregations have those members who demand that the board or pastor accede to every whim and demand. Organizations with leaders who take themselves too seriously have a lot of trouble building trust and resolving differences. Leaders need to model vulnerability and humility and yet stand firm and not let themselves be bullied by self-important members.

Is your concern based mostly on personal or aesthetic preference or are you concerned about a foundational biblical or theological issue. You might be aware of unsafe stairs or a practice that jeopardizes safety. You need to be serious about such issues, but if you find yourself upset about matters of personal preference and minute points of theology, you may be taking yourself too seriously. So be especially careful not to inflict your musical preferences on the congregation, especially if there is a strong demand for a form you don't like. I heard of a director of music who opposed offering more contemporary music, declaring "contemporary music is of Satan!" He took himself much too seriously.

Identify who might help you take yourself less seriously. My wife of fifty years, our two sons and their wives, and more frequently, grandchildren, enthusiastically fulfill this responsibility for me (though I don't exactly recall ever inviting them to take it on). Further, scripture has a way of puncturing my pomposity when I get a bit too full of myself. Psalm 146:3 reminds us, "Do not put your trust in princes, in mortals in whom there is no help." I loved the Revised Standard Version's translation of Psalm 50:9a: "I will accept no bull from your house." You can make your list of passages that puncture pomposity!

COACHING ASSIGNMENT 13: DEALING WITH DIFFERENCES

1. Assess whether your board's leaders have good fights or bad fights. What behavior do you observe both in yourself and them? How are you handling your anxiety when people differ with you? Bring to mind a recent time you were anxious. What generated the anxiety? How were you threatened? To what extent does the person or situation generating your anxiety reflect the norms of the congregation and so cause you to wonder if you are in the wrong congregation? Are some simply being curious, questioning your particular interpretation of a scripture passage or theological precept? To what extent did you deal with the anxiety creatively or shut down emotionally? What are your default reactive modes? How does this experience and your reaction

resemble other times of anxiety? What spiritual practices help you manage your anxiety? How might you handle the stress better next time? Is someone attacking the very office of pastor, regardless of who the pastor is? See the later section on dealing with difficult people for some approaches to such concerns. Do people respect one another? What nonverbal expressions of respect or disrespect do you see? Family therapists have told me that if one spouse shows significant disrespect for the other (for example, smirks, shrugs, eye rolls, or other sarcastic gestures or comments), then the odds of the couple reconciling are significantly diminished. Do they listen carefully to each other, responding to one another in ways that show that they really hear the other's point of view? Do people freely express perspectives contrary to those others express? Do they make decisions to which they are committed or do they avoid making a decision? What body language do you observe after a decision is made? Are people smiling and talking with one another or tense and clustered in small groups? Or do they just walk out?

2. Have a significant conversation with the board about how they deal with differences. Perhaps use the large floor exercises or "Guidelines for Presbyterians in Times of Disagreement." Set mutual expectations with the board for handling differences.

3. Determine which people take themselves too seriously. Explore what is behind their behavior? How might you model not taking yourself too seriously, thus showing grace?

4. To the extent possible at this point, clarify your mission and vision. In board meetings discuss what they think God is yearning for them to be and do.

DYSFUNCTION 3—LACK OF COMMITMENT

Have you ever been in a meeting where the group seems to decide something but then demonstrates disapproval with their actions? I certainly have encountered this behavior. Especially when I was in my first solo pastorate, I would propose my latest and greatest idea and people would wax enthusiastically about how terrific it was and then never follow through. They were just being nice. They hadn't bought in. How do you make sure that leaders are committed to a common course of action? There are two dimensions to this: buy-in to the idea and clarity about what's being decided. First, it's critical that every member of the board or staff has an opportunity to offer input as you discuss the issue. They need to *weigh* in before they can *buy* in! Make sure that people ask whatever questions they have, express any concerns, and make suggestions for improvement. One approach I use is to propose my idea and then invite group members to improve it. I'll smile and say something like, "I *think* this is the best possible way to resolve this problem (achieve this goal, and the like), but I realize there is a *slight* possibility that it may not *really* be the best idea in the world. What ideas do you have for improving it?" People always jump in with both cautions about and improvements to my proposal.

Then, be very clear about what it is that you are deciding. Who is going to do what and by when? How will you know whether you've done it? I'll never forget Charles, who chaired a committee in the first congregation I served. At the conclusion of every meeting, he would quickly go around the table and summarize who had agreed to do what. This exercise, which took all of two to three minutes, clarified ownership and commitment.

As the leader, you need to build ownership so that there is close to board unanimity on decisions that affect a large percentage of the congregation. Some examples might be a major change in worship style or Sunday morning schedule. But be clear: *unanimity is not the same as consensus.* Unanimity means that every single person votes yes. Sometimes there is one hold-out. Listen carefully and do everything you can to work out a mutually satisfactory decision.

Achieving board unanimity on big decisions is easier if the congregation buys in to the plan. How might you assess the level of commitment in a congregation? I have found that listening to people in small group get-togethers or town meetings helps. Present the big idea and get feedback. Ask them how this initiative would strengthen the congregation and deepen discipleship. Invite participants to envision ways in which they might get involved. Read the nonverbal responses. What's the level of excitement? To what extent do they look irritated, bored, or alienated? Do those who disagree with the idea commit themselves to try it out? You don't have to get a yes from everyone in the congregation, but you need to make sure that most people are following you as leaders. Otherwise you aren't leading. You're just going off on your own tangent.

If almost all the members of the board aren't committed to the major decisions they make, then you and the board may encounter serious problems, especially in your first year or so. I think of several relatively new pastors who responded to requests to change worship dramatically and didn't build ownership. They ran into major opposition. If you take the time and build enthusiastic commitment, you're on your way!

Tip 14: Conclude the board or staff meeting by asking people to affirm any major decision.

Summarize what you decided and say something like, "We are agreed on this, right?" Watch for any backing off from the decision and ask if the group needs to delay implementing the decision until it is clearer that this decision is what the Lord is yearning for you to make.

A colleague described a board secretary for one congregation who always sent board members a summary chart after meetings. It had columns labeled "Action," "Responsible party," and "Due date." This simple tool clarified commitment and also led board members to hold one another accountable.

TOOL 17: HOLDING A TOWN MEETING

When the congregation is considering a major change, such as trying a different form of liturgy in the worship, I find it very helpful to hold a town meeting. First, respected members of the board present the proposed changes. Then the meeting facilitator invites interested members of the congregation to ask questions for clarification. The goal of this request is simply to makes sure people understand what they are discussing. Finally, the facilitator invites suggestions for improvement.

I worked with one congregation that tried having an informal service at 8:30 a.m. and a formal service at 11:00 a.m. After experimenting for four months, we held a town meeting and invited suggestions for improvement. One man who attended the early service said that he missed singing the traditional hymns. Another man grinned and responded, "Do you suppose that we who attend the 11:00 a.m. service could swap some of our traditional hymns with some of the praise songs you sing at 8:30 a.m.? I can't get my kids to worship by 8:30 a.m., and they like the livelier songs." After the ensuing laughter, we decided to have blended worship, a mixture of musical genres, at both services. By listening carefully and incorporating suggestions, we built ownership of the changes.

COACHING ASSIGNMENT 14:
INCREASING LEADERS' COMMITMENT

Assess the leadership teams in your new congregation (board, committees, and the like). What do you observe?

- Are people clear about decisions they make as a group?
- Do individuals commit themselves to specific actions that implement board decisions?
- What body language do you observe? Are people engaged? Are some turned away from the group?
- Do people follow through on their commitments?

Assess the effectiveness of proposals you have made to the board.

- How clearly do you present the idea and any necessary changes, costs, people resources?
- How well does your proposal implement the mission and vision of the congregation?
- How do individual members of the board typically respond to your proposals?
- How have you built ownership?
- How might you build more commitment?
- How do you affirm those who take ownership?

DYSFUNCTION 4—AVOIDANCE OF ACCOUNTABILITY

Once a board achieves a sense of commitment to its decisions, what next? It's important that members of the board hold each other accountable for implementing their commitments. For example, the Christian Education Committee chairperson might say to the worship committee chair something like, "Hey, Joe, three months ago, you said that you were going to find some ways of involving youth in worship leadership. When do you anticipate we'll see more youth helping lead worship? I think it's really important that some young people are up front on Sunday mornings."

Sometimes one or two board members will actively denigrate a decision they agreed to at the board meeting or perhaps engage in passive-aggressive opposition. When that happens I urge you to figure out with board members how you will hold each other accountable for such destructive behavior. I consulted with a pastor who complained about some members of the board who rarely attended worship. When I asked the pastor how he had attempted to deal with this, he gave me a helpless look. He had no idea how to hold the offenders accountability for their behavior. He had never led the board in any conversation about mutual accountability. His assessment was that these board members were undercutting his leadership—and he was probably correct.

The previously mentioned board covenant would likely state expectations about attending worship and other meetings. I would expect board members to be in worship almost every Sunday unless they are out of town and think most board members would expect that of one another. In addition, a covenant would lay out expectations for those times when there are serious differences. One congregation with which I worked wrote the following statement of accountability:

Our Promise to Each Other on the Session

We promise to treat our time on the Session as an opportunity to make an important offering to our church.

We promise to listen with an open, nonjudgmental mind to the words and ideas of others.

We promise to discuss, debate, and disagree openly and honestly so others on the Session understand our perspective.

We promise to support the final decision of the Session, regardless of whether it reflects our perspective.

We will be open and curious to feedback. We assume responsibility for providing constructive feedback.

We will communicate openly and give others the benefit of the doubt when we perceive a breach of trust.

We will grant each other grace. [7]

This covenant was very helpful to them when a board member complained to congregational members about a board decision. When the pastor and other board members heard about his complaining, they confronted him, noting that he had signed the covenant. They held him accountable. Eventually he resigned from the board.

What methods have you used to hold people responsible for their lack of accountability, whether simply not doing what they said they would do or perhaps subverting a board decision? I have found that sometimes simply describing what I see to be very helpful. "Judy, I'm puzzled. You said that you agreed with this decision, and yet I hear that you are actively speaking against it during coffee hour. What's up? " I have found it is best to do this in private or perhaps with one other board member present to avoid embarrassing the person. However, if the person is angry and actively undercutting both your and the board's leadership, you may need to take stronger action. I address how to deal with such difficult behavior in chapter 10.

TOOL 18: PREPARING REPORTS FOR THE BOARD

A simple tool for encouraging clarity of thought and also encouraging mutual accountability is to ask each committee or team to submit a report to their fellow board members at least two to three days prior to the meeting. I encourage leaders to include the following:

- Information about what they are doing.
- Requests for action from the board. Write specific motions and include appropriate background material, so board members will know what they are voting on.
- Requests for action from other committees (or teams). Spell out what you would like from your fellow members, noting what you would like them

to do and by when. (For example, the education committee might ask the property committee to paint all the Sunday school rooms by Labor Day.)

COACHING ASSIGNMENT 15: ESTABLISHING MUTUAL ACCOUNTABILITY

Assess how well leaders hold one another accountable.

* To what extent do members of the staff or board hold one another accountable?
* In what spirit do they do so?
* How do people respond when someone suggests they haven't fulfilled a commitment?

DYSFUNCTION 5—INATTENTION TO RESULTS

In a business, results are fairly easy to identify and measure. You count the number of cars or ice cream cones you sold. You calculate the profit or loss. Results are more difficult to identify in congregations. What might leaders measure? Attendance? Membership? Spiritual growth? The size and beauty of the building?

When my wife and I went on a tour of Central Europe, we visited Melk Abbey in Austria. This abbey is resplendent with gold—our guide said that it had more gold than the Vatican! Yet it had only 15 monks and no novices. Clearly a devoted Catholic, our guide was very concerned about the abbey's future. A magnificent edifice or having lots of people in worship aren't necessarily signs of spiritual vitality. Authors of a number of excellent resources have researched what practices and norms contribute to congregational vitality. Some I especially like are *Five Practices of Fruitful Congregations* by Robert Schnase, *Natural Church Development* by Christian Schwarz, *Beyond the Ordinary: Ten Strengths of U.S. Congregations* by Cynthia Woolever and Deborah Bruce, and *Christianity for the Rest of Us* and *Christianity After Religion: The End of Church and the Birth of a New Spiritual Awakening* by Diana Butler Bass. These are cited in the bibliography.

These books and others suggest that leaders might measure:

* Worship attendance—Are we fulfilling the Great Commission?
* Hospitality—Do we welcome newcomers into our lives by introducing them to members with similar interests, inviting them to lunch or to participate in groups, and perhaps hosting them in our homes? (See more ideas below.)

- Passion and purpose—Is there a palpable sense of enthusiasm and joy in worship? Are people glad to be in worship and other congregational activities? Do members invite their friends? Are there programs and practices that implement the congregation's mission and vision?
- Amount of time and money spent helping others: Are we fulfilling the Great Commandment?
- Number of people in small groups—Are we fulfilling Jesus' commands to love one another and also to love the Lord with our mind and heart?

Leaders need to clarify what results they seek. What is the congregation's mission and vision? What are top priorities? How would they know they have achieved the results they identify? Once they are fairly clear about their desired results they can develop strategies for reaching those goals. If the board isn't clear about the congregation's mission and vision, then begin that conversation. I discuss mission and vision further in chapter 9.

Based on its mission and vision, one board I worked with set a goal of increasing its attendance 12 percent in a year. That led leaders to:

- Be more attentive to how welcoming they were to newcomers. They asked themselves if they genuinely welcomed newcomers, tried to get to know them, and then introduced them to members who had similar interests. In addition, they assessed whether members, especially leaders, would simply say, "Hi, I'm Bob. Glad you're here," and then go back to talking with their close friends.
- Assess the quality of the nursery and childcare, especially the restrooms in the children's areas. Parents, especially new parents, want the best for their babies! A nursery space that was last remodeled in 1970 is a sure turnoff.
- Encourage members to worship more often. They encouraged those who came only on Christmas and Easter to worship monthly and urged those who worshiped monthly to be present twice a month.
- Encourage members to invite friends to worship and the church school.
- Review the bulletin and liturgy from the perspective of a newcomer and make it understandable to someone who isn't familiar with their faith traditions. For example, instead of simply printing "The Apostles' Creed," they wrote, "We Say What We Believe," noting that The Apostles' Creed is a traditional faith statement used by most denominations.
- Review the worship service with the goal of making it a time to strengthen personal spirituality. For example, they added more silent time for prayer and reflection, implicitly encouraging people to pray individually. The pastor made sure that sermons pointed to how God was present in their lives.

- Assess the building from the perspective of a newcomer. Leaders took a fresh look at its cleanliness, paying special attention to restrooms, the condition of paint, carpets, furnishings, bulletin boards, and also the condition of the lawn and grounds.

Their attention paid off. They achieved their goal within eight months.

As you think about what results you want, it is important to distinguish between activity and results. The pastor who spends a lot of time reading about evangelism and going to workshops about evangelism but never meets with newcomers to invite them to be part of this congregation is involved in activities but unlikely to achieve results. A committee discussion about ways to strengthen the worship service is an activity (and most likely a critical one), but that isn't a result. Attracting more people to worship is a result. Whatever result you're shooting for, it is important to keep it simple so that members can understand and support it. Encourage members to tell friends and neighbors about what their congregation is doing and how being part of this congregation makes a difference in their lives.

COACHING ASSIGNMENT 16: ENSURING RESULTS

Assess the board's clarity about and commitment to the results they seek by using questions such as these:

- To what extent do the desired results reflect the general sense of the congregation's mission and vision?
- Are the desired results easily measured? For example, a desired result might be to increase worship attendance by 10 percent or the number of small groups from two to five.
- Are you and the board members enthusiastic about and committed to achieving these results?
- How might these results be achieved?
- Who would be responsible for what?
- Have you and board members set an approximate date to achieve these results?
- Does your timetable include interim steps required to achieve the results? For example, if your desired result is to increase the number of small groups from two to five by this date next year, a critical intermediate step would be to identify and train additional leaders within five months.
- Who might lead specific steps?
- How will you keep track of progress and celebrate that progress and achievement?

- How will you express appreciation of those who work especially hard to achieve the results?

Tip 15: Don't let the perfect become the enemy of the possible.

In your quest for results, don't fall into the trap of seeking the perfect and doing nothing until you define exactly what perfect results you want and decide on the perfect approach. Certainly you want to achieve excellent results, but don't wait to act until you have the perfect plan. There are always variables that are totally beyond your control. It is better to develop and execute a good plan, evaluate your results, and then refine your approach to get even better results. I may want to prepare a Mexican-style omelet, with sautéed onions and peppers, Monterey Jack cheese, and salsa but discover that I have Swiss cheese and mushrooms in the refrigerator. So I prepare a French omelet! The result isn't what I intended but is quite delicious! Act and then adapt.

ASSESS AND BUILD THE BOARD AND STAFF TEAMS!

Just as you assessed the trust level in the congregation and also the individual strengths of leaders, it is critical to assess and build the staff and board as teams. You need to lead together. I encourage you to use *The Five Dysfunctions of a Team* paradigm as a tool to engage in mutual self-assessment.

Trust is the foundation of effective leadership teams. If members of the staff or board don't trust one another, then there will be hidden agendas, excessive caution, and often nasty fights. This dysfunction will spread to the congregation. Use some of the tools I have presented in this chapter and chapter 3 to build trust. *Do not take trust for granted!*

Building directly on trust is the team's ability to deal with differences, to vigorously debate issues and make mutually agreed-upon decisions. Develop ways to strengthen leaders' ability to let go of their fear of conflict and fight effectively.

Then assess the commitment of both board and staff to decisions they make. Take time to make sure that virtually all of the leaders buy-in to important decisions. If they show tepid commitment, then it means they are just going along.

Encourage leaders to hold each other mutually accountable—to learn to confront one another with humor and grace when some agreed action isn't taken. Develop a board covenant if possible so that someone who engages in destructive behavior is held accountable.

Press leaders to clearly decide what results they seek.

Now to another framework for analysis: What size is your congregation and what difference does size make?

Chapter Six

What Size Is Your Church?

Size Matters

Jim was a second-career pastor. He went to seminary in his fifties after a successful business career. Following seminary he accepted a call to be a supply pastor of a congregation that had around 25 in worship attendance on a typical Sunday. Beginning his ministry with enthusiasm, he ran into some difficulty when he began pressing leaders to clarify their mission and vision and to engage in outreach. Further, he preached sermons that were similar to rather deep sermons he had been used to in his home church. Some complained that his sermons didn't make them feel good like those of the previous pastor.

Sue had been pastor of a lively congregation with around 100 in worship on typical Sundays. With only part-time staff, she was the nerve center of the congregation. She knew everyone. When people were ill, she called on them. She attended all the committee meetings. With plenty of time to study, her sermons were well developed and preached. Worship was creative. The church flourished, growing under her leadership. When she decided to seek a new call, she became pastor of a congregation of some 250 weekly worshipers in a busy metropolitan community. The congregation was well staffed, with an associate pastor who focused on education and a full-time director of music and an organist. Suddenly things started spinning out of control. Sue simply couldn't keep up with things. Pastoral calling ate up an enormous amount of time. Her sermon study suffered. People complained she was a bottleneck. Attendance started dropping.

What was happening in these situations? Sue and Jim were wandering in Wonderland. They didn't understand the norms of the new congregations.

SIZE MATTERS!

You likely entered your new congregation with considerable enthusiasm. Based on conversations with the pastor search committee and discussions with the board, you have great ideas about how to make this congregation even better. However, as you have proposed and attempted to implement some initiatives, you have encountered puzzling resistance. What is going on? Should you not have proposed your great ideas?

When, for example, might you urge leaders to add a worship service that you are convinced will increase attendance? Before taking on such an initiative, you must take time to analyze your congregation's size, how it got to that size, and the organization and leadership that are most effective in that size congregation. Otherwise you will likely make some major blunders.

In 1983, Arlin Rothauge, an Episcopalian, published a small booklet called *Sizing Up a Congregation for New Member Ministry*. He defined the terms mainline Protestants have used for over 30 years to identify congregations primarily by their size. Rothauge wanted to know why different approaches for attracting and incorporating new members work in some congregations and not others. In his research, he discovered a correlation between the success and failure of certain new-member strategies and the size of the congregation.

- A *family* church incorporates new members the way a *family* does—by birth, marriage, and adoption.
- A *pastoral* church does it based almost exclusively on the relationship newcomers develop with the *pastor.*
- New members of a *program* church are primarily attracted by the congregation's *programs*, whether for children or adults, music, study, service, support, education, or fellowship.
- What he called a *corporation* church draws newcomers with its human, financial, and physical resources for high-quality ministries that rival major secular *corporations* and that operate in a manner similar to them. (Writers since Rothauge have used the term "corporate," rather than "corporation," church.)

Alban Institute consultants have done seminal work about the effects a church's size has on its leadership and organization. Former senior consultant Roy Oswald summarizes them in his monograph, "How to Minister Effectively in Family, Pastoral, Program, and Corporate-Size Churches,"[1] Alice Mann delves more deeply into what happens when congregations change size, either growing or declining in membership.[2] Oswald's monograph is reprinted in her book *The In-Between Church: Navigating Size Transitions in Congregations.* In *Raising the Roof: The Pastoral- to Pro-*

gram-Size Transition she addresses barriers to growth and necessary changes in congregational culture for growth to happen.

How do you determine what size your church is? And why does size matter? Following are the sizes that Oswald and Mann describe, with some coaching assignments to help you consider your congregation's size, how its size has changed in the decades prior to your arriving, and implications of size and size transitions for your leadership as a new pastor. I will focus primarily on the three smallest sizes since they comprise about 95 percent of congregations in the United States.[3] Please understand that this is only a introduction to size theory; read the work of Alice Mann and others to explore size analysis in more depth.

Here is a general outline of the sizes:

- The family church: up to around 50 in worship (plus children in the nursery or church school during worship) on an average Sunday (transition zone)
- The pastoral church: from 70 to 150 present on an average Sunday (transition zone)
- The program church: from 200 to 350 average worship attendance (transition zone)
- The corporate church: 400 or normally present in worship

What are the unique characteristics of each size, and what are implications and consequences of moving from one size to another?

FAMILY-SIZE CONGREGATIONS

These small congregations operate like extended families and often are, in fact, extended families with cousins and aunts and uncles everywhere! Like an extended family, they typically have a matriarch or patriarch, some rebellious children, eccentric aunts or uncles, and many years of tradition. In rural areas they are often centers of community life. One of my clients serves a rural family-size congregation whose cemetery has graves that date back to 1810. Ancestors of some of the current members organized this congregation in 1769.

Relationships are paramount. Quality of preaching, music, and teaching are secondary. While family-sized congregations often have committees, I have observed leaders serving on multiple committees. Members of committees get much of the work of the congregation done. Their decisions are made informally in the committees but are augmented by other conversation, with the matriarchs and patriarchs having the most influence. The board formally ratifies decisions that have already been reached.

Family-size congregations are durable, having survived many newly ordained young pastors and some incompetent pastors that have been foisted on them. They have learned to deflect most ideas for changing things, because what they have been doing has worked for many decades.

Oswald notes that family-size congregations are the worst size for new seminary graduates to begin their ministry.[4] Jim, whom I mention in the beginning of this chapter, came to a durable family-size church from a large program-size church. His home church had three pastors; eleven other staff members; and dynamite music, education, and mission programs. Some of its pastors have been among the most respected in the denomination. He came to the family-size congregation with great ideas and hopes, challenging them to grow. They weren't interested. They wanted a chaplain who would be with them in times of crisis and support them in their busy lives. He lasted about two years with them.

The average tenure of pastors in these congregations is fairly short—five years or so. The most important task of a pastor new to a family-size congregation is to simply take lots of time to get to know the members and build deep trust with the matriarch or patriarch. Any ideas for change not blessed by these leaders are doomed. It is critical not to be drawn into a fight between a rebellious child or left-out sibling and those who really run the congregation. The pastor will lose every time.

Size Transition Issues

These congregations may be in a size transition. For example, think of a church that once was a comfortable family-size church out in the country. But because it is now in a burgeoning suburban area of a big city, it has grown rapidly in the past five years. The key leaders who have run the congregation aren't able to keep up with everyone. Newcomers often turn to the pastor as the key leader and are confused when the pastor cannot effect change easily. Fearful of losing their clout, long-time leaders likely will resist ideas of these newcomers as well the pastor's authority.

On the other hand, some congregations have declined from pastoral or even program to family-size over a decade or less. Some causes for this rapid decline may have been radical demographic and cultural change, conflict, or clergy misconduct or incompetence. Many such congregations have buildings that are too large for their current membership. One of my clients serves a congregation whose 60 worshipers are swallowed by a sanctuary that can hold 500. Many also have organizational structures that were suitable for the much larger congregation they used to be, but now have far too many board members, committees, programs, and mission projects. Members are burned out. Members of these now significantly smaller congregations carry a lot of frustration, guilt, and anger.

Pastors new to such congregations need to listen very carefully to the various perspectives on why the congregation has lost members. Some members might blame the previous pastor. Some leaders may feel ashamed and guilty that somehow they didn't halt the decline. Others may be in denial. And still others may like or even benefit from the congregation's being smaller. Only by understanding the differing perspectives on why the congregation declined may new pastors and leaders begin to take action to either stabilize or increase membership.

If you have been an associate pastor in a program- or corporate-size congregation and now are in a family-size congregation, it is especially important to avoid expecting them to behave like your former congregation! Members of your new congregation will certainly expect behavior from you that will contrast with your previous congregation. Take time to get to know and love them!

COACHING ASSIGNMENT 17: FOR A PASTOR IN A FAMILY-SIZE CONGREGATION

Analyze the congregations using the following questions.

- Who are the matriarchs and patriarchs? How open are they to change? How much control do they need? What happens if you cross them? What have you done and what more will you have to do in order to earn their trust and respect?
- To what extent do members behave like an extended family, sometimes very close, sometimes fussing at one another? Who are the rebellious children, the odd cousins?
- What does it take to become part of the congregational family? What is necessary for a newcomer, either pastor or lay person, to be adopted?
- What style of sermons do they expect? How long should sermons be? How varied in style? For example, do members expect a straightforward scholarly lecture, a sermon that motivates them to social action or evangelism, or one that offers pastoral support in difficult times? Do they welcome something more dramatic like a reenactment of a biblical character in a monologue or a dramatic telling of a biblical narrative such as the story of Jonah?
- What level of pastoral care do they expect of you? Do they want you to call every day on a hospitalized parishioner and visit each family annually, or do they expect that they will take care of each other and that you will focus on studying or community mission?
- How emotionally close do they expect you to be with them? Are they looking for a best friend or someone who stays at the periphery?

- How long was your predecessor there? What do members tell you about that pastor's ministry? How does your leadership style compare with the predecessor's?
- How has the church's size changed over the past three decades? (Draw a chart showing the congregation's average worship attendance (Sunday or weekly, including all services that do not duplicate attendance) by year for each of the previous 10 years and then for every third to fifth year going back 30 years.
- Was the congregation ever pastoral- or program-size? If it has been significantly larger, what emotional baggage are members carrying from the change? To what factors do they attribute the decline? What responsibility do they accept? To what extent do they blame previous pastors? To what extent are leaders ashamed of the decline or perhaps in denial?
- Are members content with the size they are, or do some want the congregation to grow? What influence do those who want it to grow have?
- What initiatives do they want you to take (e.g., changing the church's organization, remodeling the church building, starting adult classes)? What initiatives are leaders already taking? Or would they prefer that you take no initiatives?
- What has the response been when you have suggested new programs or any change? Pushback? Enthusiasm? How committed have they been to any new programs you and they undertake? What does their commitment or lack thereof tell you?
- If the church is in significant decline, are you inadvertently a hospice chaplain? What energy level is required from you and leaders to grow the congregation or even keep it viable? How much energy do you and they have?

You may also draw from interviews you have done using the Eleven Curious Questions. Then list the congregation's norms in simple, declarative sentences and reflect on how you need to lead this congregation. Develop mutual expectations and top priorities with key leaders. Communicate these to the congregation.

PASTORAL-SIZE CONGREGATION

As the name implies, the pastor is the center of this size congregation's life. Once a congregation exceeds more than 50 or so regular attendees, people simply can't know each other very well, nor can decisions be made by loose consensus or by one or two key leaders. The pastor is expected to plan and lead virtually every aspect of the congregation's life, working with key lay leaders to keep everything running smoothly. The pastor preaches most of the time, leads Bible studies and other small groups, and is communications central. Quality of preaching and teaching are important to members but so is a sense of closeness. Many pastoral-size congregations have a time of sharing joys and concerns orally in worship. Newcomers who have been in larger, less personal congregations are often attracted to this sense of intimacy. The pastor is the key minister to the sick and suffering. Though each member doesn't know every other member by name, most active members have a good idea of who people are. Regular attendees expect the pastor to be able to call everyone by name within three to four months of arriving. In general they expect the pastor to meet what I have heard parishioners describe as "my spiritual needs" (however those are defined).

Children and youth are valued. Because there often aren't enough children and youth to be herded into a group of their own, they have more interaction with adults and so they and adults know each other by name. This more frequent interaction is valued by parents and members alike. A member of a pastor selection committee told my wife and me (as we considered going to their pastoral-size congregation), "We don't have many children, but they are precious to us." After I accepted their call to be their new pastor, we observed that children were indeed very important. Our sons knew they mattered to the older members. They and other children learned how to relate with people of all ages.

Though the board makes most of the major decisions, members of pastoral-size congregations want to have a good deal of input as those decisions are made, often serving on committees. Even if 15–20 percent of the congregation is on committees, it is still important for the board to consult with the congregation on major decisions. Because of the relatively high involvement of members, it is fairly easy to get a significant percentage of the congregation involved in a building refurbishing day, a mission project, or a congregational meal. Leaders tend to be very hands-on, often micromanaging projects or doing the tasks themselves rather than recruiting and training others to do them.

If you have been an associate pastor in a program- or corporate-size congregation and now are in a pastoral-size congregation, it is especially important to avoid expecting them to behave like your former congregation! Members of your new congregation will certainly expect behavior from you that will contrast with your previous congregation. Take time to get to know and love them!

I have observed that precisely because of their dependence on the pastor, pastoral- and corporate-size congregations are especially vulnerable to poor clergy leadership; family-size congregations get along regardless and program-size often have very capable staff and lay leaders. Roy Oswald notes, "Large churches are far more vulnerable [than family size]. An exec can place an incompetent pastor in a large church and lose 200 members in one year."[5]

Oswald notes, "Clergy with strong interpersonal skills fare well in the Pastoral Church. These clergy can feed continually on the richness of direct involvement in the highs and lows of people's lives. Clergy who enjoy being at the center of most activities also do well. . . . Outgoing, expressive people seem to be the best matches for the style of ministry in the Pastoral Church."[6]

Transition Issues

Difficulties in the pastoral-size congregation arise when it grows. Suppose what had been a comfortable pastoral-size congregation has received many new members as what was a somewhat distant suburb becomes much more densely populated. The congregation has become so big that members have to make an appointment to see the pastor—and it may be several days later! Instead of visiting hospitalized parishioners every day or two, the pastor may visit only once a week and encourage a lay pastoral caregiver to visit instead. For many members of a pastoral-size congregation, a lay caregiver's visit doesn't really count as a *pastoral* visit. Those who expect prompt attention from *their* pastor are often very unhappy about the slow response. They then often place unreasonable demands on the pastor. Unless the board and pastor handle excessive demands effectively, the pastor may well begin to have emotional, physical, and family problems from the stress.

When a pastoral-size congregation exceeds more than 150 average worship attendance, there will likely be members who complain that they don't know many people anymore. The sanctuary may become crowded, so leaders are forced to add a worship service. Then those who want to know most other members are even more frustrated. "I never see the Smiths anymore; they are at the early service!" As a pastoral-size congregation grows, oral sharing of joys and concerns can take way too long, especially when someone who loves the limelight beseeches the congregation to pray for some distant relative's coworker who lives two states away! People may express concerns about "these newcomers on the board" or the unruly children at the fellowship time following worship. "Why don't those young parents watch their children?" Long-time members aren't nearly as indulgent of a newcomer's unruly child as they would have been of a child born to parents who grew up in the congregation.

With the congregation's growth, the pastor may become a bottleneck to ministry and decision making. If the pastor needs to be present in every committee meeting, then those who wish to lead may conclude that they really aren't needed, that the pastor and a few insiders want to run everything. If a congregation grows significantly, additional staff must be added if it is to continue to grow. Adding staff members means that the pastor will have to manage more relationships, take more time to build a staff team, oversee the new staff members, mentor those new to their position, and relinquish some control over an area that had been the pastor's turf (for example, pastoral care or teaching or preaching). The pastor will need to clarify roles and responsibilities. What members can expect of the pastor will have to change.

On the other hand, if the congregation has been declining, then it is important to gain some insight into the causes of the decline. Perhaps there were demographic or cultural changes, poor clergy or lay leadership, or a conflict. As the new pastor you must know what happened. For example, if one or more previous pastors betrayed the congregation in some way, a number of members will likely hold the attitude that pastors cannot be trusted. Please recall all that I wrote on trust in chapters 3 and 5. You can never take trust for granted. You must continually build and rebuild trust, especially if there have been breaches of trust. Otherwise mistrust will gum up everything. If members don't know how to fight effectively, then you help them learn to resolve differences. If demographic changes have been the reason for decline, then you need to help leaders face those changes squarely. Remember my tip that you need to describe reality as you see it and start a conversation!

COACHING ASSIGNMENT 18: FOR A PASTOR IN A PASTORAL-SIZE CONGREGATION

Analyze the congregations using the following questions.

- How has the church's size changed over the past three decades? Draw a chart showing the congregation's average worship attendance (Sunday or weekly, including all services that do not duplicate attendance) by year for each of the previous 10 years and then for every third to fifth year going back 30 years.
- What style of sermons do they expect? How long should sermons be? How varied in style? For example, do members expect a straightforward scholarly lecture, a sermon that motivates them to social action or evangelism, or one that offers pastoral support in difficult times? Do they welcome something more dramatic like a reenactment of a biblical character in a monologue or a dramatic telling of a narrative such as the story of Jonah? Or are some scandalized by such a dramatic exhibition?
- How well does the organizational structure work? Does the congregation have about the right number of formal and informal leaders? Or are there too many or too few? How easily are decisions made?

- How easy is it for newcomers to become involved? To become leaders? What helps or gets in the way?
- To what extent is the current staff made up of the right number of the right people with the right job descriptions for the size of the congregation? If the congregation is growing significantly, you may not have enough staff. If it is shrinking, you may not be able to support the current number of staff members.
- If the congregation has been formed by merging two family-size congregations, to what extent do the leaders understand the difference between family- and pastoral-sizes and hence the need for a different approach to leading a congregation? Even if the pastor selection committee told you that the congregation wants to dramatically increase its membership, don't believe it—at least for your first year. Assess how widely this desire is owned by the congregation. Leaders who come from family-size congregations have a family style of decision making. Perhaps there are matriarchs or patriarchs from the two congregations that merged to form this new congregation, and they don't want to relinquish their authority to the pastor or to a key leader from the congregation with which they merged! Explore those dynamics and ask what you need to do to help them understand the needs for a different style of leadership
- If you have come to a pastoral-size congregation from a thriving program- or corporate-size congregation, how will you guard against bringing in a more distant, CEO mindset? How will you change your leadership style to meet the demands of this congregation? If you served a larger church where the members did most of the pastoral care, are you ready and willing to provide most of the pastoral care? If you don't clarify and meet these expectations, then it is likely that members will conclude that you don't care about them. You will be in trouble!
- If you have come to this pastoral-size congregation from a family-size congregation, how will decisions be made differently? How will you meet higher expectations for preaching and teaching? How will you balance expectations that you provide immediate pastoral care with those that expect you to spend significant time studying or administering the congregation's programs?
- If the congregation has shrunk from a program church with three full-time program staff members to a pastoral-size one with a pastor and a part-time musician and secretary, what programs must you cut? To what extent is there significant denial of change? What level of guilt, grief, shame, and anger is there around the decline? How will you explore these emotions with the board?

You may also draw from interviews you have done using the Eleven Curious Questions. Then list the congregation's norms in simple, declarative sentences and reflect on how you need to lead this congregation. Develop mutual expectations and top priorities with key leaders. Communicate these to the congregation.

PROGRAM-SIZE CONGREGATIONS

People usually belong to a program-size congregation because they seek both higher quality program and a sense that they can be known as individuals but can remain somewhat anonymous if they wish. Program-size congregations usually have high-quality preaching and education. Parents know that their children are in a church school led by teachers trained by a professional church educator. The congregation usually has opportunities for members to be involved in hands-on mission, such as going on a work camp in Appalachia or serving in a food bank. Program-size congregations often have two worship services, each with a different form of worship. There are numerous groups in which members may participate, such as adult, children, youth, and bell choirs; spiritual growth groups; and vocational or age interest groups.

The pastor is typically the head of staff, with an associate pastor or educator, and one or more musicians, administrative assistants, and janitors. The pastor spends a great deal of time working with the lay leaders of the various program areas, planning, training, and making sure that all is of high quality. Because pastors of program-sized congregations need to spend more time leading leaders, preparing excellent sermons, and administering the work of the congregation, they simply won't have time to do the variety of tasks they handled in a pastoral-sized congregation.

Sue, who I mentioned at the beginning of the chapter, tried to use the leadership and pastoral care styles that were effective in her pastoral-size congregation in this new program-size congregation. There weren't enough hours available for to do what she believed was essential. She didn't realize that pastors of program-size congregations will likely not spend as much time teaching classes and having hands-on involvement with members in mission projects. Though such pastors will respond quickly in emergencies, they will provide less ongoing pastoral care. Lay leaders, such as those who are trained as Stephen Ministers, will be the primary persons to provide support and care. Trained group leaders will teach members how to care for one another in support and study groups. Pastors of program-size congregations will be much more likely to refer people who need counseling to pastoral counselors.

A program-size congregation needs to have a clear unifying sense of mission and call. While clarity of call is important for all sizes, it is essential for program and corporate sizes, since it draws members and staff together and gives direction for ministries. While the board (including staff) make decisions, they consult in appropriate ways with the congregation, perhaps through town meetings. Leaders must work continually to build and maintain trust so that they can make effective decisions. Lay leaders and staff members often oversee the various ministry areas, sometimes hands-on, sometimes coordinating leaders of smaller teams that do the hands-on work. For example, the pastor and worship committee might oversee a team that handles all the audio-visuals used in worship. There might be an IT team that takes care of the congregation's website and computer system that is under the general supervision of an administration committee.

Transition Issues

Mann, Oswald, and other experts assert that growing a congregation from the pastoral- to program-size is one of the most difficult transitions. Members of what has been a pastoral-size congregation have to adjust to not being able to see their pastor as easily or to know almost everyone. Pastors have to adjust to having less hands-on ministry with members but rather work through staff and lay leaders. All must learn to trust members and staff whom they don't know as well as they knew their pastor when the congregation was smaller. Members who want the pastor to meet their particular needs, wants, and whims will especially resist this kind of growth.

Sometimes congregations operate like a pastoral-size church even though they are program-size. One of my clients serving what was numerically a program-size church asked members of the governing board to each write a word that was a metaphor for their church. A recurring response was "family." The client (an interim pastor) noted that one has to be either born into, married into, or be adopted to be part of a family and pressed them to consider other metaphors for the congregation, such as community or body of Christ. Though this congregation had been numerically program size for at least 25 years, its long-time pastor had controlled everything. He and other key leaders led it as though it were a pastoral-size congregation.

If the congregation has declined from corporate-size to program-size, then you need to carefully explore causes for the decline. Note what I said earlier about a program-size congregation declining to pastoral size. When there has been a significant decline in membership, leaders become anxious. Sometimes they look for someone to blame, such as the previous pastor. It's critical to help them explore the multitude of factors that led to the decline and determine how to respond. Will you and leaders accept the current size as the new normal? Do leaders and most of the congregation want it to grow again? How realistic are their aspirations? How committed are they to doing what is necessary to help the congregation grow?

COACHING ASSIGNMENT 19: FOR A PASTOR IN A
PROGRAM-SIZE CONGREGATION

Analyze the congregations using the following questions.

- How has the church's size changed over the past three decades? Draw a chart showing the congregation's average worship attendance (Sunday or weekly, including all services that do not duplicate attendance) by year for each of the previous 10 years and then for every third to fifth year going back 30 years.
- How clear is the mission and vision? How does that guide leaders (both staff and lay leaders)?
- To what extent do leaders understand that the leadership style called for in a program-size congregation is different from the style required in one that is larger or smaller?
- What style of sermons do they expect? How long should sermons be? How varied in style? For example, do members expect a straightforward scholarly lecture, a sermon that motivates them to social action or evangelism, or one that offers pastoral support in difficult times? Do they welcome something more dramatic like a reenactment of a biblical character in a monologue or a dramatic telling of a biblical narrative such as the story of Jonah? Or are some scandalized by such a dramatic exhibition?
- To what extent is the staff configuration effective? One of my clients was interim pastor in a large program-sized congregation with one pastor and 10 other full and part-time staff members. It became clear that the congregation needed an associate pastor to help lead the congregation. Are there the right number of staff members, neither too many nor too few? Are the current staff members effective in their jobs? How clear are staff roles, responsibilities, and priorities? How effective is the personnel and appraisal system? See chapter 9 for more on appraisals.
- How effectively are you leading the staff, giving staff members both clear responsibility and authority to carry out their ministry? How do you oversee their work? To what extent do you trust lay leaders to oversee their ministry without intervening and micromanaging?
- To what extent do leaders operate the congregation like a pastoral-size one, even though the congregation is program size? To what extent do members expect pastors to manage everything, perhaps even making coffee for the fellowship time after Sunday worship? To what extent have previous pastors become bottlenecks, limiting initiative and creativity of staff and lay leaders?
- If the church was significantly larger, how are leaders dealing with the decline? How congruent are facilities with the needs of the current congregation? How have leaders responded to the decline? How anxious are

they? To what extent do they blame the previous pastor or other leaders? How creative are they about identifying new opportunities?

You may also draw from interviews you have done using the Eleven Curious Questions. Then list the congregation's norms in simple, declarative sentences and reflect on how you need to lead this congregation. Develop mutual expectations and top priorities with key leaders. Communicate these to the congregation.

CORPORATE-SIZE CONGREGATIONS

High-quality worship is the center of a corporate-size congregation. The senior pastor is typically an outstanding preacher. Corporate congregations feature professional-quality choral and instrumental music, with several paid musicians. Associate pastors, youth workers, educators, and other staff lead myriad ministries. These congregations have a very clear unifying vision that leaders use as the basis for decisions. The senior pastor embodies this vision in his or her words and actions, and makes sure that everyone keeps their focus.

Members can be anonymous, only attending worship, or they can build very close friendships with each other by being involved in one of many groups. One colleague who is pastor of a corporate-sized congregation told me that his goal is to be a "congregation *of* small groups, not a congregation *with* small groups." He was very clear that the primary locus of pastoral care was the intentional small group. Such congregations typically support an exciting array of mission outreach programs, ranging from hands-on efforts such as Habitat for Humanity to sending evangelistic workers to China to starting new congregations in new suburbs.

Pastors of corporate congregations typically become very prominent in the community and may even be nationally known. Roy Oswald notes, "The personage of the pastor acquires a legendary quality, especially in the course of a long pastorate. Few may know this person well, but the role does not require it. The head pastor becomes a symbol of unity and stability in a very complicated congregational life."[7]

The sheer size of the staff in such a congregation demands that the senior pastor be both a leader and a manager. Such pastors must focus on building a healthy leadership team among staff members. If the staff leadership team is caught up in squabbles, then dissonance and anxiety will spread through the congregation. Associate pastors will need to learn to serve on a team, optimally led well, but sometimes they will need to learn to manage their boss. Members of such a congregation will not usually expect the senior pastor to call on them in the hospital. Associate pastors, other staff, and Stephen Ministers will handle the bulk of the pastoral care.

More analysis of the corporate-size congregation is beyond the scope of this book. Further, a number of experts, including former Alban Institute consultant Susan Beaumont, have studied larger congregations in depth. Beaumont researched these congregations for over five years and determined that they vary widely depending on their worship attendance, number of satellite worship sites, affluence, budget, whether they have a school, and other factors. Precisely because of their uniqueness, they each require specific leadership skills. [8]

COACHING ASSIGNMENT 20: FOR A PASTOR IN A CORPORATE-SIZE CONGREGATION

Analyze the congregation using the following questions.

- How long has the congregation been this size? If the church has recently grown to a corporate size, how have leaders clarified expectations of each other and the pastors and other staff? Draw a chart showing the congregation's average worship attendance (Sunday or weekly, including all services that do not duplicate attendance) by year for each of the previous 10 years and then for every third to fifth year going back 30 years.
- How clear is the unifying vision? How clear are priorities?
- To what extent are lay leaders trained to be primary pastoral caregivers? For example, is there a strong Stephen Ministry or well-designed small group program with trained leaders?
- What style of preaching do members expect? What level of scholarship?
- To what extent does the church offer a variety of worship styles?
- What is your assessment of the variety and quality of opportunities for spiritual growth and missional service?
- To what extent is the staff configuration effective? Are there the right number of staff members, neither too many nor too few? If you are the senior pastor, to what extent is it necessary to have an executive associate pastor or church administrator to oversee support staff and other administrative concerns?
- How effective are the current staff members in their jobs? How clear are they regarding their roles, responsibilities, and priorities? How effective is the personnel and appraisal system? See chapter 9 for more on appraisals.
- How well do staff members work as a team? What kind of meetings do you have? If you are head of staff, to what extent are you a mentor for less experienced pastors? If you are an associate pastor, what can you learn

from the head of staff about leadership? How might that head of staff be a mentor for you?

- Does the congregation have a practice of bringing in outside consultants and coaches to help your staff work well together? If so, assess its effectiveness. If not, why not?
- How does the size of this church compare with the church from which you came or with other churches that have shaped you? Contrast your expectations about your role and responsibilities with those of this church.

NOW WHAT?

Size matters. The approach to leadership you used in one church won't work in a church that is a very different size. Note that size involves both what is observable—the number in attendance on an average Sunday—and the mindset and norms of the leaders, factors that are not so readily observable. If you and others try to lead a program-size congregation as if it were family or pastoral size, then you won't be able to meet all the competing commitments you face. If you come from a corporate- or program-size congregation to a family- or pastoral-size congregation, it is likely that many members will experience you as not caring for them. You won't be personal enough.

It is vital to know whether you prefer to lead leaders or be deeply involved in the lives of most members. What internal leadership template guides you as you organize and lead your new congregation? How appropriate is it to this size? Would you prefer to make decisions informally with some close leader friends or develop processes that would empower leaders to decide without much input from you? How important is having high quality music for you? I think of a few small congregations in which I have been a guest preacher whose music satisfied them but did not help me worship the Lord.

Take time to reflect both personally and with key leaders on what size your church is. Do the expectations and programs reflect the size it is now or its previous size? If the congregation has a fairly clear sense of mission and vision, do the structure and expectations work for or against achieving that mission and vision? What helps? What hinders?

Please think more about the norms that govern how your congregations does things. Consider how these norms reflect congregational size. How might these norms guide you? How likely is it that you can change some of the norms you find hard to live with?

By taking the time to clarify the size of your congregation, you will be a more effective leader. If you don't bother to do so, you'll be wandering in Wonderland.

Part II

Your Next Six Months (More or Less)

You have now been in your new congregation some six months or so. I hope you know all the leaders fairly well. You have assessed their strengths and the strength and resilience of the board and others in the leadership team. I hope you have built a deep trust between yourself and most members of the congregation.

But you have undoubtedly seen some problems. Some issues likely blindsided you. Perhaps some persons engaged in difficult behavior. Perhaps you have learned that the board and congregation are not at all clear on what God's call to this congregation is. When you encountered difficult situations, perhaps you handled them well, but there were probably those times when you reacted in ways you later regretted.

As you enter this next six months, I would like you to engage in some introspection, asking what you have learned about yourself in this congregation. What are your inner narratives? What are some of your hopes and fears? How clear are you and the congregation about personal boundaries?

These next few months are a good time for you and leaders to reflect on how clear you are about God's call to you, on how effectively you are implementing that call by doing the business of the congregation, and on how you and leaders deal with those whose behavior is sometimes problematic.

It is likely that you won't be proposing huge initiatives in these next few months but as you work through these next steps, you will grow in your ability to be the key leader in a team of committed and competent staff and lay leaders and cement your authority as an effective pastor.

Chapter Seven

What Have You Learned about Yourself?

Gremlines and Boundaries

When our sons were young and messed something up, we tried not to scream at them (too loudly). Rather, we would ask, "Now what did you learn from this?" We tried to create an atmosphere where they would learn from their mistakes.

Fast forward a decade or so and our younger son, Ben (at that point, around 20), had been leading canoe trips on the Shenandoah River. My wife and I arranged to go for a day's float with Ben. We spent a delightful day floating along, enjoying the scenery. Suddenly we came around a bend and discovered that we were being swept into a tree that had fallen across the river! Since I was in the bow (front) of the canoe and thus was closest to the obstacle, I instinctively leaned away from the tree. However, in a canoe, if one leans too far upstream (in this case, away from the tree), there is a chance water can pour over the gunwale into the canoe, swamping the canoe! Ben yelled, "Dad, sit up straight!" Immediately realizing what I was doing, I sat upright and we didn't swamp. We got around the tree, and Ben guided us to the next gravel bar so we could catch our breath. "Now, Dad," he asked, "what did you learn from this?"

One of my first tips was "to describe reality as you see it and start a conversation." In this chapter I'll be leading you to describe your *inner* realities and reflect on what you have learned from the inevitable mix-ups, misunderstandings, hurt feelings, and other rough patches that you have encountered in this first six months or so of being pastor in a new congregation.

INTERNAL REACTION AND EXTERNAL RESPONSE

Take a moment and identify some difficult situation. Perhaps you found yourself in conflict with someone. Perhaps you were over your head with competing commitments. Maybe you were sick. How did you feel, think, and respond when you were in that difficult situation? To what extent were you aware of what was going on in you? To what extent did you just react?

I encourage you to become aware of both your *internal* reactions and your *external* responses as you encounter difficult people or situations. For example, perhaps you are in a meeting of the governing board and one leader attacks another leader (perhaps you) with harsh rhetoric: "This contemporary worship stuff is the craziest idea I ever heard. We've never done anything like that around here! We're not like that big box congregation across town. We should worship God with reverence. None of this rock music garbage!" Just reading this might make your stomach knot up a bit (or maybe a lot). Maybe you have encountered such a person.

Be aware of your internal reaction. Perhaps you want to run or somehow melt into the floor. You'd like to change the subject. Or maybe you'd like rise to your feet and shout back or even hand in your resignation right then! Why bother with these idiots!

Next, what was your external response? What did your body language say about your internal reaction? That you were scared, shrinking from the situation or difficult person? Or perhaps that you were furious and were ready to bite off their heads? That you had no respect for the person who made such an outrageous comment? That you were disappointed or surprised?

Recall Virginia Satir's stress communication styles I described in chapter 5. Did you go into a default reaction, becoming a blamer, placater, computer, or distracter? Or did you respond so that you, the board, and the person had a good conversation? What did you say or do?

I am often challenged by behavior mavens who *should* all over others. Most churches have their cohort. They declare things like this:

- You should keep your children quiet during worship.
- You should wear a black pulpit robe.
- You shouldn't wear a robe; that's too high church for us.
- We should pray the Lord's Prayer using the King James version.
- The pastor should call on hospitalized parishioners at least every other day.
- Worship should last no longer than an hour.

If you find such situations difficult, what helps you? When people start *shoulding* all over me, I try to respond with questions designed to reflect my curiosity about their beliefs, motives, or tastes and also I try to encourage them to see the issue from another perspective.

For example, recently one of my doctors started ranting about government getting too involved in health care and how it will ruin doctor-patient relationships and health care in general. I responded that I'd be glad to engage in a conversation about this if he had a few minutes. Imagine my surprise when he sat down and was ready to talk a while. I asked him how well the private health care system was working for him. "Oh, we have to have four full-time employees to battle with those insurance companies!" he exclaimed. That led to a broader conversation about how important it is that poorer people get health care and doctors are able to do their work without having to hassle some insurance provider (either private or governmental) to get paid.

Another approach I often take when dealing with difficult, opinionated people is to point to salient scriptures, especially stories about Jesus. Sometimes I ask the person, "How do you suppose Jesus would have played this?" In chapter 10, I'll say more about dealing with difficult people, but for now it's important that you assess how you react internally to their difficult behavior and how you respond externally. To what extent does your response help deal with differences constructively, strengthen your relationship with the person, and strengthen the community? Or does it have the reverse effect? Be aware.

It is also important to understand your own reaction. Why does this person hook your anxieties? I will discuss this issue in chapter 10.

COACHING ASSIGNMENT 21: MONITOR YOUR RESPONSES TO DIFFICULT BEHAVIOR

As you encounter difficult people or stressful situations, be aware of your internal reaction and your external response. Keep track of these in your journal. What can you learn from how you responded? How might you respond more effectively next time?

YOUR GREMLINS AND SELF-NARRATIVES

I grew up in a small town in southwest Missouri, and sometimes I joke that I'm an Ozark hillbilly. There's a mixed message in that statement. On one level it is a joke, but on a deeper level it isn't. There is that little gremlin who says, "Bob, what are you thinking, trying to lead these sophisticated, powerful people who live in the Washington, D.C., area? Maybe you've been around a while, but you're still a country kid from the Ozarks. You don't really belong here."

Gremlins are those little green monsters that lurk in our psyches and tell us that we aren't all we think we are or that past reality is still current. I have them and believe that everyone has them. (Think of the line from Martin Luther's hymn, "A Mighty Fortress": "And those this world with devils filled should threaten to undo us.")

Sometimes the gremlins are self-narratives. It is likely you have heard of Branson, Missouri. Just over an hour from my hometown, Branson features well over 100 shows at any given time, ranging from country music to magicians to Broadway productions, as well as boating, fishing, zip-lining, and even winery touring! It's now a big tourist destination. However, when I was growing up, Branson was a small town on a lake where my dad and I went fishing. So regardless of current reality, my interior notion is that Branson is still a little country town with good fishing. That's my story about Branson, and I'm sticking to it. Why would any tourist want to go to *Branson*?

I've heard civil rights leaders bemoan the narratives that many young African American men have about themselves: "I'm just an ignorant thug and I can't learn how to read and function in the white world. I'm probably going to end up in jail anyway. So I might as well do the drug and gang scene. If I live, I live. If I die, I die." Or think about the many professional athletes who have used steroids or other banned substances. What might their gremlins have led them to think? "If I really want to be the top batter and hit the most home runs, then I have to use this stuff. Everybody's doing it. And besides, what I'm using isn't exactly what the doping commission identified. I have to use it."

What are your gremlins and self-narratives? How might you form a new narrative that counters the destructive one? What would that story say? In response to my negative narrative about being a hick from the country, my alternate, positive narrative says, "My family valued reading, good grades, and hard work. I had some really good high school teachers, got into and did well at an excellent college, had outstanding seminary professors, and have kept learning all my life. Further, based on my essential worth in Christ, I'm comfortable interacting with people of every socioeconomic status."

A tool that has helped me learn more about myself and my gremlins is writing alternative narratives. I have used this tool with both individual clients and board members. It is easy to adapt to fit different situations. While I have given it on the spot to board members on a retreat, it is more effective to assign it in advance of the gathering so participants can think imaginatively. I will spell it out below for you to use in your role as the new pastor to a parish. This will help you explore some of your self-narratives, asking to what extent they limit or lead you.

COACHING ASSIGNMENT 22: WRITING ALTERNATIVE NARRATIVES

Write three possible narratives, imagining yourself in five to ten years. Write a failure story, a mediocre story, and a heroic story. As you write, be very imaginative. Use hyperbole! Have fun. Here are brief examples of what a person might write.

1. A failure story—You really blew it; your gremlins overwhelmed you and said things that enraged your board. They fired you and you ended up homeless. Your marriage fell apart. Your health reflects your general mood.
2. A mediocre story—You muddled along and became one of those pastors described as having five years of experience repeated seven times. You feel like you are stuck in a rut even though parishioners tell you they love you. You start coasting till you retire, letting the congregation operate the way it's always done things.
3. A heroic story—You clarified your strengths, grew in effectiveness, and led your new congregation to achieve new heights. You grew intellectually and spiritually and made a real difference in the lives of the people you serve and all those with whom you interact. Your life has zest, meaning, and purpose. You are surrounded by friends and family.

After you have written the alternate narratives, take some time to reflect on them. Consider what each scenario would feel like. What would people be saying about you? Then take time to identify the gremlins and destructive narratives that hold you back. What are you learning from this? What positive forces lead you forward? How is God leading you and empowering you?

BOUNDARIES: BERLIN WALL OR BOUNDARY WATERS CANOE AREA?

Now I would like you to consider your personal boundaries. Based on beliefs, experience, and preferences, personal boundaries are the rules and practices that people develop to define the limits of acceptable behavior. They might define the personal space a person needs to be comfortable. Some people thrive on being in a jostling crowd; others cringe at the idea. They describe one's emotional and physical availability. Healthy boundaries keep people both from being manipulated by others and manipulating others.

Think of two physical boundaries: the Berlin Wall and the Boundary Waters Canoe Area Wilderness. The Berlin Wall was a formidable barrier composed of concrete walls, guard towers, anti-vehicle trenches, and other defenses. East Germans were gunned down as they tried to get to safety and freedom in West Berlin. A border fence—a system of fences, trenches, sensors, and cameras—is being erected between the United States and Mexico, and Homeland Security inspectors are on watch for terrorists who might try to breach it. Some walls are very solid—and close to impossible to breach.

Other boundaries are not so clear. Once I led a group of youth on a canoe trip in the Boundary Waters Canoe Area Wilderness in northeast Minnesota. As we paddled through the lakes along the U.S./Canada border, we undoubtedly strayed numerous times to the Canadian side of the invisible boundary between Minnesota and Ontario. One teen noted, "If anyone asks me where I went during the summer, I can say that I made a whole bunch of trips to Canada!"

Personal boundaries are sometimes porous, sometimes impregnable. I have observed pastors who seem to have no boundaries at all. They accept phone calls or drop-in visitors day and night. The pastor's family feels like they are an appendage of the church. Conversely, I have also observed pastors who, perhaps because they are very introverted or perhaps because a seminary professor told them they had to maintain a very strict separation between their congregational and private life, seem to hide behind a Berlin Wall. They make it very clear that they are not to be bothered at home. One denominational executive told me about a pastor who told church members, "Don't call me on my day off unless there's blood on the floor!"

But are there just two extremes—you maintain either very solid boundaries or no boundaries? I think reframing this question not as an either/or issue, but as a polarity to be managed is helpful. What's a polarity? It's a pair of choices that can both be stated in positive terms and appear to be *either/or* but in reality are *both/and*. You know you are dealing with a true polarity when the problems presented by one pole are resolved by the benefits of the other. For example, exercise and rest are both essential to our well-being. There are upsides and downsides to both. Each of us needs rest to let our bodies and minds recover from whatever activity we've been involved in through the day. Too much rest can lead our bodies to grow flabby, however. Not enough, and we'll be tired and unproductive. Similarly with exercise, we need to exercise our bodies to be strong and supple. Exercise helps our circulatory and respiratory systems; it sharpens our mental functioning. However, if we push ourselves too hard, we might strain muscles or otherwise injure ourselves. Exercise and rest are not *either/or*; they are *both/and*.

Think about boundaries as a polarity. One pole is to maintain very high boundaries, to be very clear about guarding one's personal space. The upside of this is that pastors protect themselves against unwarranted intrusions on family or other personal time. They are not dragged into the messiness of people's family issues on their days off. Parishioners learn they can't be overly dependent on their pastor. These pastors make clear to parishioners that they are not their mother or father or best friend.

The other pole might be framed as intimacy or personal closeness. Its upside is that the pastors can be vulnerable and open with congregational members and friends. They welcome people into their lives, building rich friendships. Their modeling promotes the deep closeness and spiritual intimacy that many people lack. Opening one's home to parishioners is a way of welcoming them into your life. Clearly there are plusses.

What are the downsides to each of these poles? Pastors with very high boundaries are sometimes seen as cold and uncaring. "She never relates the scripture passage to her own life. Her sermons are always very abstract." "He can't just relax and be spontaneous. Everything has to be scripted." Or perhaps such pastors are perceived as not interested in what members think or feel. "He's always hiding out in his study working on his sermon or taking his day off or in a clergy support group. I can't ever catch him!"

On the other hand, when pastors have very porous boundaries, their personal life always seems to take second place. Time with parishioners trumps spending time with family or good friends. Some pastors with poor boundaries slide from spiritual intimacy into sexual intimacy. Some have become predators.

Pastors need to have a good balance of both personal space and openness. They respond to phone calls that come at dinner time according to the urgency of the call. "Your son was killed in a car wreck! I'll be right there." "You're still upset about the way you and your wife are getting along? Gosh, I'm sorry, but I can't talk, since I'm in the middle of dinner right now. Send me an e-mail with some possible times we might talk, and I'll get back to you tomorrow to set up something."

Having a good balance means that you might invite parishioners into your home for special events, but being clear that you don't encourage people to drop by without giving you a call, especially if you live in church-owned housing. (Boundaries vary by regional custom. People in the northern United States might frown on a neighbor dropping by their house uninvited, whereas such visits are common in the Southern states. Further, the degree of friendship affects boundaries. We have had neighbors who have welcomed our stopping by unannounced for a late afternoon libation and snack—and we similarly welcomed them. Certainly not all neighbors were like these friends but we knew what to expect of one another.) A good balance means being willing to share some of your personal struggles with the messiness of life, not pretending to have answers to all the questions and, at the same time, maintaining those confidences that are held closely within your family. You'll find more on polarity management in chapter 10.

COACHING ASSIGNMENT 23: ASSESS HOW YOU
MANAGE THE BOUNDARY POLARITY

Assess how you handle the polarity between maintaining high boundaries and establishing no boundaries. What are the upsides and downsides of each for you? Do you have a tendency to move toward one end of the polarity? If so, which one? How might you manage this polarity more effectively? With whom will you discuss your assessment and plan?

MANAGING YOUR ANXIETIES

I once had a bad reaction to a colonoscopy that resulted in eight weeks of debilitating daily bouts of diarrhea. I lost 20 pounds in those two months! The gastroenterologist who had administered the test tried several remedies, none of which helped. So I found a new doctor who, after hospitalizing me for dehydration, correctly diagnosed my problem and put me on IV steroids and other fluids. I was doing much better within a few days, but was still weak and physically stressed. Then a week later my brother, who lives some distance away, was rushed to the hospital. Discovering he had blood clots in both lungs, doctors kept him in the hospital for 10 days. Predictably, my anxiety kicked in. He was single and not in good health, so I called and talked with his doctor, nurse, and discharge planner, laying out what I thought were important requirements for his return to his apartment. I thought I had assurances that they would do what I believed was necessary. After his discharge, I discovered to my dismay that the hospital personnel did virtually none of what I deemed necessary for a proper discharge. Marshaling all my experience in human relations and ability to be a nonanxious presence, I phoned my brother and exploded at him because *he* didn't make sure the hospital did what *I* expected!

He hung up on me, and I became a case study in how *not* to handle anxieties!

In reflecting on my behavior, I recalled members of my congregation, including leaders, who were having difficulties either at home or work and who then behaved badly at church. My experience was a great reminder that outside stresses often engender anxiety that can then resonate through the congregation. Outside stresses create messes! Odds are that you have at times been under outside stress and it played itself out in your leadership (or lack thereof). Or a lay leader or other staff person brought in garbage from outside and dumped it on some unsuspecting soul.

What have you learned about handling your anxiety and stress? It's important to be aware when you are behaving reactively, spreading anxiety, and generally stirring up the system. When that happens, be curious. Ask what stressors are sabotaging your effectiveness.

What approaches have you used that have helped you manage outside stresses more effectively? What have you learned from these successes and failures? I have seen both pastors and laity who don't take care of themselves, eating and drinking and working too much. Either their bodies wear out and they die prematurely, or perhaps their families fall apart. Do you engage in healthy physical activity? How does this help you deal with difficult situations? I have one friend who finds his time exercising at the YMCA absolutely essential not only for both his physical and mental health, but for his spiritual health. "It is my time to meditate!" he declares.

What is your body telling you? Do you have stress-related pain—in your neck, back, elsewhere? Common slang about difficult people is often very revealing. *He is a pain in the neck! She gives me a headache! When he was ranting and raving, I felt like throwing up!* Listen to your body. What do you learn about your internal reactions and external responses to stressful situations? What helps?

As you reflect on how you handle stresses, be aware of what spiritual practices anchor you. Reading and reflecting on the daily lectionary passages gives me perspective and clarifies my thinking. Walking for 30 minutes while singing Taizé chants also eases stress and draws me closer to God. What helps you deal with anxiety and stress? I will address spiritual practices more in chapter 11.

MANAGING COMPETING COMMITMENTS

Stress is also created by the pulls and pushes from the web of competing commitments in which we live. Each one of us must manage our competing commitments. Here are some examples, but feel free to expand the list:

- work—with its own set of competing commitments
- personal intellectual growth—reading and study
- family—especially if you're married and have children, but most of us have commitments to extended family
- friends who function like family
- community—neighbors, schools, coaching a child's team, and so forth
- your relationship with God, your continuing spiritual growth
- involvement in recreational activities such as clubs or teams
- financial security
- attaining the proper socioeconomic status with the right job, car, and house in the right neighborhood

How does a busy pastor balance all these competing commitments? I recall earnest teachers admonishing us seminarians (in the late 1960s) to avoid working more than 40 to 50 hours a week and becoming workaholics like pastors were in the 1950s. I suspect professors still give seminarians the same caution. I found that was much easier for a seminary professor to say than a busy parish pastor to do! However, if you don't balance the competing commitments fairly well, you are likely to be very stressed. I recall a time a few years ago when I was pastor of a very active congregation. Here were some of my competing commitments:

- preaching excellent sermons and leading an intense, long-term Bible study
- organizing small groups
- being the primary provider of pastoral care
- being a loving, attentive husband to my wife, who worked outside the home, making sure we had time to go out on dates and enjoy each other
- spending time with my two sons, attending school and extracurricular events, helping with Boy Scouts
- going on vacation with family and keeping in touch with extended family
- serving on the parent-teacher association board at our boys' elementary school
- serving on three committees or task forces of the presbytery
- fixing up and maintaining an older house, doing lawn care, creating a vegetable garden and raspberry patch, and sharing cooking, laundry, and other daily tasks
- maintaining some sense of spiritual wholeness

I still remember the time when I made three announcements at one presbytery meeting and realized I was doing way too much in the denominational organization. I also saw the weeds in the garden and the unfinished projects around the house. It was clear that I had too many competing commitments. So I resigned from two presbytery responsibilities and trained some lay pastoral caregivers. Spending time with family and doing an excellent job at my congregation were highest priority. The weeds? I used more mulch the next year!

Following is an assignment that might help you clarify and learn how to balance competing commitments. I ask you to explore what is important about each commitment and why.

COACHING ASSIGNMENT 24: ASSESSING YOUR COMPETING COMMITMENTS

List the competing commitments you are balancing. For each one, ask yourself the question, "Why is this important?" at least seven times. Discern what are the four or five most important priorities. What do you need to let go of? How might you handle some other responsibility differently? Might you delegate something to someone else? With whom might you discuss your priorities? (If you're married, you better discuss these with your spouse!)

Assess how you handle your gremlins, anxieties, competing commitments, and stressors. What behaviors and activities are helping, and what are not? Determine how you can handle them more effectively and make a plan. Describe your commitment to change your behavior and attitudes to your spouse, a trusted friend, or coach. Write them in your journal. For example, you might commit yourself to walk three times a week for at least 30 minutes and work out at a gym. Or you might commit to keep Friday night open for family or friends. Then share your commitments with someone who will hold you to your best intentions. Arrange with that person how he or she will hold you accountable.

ESTABLISHING A SUPPORT NETWORK

People who hold you accountable are part of your support network—friends, family, and peers who know you and care about you. You enjoy being with them and they with you. You can be candid with one another, disagreeing in good spirit.

Pastor friends have long been part of my support network. For a number of years I met regularly with a group of pastors who studied a variety of new books, ranging from fairly heavy theology to spirituality to economics and faith. Many pastors love their lectionary study groups. Some pastors get together for one week each year at a mutually convenient place, perhaps a seminary, and plan sermons for the next year. Clergy colleague groups, especially if they span theological lines, are wonderful venues for support if you take time to build trust.

One caution: ideally pastors would have good relationships with judicatory executives. An insightful judicatory leader could help defuse problems and envision creative possibilities. However, my sense is that judicatory leaders can rarely really be pastors to their pastors, in part because they spend so much of their time dealing with crises. In addition, because they often have considerable say over whether a pastor gets a new position or not, it is difficult for a typical pastor to be very open to a denominational executive.

Though I always had good friends who were members of the congregations I served, it's important for pastors to also have friends who are not connected with the congregations they are serving. My wife and I typically have had friends drawn from other circles, such as from our sons' schools, based on mutual interests, and extended family. Whatever the source of the friendship, I have learned that having a good time with long-time friends mitigates whatever is bothering me at the moment and gives me new energy. What have you learned about making and maintaining friendships? To what extent do you use some of the newer social media to keep in touch?

A trained coach can be wonderful support. A coach can listen carefully, ask you powerful questions, call you to account, and help you design approaches to achieving whatever you want to achieve!

COACHING ASSIGNMENT 25: ANALYZE YOUR SUPPORT NETWORK

List everyone you can think of who is in your support network.
   Now, scratch off the following:

- members of your current congregation
- denominational superiors
- any pastors with whom you feel particularly competitive, whom you somehow resent, or whom you sense resents you
- friends or family who are emotionally and financially very dependent on you or on whom you are very dependent. (Of course, you wouldn't scratch off a stay-at-home spouse whom you support financially, but from whom you receive considerable love and support!)
- anyone with whom you can't be candid

Review who is left and decide if you need to expand your support system. If so, with whom might you intentionally develop a deeper friendship? What have you learned about the strength of your support system, and how you might strengthen it?

WHAT HAVE YOU LEARNED SO FAR?

One thing I have learned is that life has a way of sweeping me around a bend in the river and into a fallen tree from which a snake is about to drop into my canoe! We never know what's around the proverbial corner except there is almost certainly something that will cause us stress. If we aren't aware how we react and respond to stresses, then we can inadvertently get ourselves in deep trouble. Our gremlins will lead us to say or do something we will regret.

On the other hand, if we are aware of our gremlins then we can respond to the inevitable stressors with curiosity and creativity and even love. Rather than dismissing difficult people as jerks, we can ask questions that will show interest and draw out their concerns. By implementing our heroic narrative, we might hear some valid concerns, gain new perspectives, and even work together, building on their energy.

Please take some time and reflect on what you have learned about how you handle stress and stressful people, especially in this congregation. What are your usual responses to stress? How do you manage your anxiety? How do you manage the boundaries, competing commitments, and other polarities you inevitably have to deal with? Who is in your support network? How might you strengthen your relationships with those in your support network?

How strong are your spiritual practices? How do you draw daily strength and support from the Holy One who gives you life? How does God guide you through scripture and prayer? How does the Holy Spirit help you envision a heroic life narrative? Pray and write in your journal.

Taking time to learn to handle your reaction and response to unexpected stress will make you a much more effective leader.

Chapter Eight

Where Are We Headed?

Assessing the Congregation's Mission and Vision

Chapter 6 of *Alice in Wonderland* portrays Alice continuing her explorations of Wonderland. Suddenly she encounters the Cheshire Cat sitting on the bough of a tree.

"Would you tell me, please, which way I ought to go from here?"
  "That depends a good deal on where you want to get to," said the Cat.
  "I don't much care where," said Alice.
  "Then it doesn't matter which way you go," said the Cat.
  "—so long as I get *somewhere*," Alice added as an explanation.
  "Oh, you're sure to do that," said the Cat, "if you only walk long enough." [1]

Perhaps you and others in your congregation are very clear about who God is calling this congregation to be. You have a clear sense of your destination. Or perhaps like Alice, you are wondering which way you ought to go. Perhaps you feel like you and leaders of the congregation are just exploring, hoping you'll know when you've reached your destination. Perhaps there are many purposes competing for priority.

In chapter 5, I noted that leadership consultant Patrick Lencioni declares, In order to successfully identify their organization's purpose, leaders must accept the notion that all organizations exist to make people's lives better. . . . Nonetheless, every organization must contribute in some way to a better world for some group of people, because if it doesn't, it will, and should, go out of business. [2]

It is time to assess your congregation's mission and vision and ask, "What is *God* yearning for your congregation to be and do in this particular place at this unique time?" Your congregation's purpose *isn't* what *you and other leaders* want the congregation to be and do. Rather, it is what *God* yearns for.

Does the congregation have mission and vision statements? If so, how were they developed? Perhaps a study had been done prior to the former pastor's leaving or a self-study was done during the interim period. Assuming current mission and vision statements exist, how do you assess them? If they are not clear and compelling, then how and when do you update them?

What do I mean by the terms "mission and vision?" In their book *Holy Conversations: Strategic Planning as a Spiritual Practice for Congregations*, former Alban Institute consultants Gil Rendle and Alice Mann define them this way:

- *Mission Statement*: "A mission statement is a statement of identity and purpose."[3] It declares what God is calling your congregation to be, your reason for being. It should reflect some of the key concerns of your congregation and culture. It captures your DNA.
- *Vision Statement*: "A vision statement is a word picture of what our congregation would look like if we were, in fact, able to fulfill our mission statement."[4] A good vision statement declares what the congregation will emphasize in the next three to five years as it seeks to live out its mission. For example, a congregation in a troubled urban community might envision a network of mentoring groups for young people.

These definitions are similar both to those used by Lovett Weems in his book *Take the Next Step: Leading Lasting Change in the Church.*[5]

Further, these definitions are similar to those used in business and the public sector, so members who have done vision and mission work in other settings will likely understand the process. Having said this, I recognize that some congregations define "vision" in the way that I just defined "mission" and vice versa. What is important is that leaders and the congregation have a clear sense of God's call to them.

Rendle and Mann note that these statements are both axiomatic and unique. An axiomatic statement that might work for virtually any congregation would be, "God is calling First Church of Metropolis to praise God, proclaim the good news of Christ, and serve God's people." According to Rendle and Mann, "The unique states what is important to the particular congregation because of who it is, where it is located, and the historical moment it is in—all of which separates this particular congregation from other congregations of other locations, gifts, and times."[6]

Following Jesus will take very different forms in a small town in farm country, a wealthy suburb filled with jaded, overworked professionals, a culturally mixed urban neighborhood, or a university community adjoining an area of extreme poverty. An effective mission and vision study process leads a congregation to discern some of what God yearns for that congregation to be and do. Participants ask, "What kind of people is the living Lord hoping we will be here and now? How will that identity and purpose be manifest in action?"

One congregation I worked with included this in its vision statement: "God is calling UCP in the next three to five years to . . . enliven worship, building on our rich tradition while exploring new ways of experiencing God." This statement helped them build on a tradition of creative worship that incorporated dance, varying instruments, traditional and contemporary music, and different forms of preaching. The pastor and musicians knew that the congregation wanted them to be innovative and not have the same style of worship Sunday after Sunday.

I think that mission and vision statements are best written in the first person plural, that is, "We believe God is calling us to . . . ." When they are written this way, members may voice them in liturgies or other meetings, thus affirming God's call to them as members of a community. When I served a congregation as pastor, I often replaced the affirmation of faith with the mission or vision statement, which we read in unison.

Having reviewed these definitions, what do you conclude about your congregation's mission and vision statements? Are they good enough for now? Or do you and leaders need to lead the congregation in conversations to better discern God's call?

Notice that I use the term "conversations." When I coach a client I am curious and listen attentively. I ask lots of questions. My goal is to spark insight and creativity. I never quite know where the conversation will lead, however. Similarly, Rendle and Mann observe that congregational conversations about where God is leading won't be predictable and cannot be controlled. I have often been surprised by someone unexpectedly speaking God's truth to me and other leaders. As Presbyterians debated in the 1970s whether baptized children could receive the bread and wine of the Lord's Supper, I recall a seven-year-old boy who, wishing to receive communion, exclaimed to his grandmother, "But Grandma, I love Jesus too." I think of the wise older choir member observing to his peers, "We aren't going to be on this earth much longer, and we need to adapt our music to reflect the tastes of younger folks." These were holy moments, full of God's presence. Rendle and Mann observe that "conversation is *holy* because, at its best, it is about a people's understanding of their identity as a faith community, their sense of purpose, and their relationship with God."[7]

This process is one of discerning how God is leading. It assumes that God is alive and well and loves us and sends the Spirit of Christ to us to bring us into deeper understanding and relationship with God. The Holy Spirit helps us see those who need good news with the eyes of Jesus. Discernment involves deep, prayerful listening for the voice of God speaking through scripture, the wisdom of children and scholars, the voices of neighbors, and the insights of faithful friends. Discernment involves individual prayer and study and conversation in small groups and the larger congregation. Discernment of God's leading doesn't happen through simple majority votes or decisions by a board. Further, our discerning God's yearning is always partial. Recall 1 Corinthians 13:12: "For now we see in a mirror, dimly, but then we will see face to face. Now I know only in part; then I will know fully, even as I have been fully known."

Danny Morris and Charles Olson, in their book *Discerning God's Will Together: A Spiritual Practice for the Church*, note, "Discernment creates the capacity to see. To discern is to see through to the essence of a matter. Discernment distinguishes the real from the phony, the true from the false, the good from the evil, and the path toward God from the path away from God."[8]

Leaders and people humbly and prayerfully attempt to see what path God has in mind.

How might you assess your current mission and vision statements? Have leaders attempted to discern God's yearning? Here are some suggestions:

A. ASK CURIOUS QUESTIONS

The Eleven Curious Questions interviews included the questions:

1. Complete this sentence: "God is calling this congregation to be . . . "
2. What do you think God wants your congregation to emphasize in the next three to five years?

Based on responses to these questions and what you have observed, how clear are leaders of the congregation about what God is yearning for this congregation to be and what its priorities are for the next three to five years. If their responses are pretty unified, then that's a good indication that they own the statements. If responses are widely varied, then that's a clue that the statements don't guide the congregation and reflect its sense of God's call.

B. ASK HOW THE WIND IS BLOWING

Joan Gray, a former moderator of the Presbyterian Church (U.S.A.), asks leaders to consider how the wind of the Holy Spirit is blowing. In her book *Spiritual Leadership of Church Officers*, she notes that a symbol of the early church was a sailboat.[9]

Notice it wasn't a rowboat. Many congregations are rowboat churches. Leaders and members believe that where they go and how fast they get there depends completely on them and their energy. When they run out of energy, they simply drift.

Leaders in sailboat congregations, on the other hand, sense which way the wind of the Holy Spirit is blowing. They catch that wind and draw from the Spirit's power. These are churches that develop ministries and liturgies that touch the hearts and spirits of people who are hungry for meaning and hope. These are congregations energized with the possibility of making the world better. These are congregations filled with hospitable groups that welcome searchers.

How is the wind blowing in your neighborhood? Who are new residents? What issues are crying for attention? Are these new residents seeking authentic community? A congregation that welcomes spiritual explorers? A community that offers healing in body and spirit to those who have been crushed?

To what extent is your congregation a rowboat church or a sailboat church? Are leaders burned out, refusing to come back on the board or to take other responsibilities? Or are they inspired by and filled with Spirit? I suggest you introduce this metaphor to the board, describe what you observe and have a conversation with them about how they see themselves and the congregation.

How do your mission and vision statements catch the power of the Holy Spirit's wind?

C. ASSESS THE CLARITY, USEFULNESS, AND OWNERSHIP OF THE STATEMENTS

There's a Dilbert cartoon in which the pointy-haired boss tries to clarify Dilbert's plan. The boss asks Dilbert how his plan fits with corporate strategy. Dilbert admits he doesn't know the strategy and asks the boss if he does. Here's the response:

"It's something about leveraging our platforms. Does your plan leverage our platforms?"

"I can rewrite my plan so that it seems as if it does."

"Good, go back and do that. There's no point in having a strategy if you aren't going to pretend to follow it."[10]

One of my colleagues consulted with an organization that printed t-shirts that declared, "We will leverage our mission!" A web search quickly surfaces many similarly vague mission statements. Statements of mission and vision do no good if they are so nebulous that nobody can understand them or if they are so general they could apply to any congregation. They must be clear, widely owned, and useful in guiding anyone who makes a decision related to the congregation.

How might a statement guide leaders? The congregation I served in Columbus, Ohio, included the following in its statement:

> Responding to God's love and leading in Christ, we commit ourselves: to be in the creative center, offering an alternative to empty secularism and to religious rigidity.

We—staff, leaders, and members—were declaring that we were theologically centrist. We were firmly anchored in our faith in the God we knew in Christ and the Spirit and, at the same time, open to new understandings of scripture and God's call to us. This statement helped guide me in my sermon preparation and musicians and educators in their choice of offerings.

A congregation that has as its top three priorities empowering members for their daily work, broadening the options for worship, and strengthening outreach to people in need could say no to a request from a group that wanted a venue for folk dancing every week. Not that folk dancing isn't a great activity, but letting such a group tie up a sizeable space weekly would not be consistent with its vision. In this congregation the director of music should have the authority and resources to identify and employ musicians who would help lead another style of worship. Mission and vision statements need to be specific enough to be useful.

You still need to ask how widely owned are these statements. Members of the congregation need to be committed to the mission and vision. If a mission and vision study is done by just a few people, then it will likely end up forgotten on a shelf and have no impact on the congregation. As you talked with people about the current statements, how well did they know the statements and understand their implications for ministry?

Good mission and vision statements focus and energize members of a congregation. People say, "Yes! That's us!" They reflect a congregation's uniqueness. The process will also build trust and ownership. Members will have effectively dealt with competing commitments. Clarity about objectives will lead to better results.

In assessing your congregation's statements be curious about their clarity and usefulness, and the degree of congregational ownership. (You will find examples in Appendix G.)

D. ASK WHERE THE CONGREGATION IS IN A TYPICAL CONGREGATIONAL LIFE CYCLE

Rendle and Mann describe the typical life cycle of congregations. [11] The stages are:

- Birth—This is a time of great excitement and energy. Organization is fluid. The Spirit is moving!
- Formation—The congregation's identity is formed. We ask the big questions: Who are we? Who is our neighbor? Why do we exist?
- Stability—We get organized, build a *real* church building. We set up formal structures for doing things—worship, education, mission, fellowship, and evangelism. Sometimes we work on spiritual formation.
- Decline—If the congregation doesn't work intentionally on renewal and spiritual development, then decline begins. Old timers focus on their heritage, the building, and recruiting younger members just like them. Attendance and membership drop. People blame one another or demographic changes for the problems, but they take no action.
- Death—If no action is taken, then the congregation ends up with a bunch of loyal older members who run the show until they die or run out of steam. Some of my clients describe leaders who say, "We're old and tired. We just can't do this anymore. Find some younger people to do the work for us."

It is important to understand that this cycle is not an inevitable progression. Leaders need to ask if they're on a downward curve and, if so, how they might reverse the trajectory. If they're doing well, they should ask themselves what they need to anticipate. By being open to the power of the Spirit, they can grow in spirit, gain new energy and rebirth. They can shift to a new time of formation. But such an effort requires the right leaders and lots of effort and intentionality.

DECIDING WHAT'S NEXT FOR MISSION AND VISION STATEMENTS

As you assessed the mission and vision statements, here are observations that you may have made:

1. Members and leaders are very clear on the congregation's mission and vision statements and are actively implementing them.

2. Leaders are unified in their support of the current statements and are implementing them to some extent. Members have a vague understanding of the congregation's sense of mission and vision.
3. The pastor selection committee or another group did a mission study prior to searching for a pastor but didn't involve the congregation at all. Leaders and members don't seem to know about and agree with what was written and presented to you as the wish of the congregation.
4. Leaders and members of the congregation are in conflict, disagreeing about priorities.
5. Leaders and members don't have a clear sense of the congregation's mission and vision but enjoy each other. However, you heard several people say that the congregation is in a bit of a rut and something more needs to be done to generate direction and energy.

Now what might you propose to the board? Is it wise for you to encourage a major mission study initiative in your first year or two as pastor of this congregation? Since I think leaders should regularly work to discern God's yearning for their congregation in light of ever-changing community and culture, my general answer is "yes!" However, your approach will differ depending on the situation.

Plan A—Do an In-Depth Study

First, imagine that you have observed that your congregation is described by one or a combination of scenarios 3 to 5 above. In these scenarios members of the congregation neither know about nor have bought into the official mission and vision statements. In these cases, I recommend that the board and congregation engage in a vigorous mission and vision study process. I have led such mission and vision studies as an interim pastor and as a consultant. Done well, they lead to people getting to know one another better, most of the congregation doing significant study of foundational biblical passages, and leaders and members agreeing on clear emphases for the congregation. In congregations where there has been some conflict, these studies help people build trust and have common language to describe God's call to them. This kind of study pushes those who disagree to look at each other and the congregation from fresh frames of reference. For example, when studying and discussing the Great Commission and Great Commandment, members will be led to reflect on who are those in the community that Christ is calling them to reach out to. Such a study usually takes at least six months. In the following section I will describe a shorter process for congregations who fit scenarios 1 and 2.

There are many approaches to doing a depth mission and vision discernment study. Here is a process that draws from what I have done and what Rendle and Mann describe in *Holy Conversations*. There are three phases: [12]

1. Getting Ready

You have already begun this step in your assessment of the current mission and vision statements and determined that the congregation needs to do a new study. Now it is time to involve the congregation. You and leaders need to interpret the urgency for doing such a study process using various methods, such as sermons, newsletter articles, congregational e-mails, and town meetings. Stress that everyone needs to be much clearer about who God is yearning for the congregation to be and what it needs to emphasize in the next three to five years.

You and other leaders will likely be generating changes as a result of this study, and so it is critical to prepare the congregation for possible changes. People don't like surprises, especially if the surprise requires them to change their behavior! For example, a study might indicate that the congregation needs to add a worship service whose style is different from what it currently has. Some members or staff might dislike and resist this proposed change.

You and the board then need to select a mission and vision discernment team (DTeam). I have found that a group of seven to nine respected members of the congregation is a great size. This size is large enough to have variety of perspectives and also to oversee the detail work demanded. It is small enough to work effectively. Seek a combination of long-time and newer members with a mix of ages. Newcomers bring their fresh ideas and insights. Longer tenured members help capture the essential norms of the congregation, recalling the heroic stories that will help guide the congregation into its new future. While not essential, it is very helpful if one of the members knows a lot about community demographics and trends. I have found realtors and school district administrators to be very helpful. I think it is critical that the pastor serve on this team. If pastors aren't key leaders in the process, then it is unlikely that they will help implement the priorities that are decided. However, because pastors have more than enough to do, it is best that the team be chaired by a well-organized lay leader. Depending on how nimble the congregational system works, my experience is that this preparation will take around a month.

2. Collecting Data

Once a team is assembled you or an outside consultant will need to train them in how to lead a mission and vision discernment process. Team members need to understand that they are engaging in a spiritual discernment process; they aren't doing commercial market research. They (and you) are trying to discern God's leading. Whoever is leading the preparation will help them design a process to study both the congregation in more depth and to see the community with fresh eyes.

Then the team begins collecting and studying data. Team members will study foundational scripture passages such as the Great Commandment and Great Commission. I think that they should study one or more books on what makes for vital congregations. One example I discuss below is Robert Schnase's *Five Practices of Fruitful Congregations.* The team not only can use it as a resource for their own thinking, they can easily adapt it for small group study. While there are many books on congregational vitality, I find that leaders and members readily understand this book.

Team members will study demographic trends in the community, identifying population projections and assessing the extent to which the congregation is similar to the community. They should find out how community leaders in governmental and the private sector are responding to any trends. What do congregational planners need to know? For example, are there plans for new housing developments, highways, or schools? Is a long-time major employer expanding or closing? Be curious.

The DTeam will review the congregation's history and have conversations with all who will participate about the congregation's story and its current practices and norms. Push to involve at least half of the worshiping congregation in the discernment process. One enjoyable exercise is to have a congregational meal at which a timeline is posted, listing pastors and some key events in both community and congregational history. Ask participants to note when they joined the congregation, indicating other significant events for them. Encourage them to reflect on what they learned about themselves. Particularly help them recognize times when they have met a significant challenge. Help them see their strengths and challenges using a SWOT analysis. I describe the SWOT (Strengths, Weaknesses, Opportunities, Threats) in Tool 20 below.

In addition to large group events, I like to engage each participant in a series of small-group gatherings in which they study key scripture passages and reflect on how they think God is leading the congregation. When members meet in small groups of seven to ten in homes or the church building, I hear people say things like, "You and I have been coming here for 15 years, and I never realized that you attended that university too!" "I didn't know you worked for the XYZ corporation, too." "I was really moved by your story of how your faith strengthened you." Small-group study enriches relationships and helps people see the congregation and its call in fresh light. To conclude their last gathering, I recommend that each small group identify 10 top priorities for the congregation for the next three to five years. See Tool 21—Discernment through Small Groups and One-Day Leader Retreat for more details of how to do this.

As data are gathered and analyzed, there should be ongoing conversation with the congregation through town meetings, announcements and articles, small groups, and other venues. The key idea is that discernment involves a lot of prayerful listening. It's important to listen for God's voice through scripture, through the voices of members of the congregation, through voices from the community, and voices of those with particular insight into where Christ might be leading.

This phase of the process will take three to five months, depending on the time of year, how busy people are, the complexity of the congregation, and the urgency to complete the study.

3. *Shaping the Future*

Now the DTeam evaluates the data gathered in its research, in congregational gatherings, in the small groups, and in other conversation. They put these pieces of data into a coherent report. The report summarizes historical and demographic findings. It assembles the various suggestions for priorities into clear declarations, each saying something like, "We believe God is calling St. John's Congregation to embody good news to the homeless in our community." Then the DTeam develops a process to involve leaders in a conversation about the meaning of the data. How do they feel the Holy Spirit wind blowing? What opportunities present themselves? What are crying needs?

I have usually led an all-day retreat at which leaders identify the top five or six priorities for the next three to five years and also write beginning drafts of a statement of identity and purpose. These retreats bring out a lot of enthusiasm and hope. They build on the congregation's history and project what might be. See Tool 21—Discernment through Small Groups and One-Day Leader Retreat that follows.

Following this retreat, the DTeam refines and presents its report and proposed priorities to the congregation for conversation and suggestions for improvement. Incorporating input from these additional conversations, the DTeam presents another draft to the board, which votes to approve the mission and vision discernment report and adopt the mission and vision statements. Board and staff members will then discuss how to implement the mission and vision statements in their areas of responsibility.

After they are adopted, you and leaders must then embed these statements into the consciousness of the congregation. Use them in liturgy, post them on bulletin boards and discuss them in committee or team meetings. Get people talking about these statements and how they, in fact, capture your purpose and immediate priorities. I have found these full mission and vision discernments processes to be very energizing for a congregation. Both leaders and members are much clearer about their identity and priorities.

As I said when I introduced this section, I recommend this process for congregations in which there has been no significant mission and vision discernment process, especially when the congregation is in conflict or is stagnant. While such a process is time consuming, it is time and energy very well spent. Taking the six months or so to have a significant congregational conversation involving leaders and members helps pull everyone together and clarify direction.

Despite this expenditure of time and energy, it is vital to recognize that what you have developed won't ever be a *final* statement of mission and vision. Circumstances and communities change in very unexpected ways! Rendle and Mann note that congregations clarify their mission and vision through successive approximations. Leaders take initiatives, evaluate, learn, and then take new initiatives. Keep asking, "What did we learn from this?"

I have found that as leaders and members engage in setting priorities for their vision, they become much clearer about their identity. Rendle and Mann observe, "Discernment is said to function like the headlights of an automobile on a dark evening. They don't show you where you eventually end up. But they will illuminate the next part of the road."[13]

Plan B—A Shorter Process to Clarify Existing Mission and Vision Statements

What if your assessment of existing statements showed general understanding (scenarios 1 and 2 above)? Might you lead a process that helps your congregation be significantly clearer on its priorities in significantly less than six months? Yes.

If the congregation has done a mission and vision discernment in the past five years and is reasonably clear on its identity and purpose, then some small group study and a one-day leader retreat would likely be sufficient to identify the top priorities for the next three to five years. Similar to Tool 5 that I described in chapter 2, I outline such a process below in Tool 21— Discernment through Small Groups and One-Day Leader Retreat. This process involves some preparation by the DTeam. They simply develop a discernment process and follow-up plans. The congregation can do an adequate mission/vision study in two or three months.

SO WHAT?

Robert Bruner, dean of the Darden School of Business at the University of Virginia, wrote a provocative article asking, "What Business Are You In?"[14]

He notes that too many businesses define their focus too narrowly and so limit possibilities. Once upon a time, for example, railroad leaders declared that they were in the railroad business rather than the transportation business.

Consequently the railroads let autos, trucks, and airplanes fill the need for transportation services that they might have provided had they defined themselves more broadly. He cites William Neukom, CEO of the San Francisco Giants, who observed that the Giants are

- in the entertainment business
- in the customer service business
- in the talent management business
- in the community service business
- stewards of a quasipublic trust

Regardless of whether you do an in-depth mission and vision discernment process or one that is shorter, I urge you to work with leaders and members to clarify what "business" you are in and how God is leading you at this stage of your congregation's history. With the abundance of good research that has been done on what makes for vital congregations, leaders have no excuse for wringing their hands and declaring that "nothing we try works." Working through a good mission and vision process will build unity and energy in the congregation. It will provide a sense of clarity that enables both pastor and leaders to say yes to some ideas and no to others.

How is God yearning for your congregation to make the world a better place, to make a difference in people's lives? Be curious, study, pray, listen, discern. Taking such time for discernment may take a few months or longer, but it is time well spent. Done well, such a process builds excitement and direction. Leaders can make decisions more quickly. Members will think more creatively and take new initiatives consistent with the mission and vision you discerned.

Are you in the "maintaining First Church the way it's always been" business or in the business of leading people to know and love the Lord and making the world a better place by serving God wherever they may be? Your mission and vision statements say what business you're in.

There are many excellent books on developing a mission and vision. See the annotated bibliography for a list of some resources I particularly like.

Tip 16: Use Robert Schnase's book* Five Practices of Fruitful Congregations *as a framework for doing a mission vision discernment.

Robert Schnase, United Methodist Bishop of Missouri, summarizes a great deal of research in this book. I have found that congregational leaders can quickly understand the five practices he describes and have good conversations about how they might implement these practices. The practices are

- Radical Hospitality

- Passionate Worship
- Intentional Spirituality
- Risk-Taking Mission
- Extravagant Generosity [15]

Note that Bishop Schnase uses the word "practices." These are not simply programs or activities. The idea is that they are spiritual practices, built into individual's lives and the congregation's life. Developing a spiritual practice is like developing a fitness practice, optimally exercising every day. I have found that as I have engaged in (nearly) daily exercise to promote strength and flexibility, I feel better and have more energy. I have heard friends describe exercise as a "positive addiction." Similarly, I find that when I read the daily lectionary online and reflect and pray through the scripture passages, I focus on God's love for me and others and on God's call to me to serve. A practice becomes part of the DNA of a congregation. Schnase notes, "Repeating, deepening, extending, teaching, and improving these practices should fill church agendas, guide church boards, and shape leadership training. Vibrant, fruitful, growing congregations are those that naturally practice these qualities and constantly seek ways to develop them further." [16]

Here's an overview of the practices with my observations.

Radical Hospitality

Most congregations describe themselves as "friendly." But that friendliness too often simply means that a bunch of best friends enjoy getting together and catching up on Sunday morning. In my visits to congregations, I have found that at least half of the time nobody comes up and greets me in the coffee hour after worship.

Members of congregations that practice radical hospitality are eager to welcome a guest into their lives. They don't ignore you if you are a newcomer. They don't say, "Hi, I'm Bob. We're so glad you're here," and then turn and start talking with a friend. They invite you to join them and other members for coffee and cookies after worship and introduce you to members with whom you might have something in common. Perhaps they will encourage you to come with them to an adult class or small group. Depending on local customs, they might invite you to join them and friends for lunch at a nearby restaurant. They are intentional about including newcomers.

Says Schnase, "Hospitality is a quality of spiritual initiative, the practice of an active and genuine love, a graciousness unaffected by self-interest, an opening of ourselves and our faith community to receive others." [17]

Passionate Worship

The second of Schnase's practices is passionate worship. Schnase writes, "Passionate Worship means an extraordinary eagerness to offer the best in worship, honoring God with excellence and with an unusual clarity about the purpose of connecting people to God."[18]

When I think of worship that is passionate, I think of congregations across the theological spectrum. I think of a packed traditional service in one congregation. It has a great choir, dynamic preaching, and a superb children's and youth music program. People are excited to be there. They praise God! I think of a much more evangelical congregation I visited with worship led by a praise band. The worshipers sang enthusiastically, clapping and swaying. The pastor's sermon was engaging and solid. They were passionate about their faith. My wife and I spent five days at Taizé, that wonderful ecumenical community of reconciliation in France. Some 5,000 young adults in their teens and twenties gathered four times per day for worship, passionate in their sung prayer.[19]

Worshipers who are passionate radiate God's love, grace, and hope. They sense the presence of the living God as they unite in song and prayer. The listen expectantly to scripture and sermon, seeking God's good news and guidance. Worship is a high priority for their lives. It isn't just something they do. Passionate worship is a spiritual practice.

Intentional Spiritual Development

Schnase asserts that fruitful congregations involve members in many opportunities to grow spiritually. They pray and study the Bible together in small groups, adult classes, board and committee meetings, choir practices, and service projects. It is in these groups that disciples are really formed. Here is where people deepen their relationship with a living Lord.

I have led groups that helped people apply their faith to their grieving, to their work, to politics and parenting. I love retreats that have a good mix of intellectual content, time for prayer, and time for building deep relationships. I have previously mentioned the *lectio divina* and Word/Share/Prayer tools (see Appendix E) for beginning meetings. The possibilities are unlimited. The key is intentionality.

Risk-Taking Mission and Service

Schnase's next category includes what many congregations describe as mission and adds an element of risk. He adds the prophetic to the altruistic. Many congregations encourage members to help with food or clothing banks, provide lunches or emergency aid for homeless persons, or send young people on a work camp in a city. These actions are important. They fulfill the

Great Commandment to love neighbor as self but they aren't particularly risky.

Schnase says, "*Risk-taking* steps into greater uncertainty, a higher possibility of discomfort, resistance, or sacrifice. Risk-taking mission and service takes people into ministries that push them out of their comfort zone, stretching them beyond the circle of relationships and practices that routinely define their faith commitments."[20]

Think of some scripture passages that press Christ's disciples into action:

- "Love your neighbor as yourself." (Mark 12:28-31)
- "As you did it to one of the least of these, you did it to me." (Matthew 25:40)
- "This is my commandment, that you love one another. No one has greater love than this, to lay down one's life for one's friends." (John 15:13)
- "So, faith by itself, if it has no works, is dead." (James 2:17)
- "He has told you, O mortal, what is good; and what does the Lord require of you but to do justice, and to love kindness, and to walk humbly with your God?" (Micah 6:8)
- "Take away from me the noise of your solemn assemblies. I will not listen to the melody of your harps. But let justice roll down like the waters and righteousness like an ever flowing stream." (Amos 5:23-24)

The Bible is clear: the Lord expects followers to care for each other and others, even to the point of sacrificing oneself.

I think of some vigorous congregations that engage in risk-taking mission:

- Despite opposition from many neighbors and some county officials, Trinity Church provides meals and hospitality for day laborers in its suburban location.
- Western Church hosts a breakfast program for 5,000 homeless people every year in Washington's Foggy Bottom, near the Watergate Apartments, Kennedy Center, and State Department.
- Neighborhood congregations in The Ohio State University area of Columbus, Ohio, sponsor a helping-hands program led by paid staff and client volunteers. Middle-class members of the sponsoring congregations work with the staff members, most of who are also clients of this helping hands program, to provide food, clothing, job counseling, and many other services.
- Many vital congregations send young people and adults to work camps to an underdeveloped country, where they live in very primitive conditions, working with and learning from fellow Christians there. Definitely out of

their comfort zone, many people come back with a new understanding of discipleship.

You can make your list of vital and sometimes risky mission activities. These put flesh on admonitions to care for others. What Schnase and other researchers have found is that when members of fruitful congregations get out of their comfort zones to care for others, they grow spiritually and are more compassionate. Newcomers are drawn to congregations which act on rather than talk about these foundational biblical passages.

Extravagant Generosity

Schnase observes, "[Countless followers] have discovered a truth as sure as gravity, that generosity enlarges the soul, realigns priorities, connects people to the Body of Christ and strengthens congregations to fulfill Christ's ministries. Giving reflects the nature of God."[21]

In his fifth practice, he stresses how important it is that followers of Christ place God above their own desires. He unapologetically urges people to tithe, noting that when people set their priorities so they tithe, "The practice of tithing blesses and benefits the giver as much as it strengthens the mission and ministry of the church."[22]

What is the giving level in your congregation? To what extent are people giving sacrificially? Are they giving anywhere near a tithe? Are you? Tool 19 will help you calculate the rough percentage of their income that members of your congregation are giving and so have a sense of how committed members are to Christ and their congregation. I described this tool to the finance committee of a congregation in a very wealthy Washington suburb. They were having trouble getting members to give enough to meet their budget. After quickly doing the math, they started laughing. They were embarrassed at the lack of financial commitment to the congregation. Their members did *not* practice extravagant generosity!

I recognize that most members don't give charitable contributions exclusively to their congregation, but it's critical to challenge them to ask what God is leading them to give to do the work of Christ. How is the Spirit of Christ leading them to deeper gratitude and generosity? There are many scripture passages that lead disciples to extravagant generosity.

Schnase's book and supporting material present the practices in a way that is easy to understand and at the same time challenges members of a congregation to assess and strengthen their congregation's vitality. There are numerous resources for engaging a congregation in studying these practices. Cokesbury Publishing has a prepackaged kit. Others are available online. Several colleagues and clients who have used this process have found it helped their congregations significantly clarify their mission and vision and generate energy and direction.

TOOL 19: A PERCENT CONTRIBUTION CALCULATOR

Here is a simple formula for calculating roughly what percentage members of your congregation are giving to do the work of Christ:

- RPG = TG/(FU x MI)
- RPG (rough percentage giving) equals
- TG (total giving to the congregation)
- divided by FU (number of family units in the congregation) times MI (median income of the community).

Multiplying the median income of the community by the number of family units in the congregation gives a rough estimate of the gross income of all the members. You and your leaders can decide to what extent the congregation is roughly representative of the community and adjust accordingly. Then, divide the actual giving by the gross income, and you will have an idea of how sacrificially people are giving.

Imagine a congregation in a Washington, D.C., suburb that has 150 giving units. Multiplying 150 x $100,000 (the rough median income of Washington suburbs), the gross income of its members would be around $15 million. If they are giving $1.5 million, they are tithing. The $750,000 would represent 5 percent.

TOOL 20: SWOT ANALYSIS

SWOT is an acronym for strengths, weaknesses, opportunities, and threats. The strengths and weaknesses of a congregation reflect its internal resources. Opportunities and threats represent the opportunities and threats in the wider community and its culture. Board members might do a SWOT analysis as part of a one-day retreat, simply putting items on newsprint. However you and other leaders may decide you need more data to adequately analyze the opportunities and threats. Indeed, ignorance of or blindness to outside opportunities and threats may significantly undermine any discernment or planning process. By doing a SWOT analysis, leaders can often identify some immediate needs or challenges to which the congregation can respond. They might identify previously untapped resources from which they can draw.

Here is a partial example of what a strong, pastoral-sized congregation might identify in its SWOT analysis.

Leaders reviewing such an analysis might decide very quickly that they might want to focus on the many new young adults in the community. They might have mentoring groups for young professionals, involve twenty-somethings in ministries to immigrants, and be very intentional about strengthening and expanding small groups. Perhaps a second worship service utilizing more contemporary forms of worship would be started. If current members increased their giving to the 5 percent level, another musician or educator might be employed. However, the pastor would need to learn some new leadership skills, taking care not to micromanage.

Table 8.1

Strengths	Weaknesses
• 140 regularly in worship; 90 in children's church school and weekday activities	• Older building with impending replacements and repairs
• Excellent adult choir and growing children's music	• Outdated computers
• Three small groups involving 20 people	• Cumbersome organization
• Pastor is excellent preacher—does great pastoral care	• Pastor sometimes doesn't have enough time for adequate pastoral care
• Pastor has many ideas for initiatives	• We have a net loss of eight members per year for each of the past five years
• Excellent administrative assistant and musician	• The median age of our leaders is 60; younger members are reluctant to commit themselves to serving on board
• Mission outreach respected in the community	• More families with both spouses working means less time for volunteering
• Two vigorous adult classes	• Women's group is struggling
• Budget has been in the black for 10 years.	• Estimate of percentage giving indicates members give about 3 percent of their income.
• Ten regular volunteers with community food bank	• Leaders tend to rely on pastor too much for new ideas
• We sell fair trade coffee as a way to care for farmers in Mexico	• Pastor tends to micromanage at times
• Mission giving to higher judicatory is at least 10 percent of budget/year	• Church education leaders getting tired
• Lots of long-time hard workers	

Opportunities	Threats
• Many new younger families in community as older persons either die or move	• Changing demographics—immigrants moving into community who are of different religions or denominations (This could also be an opportunity!)
• New restaurants and commerce stimulating community	• A more secular culture with increasing competition for Sunday morning activities
• Increasing property values	• Many younger adults say they are spiritual but not religious, many say they don't like our music
• New condos being built within three blocks of our building	
• Many young adults in nearby apartments seem to be hungry for spiritual nourishment	

Here is a caution: don't use SWOT analysis as the only tool to set priorities. It is one of several tools and approaches.

TOOL 21: DISCERNMENT THROUGH SMALL GROUPS AND ONE-DAY LEADER RETREAT

Here is an outline of a process for a relatively short mission and vision discernment process.

1. Establish a DTeam (Discernment Team)

An effective team has seven to nine members, including the pastor. This DTeam decides whether they can use results of a mission/vision discernment that was done in the past two or three years or might better conduct a short discernment using Schnase's *Five Practices of Fruitful Congregations*.

DTeam does an initial SWOT analysis, reads the *Five Practices*.

DTeam gets buy-in from board for doing the short discernment exercise, publicizes initial plan to congregation.

2. Organize Small Groups to Discern God's Leading

Option 1: Use Five Practices

a. Develop a process. The DTeam develops the process and timetable for working through the practices, coordinates with worship and education leaders. Then, based on the desired number of participants in small groups, it determines the number of groups needed for each of the practices, so that each group has seven to 10 participants. Thus, if a congregation averages 200 in worship on Sunday, the DTeam might have a goal that at least 100 members be involved in one of the groups. That would mean that the DTeam would need to set up 11 or 12 small groups.

Members of the DTeam identify hosts for the groups. Hosts prepare the setting for the meetings, providing simple refreshments. DTeam members and other respected leaders lead the groups. Meeting at varied times during the week, some groups meet in homes, some at the church building or other convenient locations. For example, one group might meet for six successive Wednesday evenings at Mary and Joe's home; another group might have a light lunch after worship in the church building on six Sundays. Set up several ways in which people can sign up for a group, for example, on registration sheets after worship, by e-mail to leaders, or by calling the church office.

Publicize the program and sign up people for groups. Orient group leaders.

b. Lead the Congregational Studies The pastor or pastors preach five successive Sundays on each of the Five Practices.

Engage the congregation in the Five Practices process, attempting to involve half of the worshiping congregation in one of the groups (with each group having eight to ten participants).

Each small group gathering should begin with a trust-building exercise. For example, in the first session, participants tell briefly about themselves (where they are from, how they spend their time during the week, and something about their family). The second week they might say how long they have been part of this congregation, what drew them here, and what they value about being a member.

At conclusion of the six weeks, each group identifies what it thinks are the top 10 priorities for the congregation for the next two years.

Option 2: Set Priorities Based on Existing Mission and Vision Statements

a. Develop a Process The DTeam studies the current mission and vision statements and the work that was done to develop them. They then develop a process for members to meet in a series of three small group meetings to study foundational scripture passages and the current statements, coordinating with worship and education leaders. Then, based on the desired number of participants in small groups, it determines the number of groups needed for each of the practices, so that each group has seven to ten participants (see Option 1a above.) Similarly identify leaders, hosts, and times and places for the groups to meet.

Publicize the program and sign up people for groups. Orient group leaders.

b. Lead the Congregational Study Groups The pastor or pastors preach at least three to five successive Sundays on foundational biblical passages. Even better would be for the pastor to preach on key passages for two months or so, both during the preparation for the study groups and while they are meeting.

The congregation engages in the study process, attempting to involve half of the worshiping congregation in one of the groups. At the conclusion of the three to four weeks, each group identifies what it thinks are the top 10 priorities for the congregation for the next two years.

3. DTeam Identifies 15 to 20 Top Priorities

The DTeam gathers the input of the various small groups and combines and summarizes the various suggestions into declarations phrased: "We believe God is calling our congregation to . . . ." For example: "We believe God is calling Christ Church to strengthen our outreach to families with children and youth." The DTeam should have a maximum of 20 priorities to offer to

leaders at a retreat. Be careful to combine the various group recommendations into fairly concise declarations. It is confusing to have two or three
declarations that say essentially the same thing. So, for example, in addition
to the example above, the team would not have one saying, "To double the
size of the youth group." The latter could be a more specific goal that would
flow from the priority. The declarations of priority would be concise enough
to focus energy and action but broad enough to allow for creativity.

Print each declaration on an 11 in. x 17 in. sheet of paper, and list all of
them on handout sheets for those who participate in the leader retreat.

4. Hold a Leader Retreat

Hold an all-day retreat for leaders. These leaders would be both those formally elected and other respected leaders. Try to get at least 20 percent of the
worshiping congregation at this retreat. Here is a possible outline.

9:30—Gathering

Group building using one of the trust building exercises outlined in chapters
2 and 5. (Provide name tags and refreshments in a comfortable setting.)

9:50—Summarize What Has Been Discerned So Far

DTeam leader, members of the team, and pastor present a summary of the
Five Practices material and the SWOT analysis. Invite participants to offer
additional perspectives. Note what the congregation is already doing well.
(Remember my tip to catch them in the act of doing something well!)

10:45—Break

11:00—Introduce Possible Priorities

Post 11 in. x 17 in. sheets with the declarations and distribute lists of declarations during break. DTeam leader and others present them to the group.
Invite participants to refine the declarations and suggest additions. Invite
participants to briefly advocate for the priorities they think are especially
critical.

11:45—Set Priorities

Give each participant 10 colored adhesive dots with the following assignment:

*Place your dots on what you believe are the top priorities for our congre-
gation. What is God yearning for us to emphasize? You may vote however*

you wish: place all 10 dots on one declaration, two each on five declarations, or whatever you prefer.

I have done this dot exercise many times. Five or six priorities have always risen to the top. By simply seeing the concentration of dots, participants get an immediate sense of what this group of leaders think are the top priorities.

Noon — Lunch

During lunch, members of the DTeam review the declarations and reorganize so that the top four to six are front and center.

12:45 — Discuss the Apparent Priorities

In the total group, discuss the results of the priority-setting exercise. Clarify and reword any declarations as necessary. Get general consensus on the top four to six priorities. If possible, narrow these to the top three.

1:00 — Identify Possible Immediate Steps to Implement Priorities

Divide into small groups, perhaps by committees of the congregation. Ask each group to review these top priorities and identify some possible next steps to take to implement this priority. The pastor should identify personal steps to take.

1:45 — Receive Reports from Groups

Invite a representative from each group to describe action steps their group or committee will take in the next three to six months.

2:00 — Develop a Communication Plan

Discuss how these priorities will be communicated to the congregation. The DTeam and pastor should be the primary persons to communicate them, but other leaders should make commitments to tell the groups they lead and others about the priorities.

2:30 — Reflect on What Priorities Tell You

In the total group reflect on what these priorities tell you about your identity and sense of purpose. List key insights that emerge. Compare these insights with any mission statement that you have.

3:00—Adjourn with Prayer

5. Convene the DTeam to Review and Refine Priorities Set at Retreat

The DTeam reviews and refines the priorities and insights about identity and purpose that emerged from the retreat, phrases them as Mission and Vision Statements, and presents them to one or more town meetings for review and suggestions for improvement. Your objective is to get significant buy-in from members of the congregation. Participants should say things like, "Yes! That's what we should focus on!"

After further review, the DTeam brings mission and vision statements to the board for approval. The board makes any final adjustments of the priorities.

The DTeam writes more formal mission and vision statements that can be used in worship.

6. Board and Team Members Publicize the Revised Mission and Priorities

Leaders encourage their groups to identify how their group, committee, or team might implement the priorities. The board should make sure that the priorities are guiding decisions.

Tip 17: Be on the lookout for low-hanging fruit.

Clarifying priorities will almost certainly show there is already significant momentum towards implementing a priority. If so, by all means encourage leaders to implement the priority quickly. Some quick wins will build the congregation's confidence in you and their leaders. For example, if finances have been a problem and the congregation has a history of lackadaisical stewardship programs, then you can introduce a proven program that will generate more enthusiasm and giving. If several people have already been asking for a spiritual growth group and one of the top priorities identifies building spirituality, then a group should be set up as soon as possible.

Be alert to what you and other leaders can do promptly to implement the vision you have discerned!

Chapter Nine

How's Business?

Leadership and *Management*

"Pastor Smith was such a great guy, but he had both feet planted firmly in the clouds. We never could figure out where he wanted us to go."

"Pastor Susan wasn't all that good with finances, but she made sure that the finance committee had really solid members. We were always very clear about our finances."

"All these committees are getting me down. I feel like I'm running from one meeting to another."

"I can't change a light bulb without going through the property committee and the board! How can this size congregation have so much bureaucracy? We're as bad as IBM!"

I didn't go to seminary to be manager of a business. The year I spent in a management training program for AT&T (two years out of college) made me very clear that handling administrative detail would bore me out of my mind. I suspect that few pastors feel called to oversee the daily operations of a church. Most of us envision serving Christ through preaching, teaching, pastoral care, and ministry in the community.

Maybe the church isn't a business, but pastors and leaders need to lead and manage it well. We can't spend money we don't have or only anticipate having. If we have a building, we have to take care of it. If the congregation has employees, then they must be treated with respect. And the pastor has to set the tone.

LEADERSHIP AND MANAGEMENT:
MAKE A CLEAR DISTINCTION

John Wimberly, long-time pastor of Western Presbyterian Church in Washington, D.C., has written a very helpful book, *The Business of the Church: The Uncomfortable Truth That Faithful Ministry Requires Effective Management*. He makes a clear distinction between leadership and management, noting that most pastors and other staff have to do some of both: "A *leader* is a visionary. She has a dream of what her congregation can be. He is a motivator. A *manager* is a person who can transform a vision into reality. She is a master at implementation. He gets the job done."[1]

Former Alban Institute Senior Consultant Dan Hotchkiss, in his book *Governance and Ministry*, makes similar distinctions between overseeing the congregation as a whole and hands-on work. Governance has to do with policy and vision (i.e., leadership). He writes, "Governance means 'owning' the congregation, exercising ultimate control of its human and material resources and ensuring that it serves its mission." Ministry involves implementing the specifics of a vision (i.e., management): "Ministry is most of the rest of what a congregation does—achieving the inward and outward results the congregation exists to achieve."[2] Lay leaders may do both but often focus on one area. Put another way: leaders help the congregation envision and clarify what are the right things to do, and managers make sure they are done right. As pastor, you need to be clear which hat you are wearing.

Much of what I have written thus far has focused more on various aspects of leadership: building trust, strengthening the leadership teams, and discerning God's call to the congregation. Now we need to look at both leadership and management. Let's begin by reassessing the congregation's organizational structure. Do staff, board, committees, teams, and other groups work well together, or are people frequently at odds or ineffective? Start with the governing board.

What happens in normal board meetings in your congregation? Are you and board members energized, or are you drained? I have been to (and early in my career, led) board meetings that "wasted hours and took minutes." One committee chair after another would read a report, often regarding minutiae that few cared about. Rarely were there substantive theological discussions or attempts to discern God's leading. Intentional spiritual practice was restricted to bookend prayers. How much better it is when board members spend significant time reflecting on how God is leading their congregation. Perhaps they study a scripture passage that speaks to their current situation. They reflect on their sense of mission, vision, and values. They learn how to say yes to teams or committees whose ideas and proposals are clearly in line with the church's direction and how to say no to proposals that don't fit.

Board meetings are not productive when members are not clear about what they are attempting to accomplish. Assuming that your board members are among the most respected leaders of your congregation, help them focus on governance. Studying books on church renewal and engaging in deep Bible study, they might discuss:

- the purpose and meaning of worship and how varied forms help different generations worship most authentically
- the importance of hospitality and how your congregation might be more hospitable
- changing culture and demographics in the community and how the congregation might respond
- how congregational care and communication might be strengthened by using new social media

The objective of such discussion would be to further clarify the congregation's sense of purpose and to develop longer-term goals. In addition to dealing with leadership challenges, however, most boards in program-sized and smaller congregations also attend to ministry details. Optimally the board will oversee the details of ministry through its committees and teams, but usually the board gets into the details of some issues. I urge you to press for the board to focus more on leadership than management.

How do you make sure there is a good balance between a focus on leadership and attending to the details of ministry? You start by setting the agenda, perhaps designing it yourself in consultation with key lay leaders. I have been guest moderator for some boards who seem to have the same agenda every meeting. The clerk reads the minutes, and the treasurer gives a budget report. Then comes old business, and then each committee reports in alphabetical order. I find such meetings painfully boring and sense most leaders do too. They focus too much on the details of ministry and ignore the priorities of the congregation. Thus, to ensure that the board deals with important governance issues, consult with leaders, so that, following 20 minutes of trust- and community-building activities, the most important items are at the beginning of the agenda. Remember to use Tool 18 describing effective board reports. Focused board reports promote clarity and saves time for more important conversation about how God is calling the congregation to serve and how specific ministries might be strengthened to accomplish its mission and vision.

To strengthen leadership, Larry Osborne, lead pastor of North Coast Church in San Diego County, advocates having a second monthly board meeting in someone's home, studying scripture, theology, and mission.[3] One of my clients tried this and in the first meeting made a significant breakthrough in understanding the culture and history of the congregation and built deeper trust between himself and members of the board. Such a second meeting would be particularly helpful if there has been conflict in the congregation and mistrust among members of the board, or if the board has little idea of what it means to be a board.

I recommend having board retreats at least twice a year to deal with larger leadership issues, such as priorities for the next year, staffing patterns, changing worship forms or adding a new worship service, or setting up a comprehensive small group program. Such retreats are wonderful venues for bringing new members on to the board, especially if you can get the board away for an overnight gathering.

What is important is that you and board members are clear about the distinction between leadership and ministry. The work of ministry—the hands-on stuff of teaching church school, singing in the choir, making sure the building is taken care of, handling financial details—is done by myriad smaller groups. Traditionally these ministries are overseen by committees, with members of the committee doing much of the work. In more traditional congregations, this model works reasonably well, but my clients have noted that it is much more difficult than it was even 15 to 20 years ago to get people to serve on committees. They describe people who say, "I'm glad to do a job, but don't make me come to a committee meeting!"

Responding to this attitude, some congregations are leading the work of ministry through semi-autonomous ministry teams. These groups are more than committees, in that members are intentional about building deep relationships and growing spiritually, as well as doing a ministry task. These teams have clear responsibility coupled with authority and appropriate funding. For example, a landscape ministry team might make sure that the grounds of the church are well managed. Typically led by a layperson, the group oversees lawn care, raking of leaves, snow removal, and other lawn and landscape tasks. Such a team would also take time for Bible study, prayer, and fellowship.

Ministry teams can lead virtually every dimension of the congregation's life:

- Communication—newsletter, website, and other media
- Information technology
- Children's education
- Youth ministry
- Traditional worship
- Contemporary worship
- Mission in the community
- Special ministries with retirees or newlyweds

The possibilities are limitless.

E. Stanley Ott, church transformation consultant and head of the Vital Churches Institute, notes, "The beauty of ministry teams is that the team experience of friendship and fellowship is such that its members don't feel that their meetings are interrupting their lives. Instead, each member can say, 'The team has become a *part* of my life. . . . I belong here.'"[4] Ministry teams—trained, supported, and coached as Ott recommends—become life-giving communities of faith. I served in one congregation with ministry teams. The team leaders, who were not on the board, met for a light supper before an all-committee night, updated each other on their plans for the coming month, and coordinated as necessary.

The key is to be clear about what big issues the board needs to address and what details need to be handled by teams or committees. Obviously the board needs to know what committees and teams are doing but they normally should not spend much time discussing details. Ott describes a "loose-tight" balance: "For a ministry team, 'loose' means that the congregation gives the team tremendous freedom to plan and carry out its vision for ministry. 'Tight' means that the team aligns its ministry with the defining vision and practices of the congregation."[5]

The various groups will be clear about authority, responsibility, and accountability when the board sets clear policies. A policy is simply a statement that guides many decisions over time, whether these decisions are made by staff, board, or teams. Examples of policies might be that the property committee can spend whatever funds it is allocated for the year or that the administrative assistant (AA) may authorize payment of office expenses under $500. Hotchkiss strongly urges congregations to develop clear policy books. He cites John Carver's comparison of policies and mixing bowls. Carver, a consultant to nonprofit organizations, says that there are various levels of policy, like nesting bowls. "The largest policies in a given area announce the most general principle or goal the board wishes to achieve."[6] Then come the lower-level, more specific policies that spell out authority, such as the AA's being able to buy office supplies.

Hotchkiss asserts that boards have a foundational policy that "if it's a policy, it's in the book; if it's not in the book, it's not policy."[7] Since more discussion of such policies is beyond the purview of this book, I encourage you to read *Governance and Ministry*. Following Hotchkiss's counsel will help clarify who does what and make board meetings better, so you won't be reinventing the wheel. You can spend more time on substantive issues.

Make clear distinctions between governance and ministry. You will sometimes be wearing your leadership hat and sometimes wearing the manager hat. Be aware of which skills are needed. Always keep the big picture in mind when you are attending to the details. When discussing details of ministry with teams and staff, frame discussion in light of the congregation's mission and vision.

Tip 18: Limit the size of the governing board to about 10 members.

How large is your governing board? I think that nine to twelve is about right for churches averaging more than 100 in worship. Forming a strong leadership team is much more difficult when the board gets larger than a dozen. I think it isn't a coincidence that Jesus had 12 disciples. I have seen churches with 18 or 24 or 30 people on their governing boards. When boards are that large, members tend to represent constituencies in the congregation and then to micromanage their area of responsibility. Further, members of the church easily begin to think, "We elected a good strong group of leaders. They and the pastor can do all the work." Also, somewhat paradoxically, the larger the board, the easier it is for a pastor to control things. Members of the board are so focused on their specific responsibilities that only the pastor knows what's going on everywhere. When a board is too large, the dysfunctions I discussed in chapter 5 can quickly spin out of control. Large boards are often made up of people who don't know each other well. This means they often don't trust each other enough to communicate effectively or to fight effectively and fairly. While they may achieve some positive results, too often mediocre ideas don't get voted down or improved. Members of the board don't buy into decisions, and little gets accomplished. You will have a stronger leadership team with a smaller board. Having said this, be very careful that the board doesn't isolate itself from the congregation. Make sure that board members talk with members and staff, are active in the congregation's community, and offer opportunities for congregational input regarding important decisions.

Tip 19: Have an all-committee or ministry team night.

In all but one of the congregations I served, committees met at times that were convenient to the members of each committee. Further, in these program- and pastoral-size congregations, committee chairs typically expected me or other program staff to attend all committee meetings. In one congregation, however, all committees met the same night of the month. The members would gather at 7:00 p.m. I led a short devotional, participants raised a few concerns or top priorities, and people moved to their committee meetings. Based on prior conversations with committee chairs, I met with committees that needed my input. Since neither I nor the director of education were expected to be at every committee meeting, we couldn't lead the meetings. This arrangement strengthened the authority of the committee chairs and prevented staff dominance. Further, if two committees were working on a joint project, they met together for a portion of the evening. For example, the education committee might meet with the worship committee to review plans for the vacation Bible school and the special worship culminating the vacation Bible school session. Obviously the meetings don't have to be in the evening. They can be on a Sunday afternoon, a Saturday morning, whenever is best.

COACHING ASSIGNMENT 26: ASSESS HOW CLEAR DISTINCTIONS ARE BETWEEN GOVERNANCE AND MINISTRY

Clarify whether staff and board members are clear about the distinction between leadership and management and doing both well. Based on the congregation's mission and vision, does the board give appropriate authority, responsibility, and resources to committees and ministry teams?

ASPECTS OF MANAGEMENT

Let us examine some aspects of ministry and management that are important for you to know about. You may be great at seeing the big picture and casting a vision. You may write clear and compelling sermons and teach stimulating classes, but if you ignore the support infrastructure, then you may well find yourself in some difficulty. Be clear, I'm not advocating your overseeing all the details of these aspects of management, but you need to understand the basics and make sure that sound policies govern these areas. In his discussion of congregational management, Wimberly uses a systems approach, noting how three interlocking inputs—finances, facilities, and personnel—combine to produce the ministry outputs of proclamation, pastoral care, program, and mission.[8] Consider these aspects of your congregation.

A. Finances

How clear are you about the finances of the congregation? How clear are other leaders? Are there adequate guidelines and controls so that finances are handled responsibly?

What if the church treasurer gives reports that a certified public accountant can barely understand, much less someone who doesn't specialize in finance? And what if you discover that there are substantial funds invested in ways that the board had no say over? Or that trustees had been battling with the board for years over how much to put in reserves? Or that a staff member had been misappropriating funds?

In most congregations the board has primary fiduciary responsibility. While members of the board neither need to (nor should they) get into every financial detail, they must understand the finances of the congregation in a general. I have known a few pastors who had business or accounting backgrounds. If you have such a background, you can probably skip what I write here—and could likely improve it. However, if you don't have training in finance, here are some concepts I have found important.

In order for you and members of the board to clearly understand congregational finances, the finance committee or its equivalent need to provide clear reports to the board. There are three general reports that you and other leaders need to make informed decisions concerning virtually any issue you face:

- an income statement
- the cash flow report
- the balance sheet

1. Income Statement

An income statement, sometimes called the operating budget, summarizes income and expenses, typically with one column showing the previous month's income and expenses, another showing income and expenses for the year to date, and a third showing the annual budget. The income statement will indicate whether a committee's expenses are over or under budget and whether income for the year has covered the expenses. These statements are typically divided into ministry areas. For example, expenses might include sections for staff, education, property, and so forth. Each of these would be further divided into line items. So, for example, the property category might include utilities, building maintenance, and furnishings.

Such reports need to be both accurate and easy to understand. Thus, each committee category should have as few line items as reasonable. So, for example, there might be a line for building maintenance. This line would summarize expenses for repairing furniture, buying floor wax, and other maintenance expenses. Committee chairs would review the specific expenses. If treasurer's reports are too detailed, neither pastors nor board members are likely to read them.

2. Cash Flow Report

The cash flow report simply shows how much cash the congregation has at the end of the reporting period. This is like a typical household's checkbook. You know what your balance is and whether you have the funds to take that vacation or not. Often the income and cash flow statements are combined into one statement that the board can easily understand. Regular, clear financial statements make sure that board members know that members' contributions are handled properly.

Tip 20: Base income statements and cash flow reports on prior years' experience.

Basing reports on prior years' experience simply means that planners take into account typical variations in income and expenses. The chart below illustrates a possible scenario. Typically, income varies widely from month to month, with giving in the summer being less than in the academic year. In some congregations, December's giving is dramatically higher than any other month because some people wait until the end of the year to give most of their offering, and expenses vary too, with expenses for church education material being higher in August or September, utility costs being higher in the summer for air conditioning or in the winter for heating, and worship expenses might be higher around Christmas and Easter when special musicians are hired.

When the finance committee simply pro-rates income and expenses in 1/12 increments, they can draw incorrect conclusions as they review income and expenses. In such arbitrary calculations, if the winter's fuel bills are higher than the 1/12th budgeted, leaders may panic at seeing the utilities expense being way over budget, when in reality these expenses are fairly normal. In table 9.1 shows that prorated utility expenses would be $6,667 at the end of April, but would be $7,600 based on experience.

3. Balance Sheet

The balance sheet shows both the value of the congregation's various assets and its liabilities. Assets would include the value of the building and its property, furnishings, office equipment, other congregational real estate, bank accounts, investments, and other funds. Depending on how likely it is that members give to the congregation what they pledge to give, their promises would also be considered assets. Liabilities would include the mortgage or other outstanding loans, any unpaid obligations to staff, tax payments due, and so forth. A balance sheet is intrinsically less accurate than the income and cash flow reports because it isn't possible to know exactly what the building and property are worth. However, reports can include a current estimate of these values plus current values of other funds.

To help make sure all is done according to accepted accounting practices, Wimberly advocates employing a bookkeeper to make "adequate journal entries. These entries are simple to make, but they are a nightmare to correct if made incorrectly."[9] See Wimberly's book for a much more thorough treatment of balance sheets and other accounting issues.

Table 9.1

Month	Estimated Monthly Income (1/12 of budget)	Estimated Total Income (based on 1/12 increments)	Estimated Income Based on Experience	Monthly Utilities (1/12)	Monthly Utilities (experience)
January	16,667	16,667	16,000	1,667	1,900
February	16,667	33,334	18,000	1,667	2,300
March	16,667	50,001	19,000	1,667	2,500
April	16,667	66,668	26,000	1,667	1,600
May	16,667	83,335	18,000	1,667	1,200
June	16,667	100,002	16,000	1,667	1,200
July	16,667	116,669	10,000	1,667	1,600
August	16,667	133,336	8,000	1,667	1,800
September	16,667	150,003	12,000	1,667	2,000
October	16,667	166,670	18,000	1,667	1,200
November	16,667	183,337	17,000	1,667	1,200
December	16,667	200,000	22,000	1,667	1,600
	200,000	200,000	200,000	20,000	20,000

4. General Policies Regarding Finances

Make sure that there are adequate controls over those who handle finances. Having multiple persons count the weekly offerings helps protect the congregation against embezzlement. Having a separate team perform sample audits of finances also ensures adequate controls.

Make sure that you and other leaders are clear about how the various congregational funds are invested. Determine how bequests are handled. Are they restricted or not? How might leaders guide those who wish to make bequests to the congregation? In general, I have encouraged those who wish to leave the congregation a bequest to make it as flexible as possible, consistent with their wishes. So, for example, someone who wants to support a youth program might designate it for ministry with youth rather than to support youth mission trips to Kentucky.

Should the congregation have a reserve fund to handle major expenses, such as repair or replacement of the roof or heating, air-conditioning, electrical, or plumbing systems? I think it is important to build reserve funds to handle both expected and unexpected expenses. However, sometimes a capital improvement fund drive is necessary. Initiate a conversation with leaders about how the congregation might anticipate and deal with major expenses.

The policy book I discussed earlier should spell out financial policies. Further, the policies should be based on the priorities of the congregation. Don't let fearful leaders tie up funds that could be profitably used for ministry, especially if the congregation is declining. An interim pastor colleague working with a declining congregation discovered that the congregation had some $750,000 in reserve funds. "Those are for a rainy day," one leader explained. This pastor exclaimed, "My friend, it's raining!" After facing reality, they used some of those funds to dramatically increase handicapped accessibility, brighten the entryway, and make other helpful improvements. Their leadership helped turn the congregation around.

Tip 21: Follow the KISS principle.

Perhaps you have heard the KISS acronym: Keep It Simple Stupid! (Or some say "Keep It Sweet and Simple.") Most pastors and board members are not trained financial managers. Make sure reports are simple enough to understand and yet detailed enough to adequately describe the congregation's financial status.

Tip 22: Ask financial leaders to tell you about any who have stopped giving altogether or who have significantly increased or decreased their giving.

I think it is good for the pastor to generally know what members give but recognize that many congregations have a policy against the pastor's knowing any details about individual contributions. Stress that not giving or giving only a token amount is a spiritual and pastoral issue. When someone stops giving, it's a signal that something is wrong. You need to check out what's happening with the person or family. They could be unhappy with the congregation or you. There might be a major illness draining their funds. Someone may have lost a job. You can't guess, but you can care—if you are notified.

B. Facilities and Infrastructure

If a congregation is going to have a building, it must be maintained or deferred maintenance will haunt you. Further, poorly maintained buildings and grounds are a turn-off to prospective members. So be sure that those who oversee the property are competent and committed. If they are not able to take care of the building, then I suggest you describe the reality you observe and explore other ways of handling the maintenance, such as employing a building manager. Please review what I wrote in chapters 1 and 4 about assessing the building and leadership.

Infrastructure would include technology such as computers, photocopiers, telephones, audiovisual systems, and the website. Work with knowledgeable members to assess how well these various technologies are supporting your ministry. Two cautions: don't get bogged down with a well-intended member who knows something about IT or website design but not enough to be really effective. Several of my clients have groaned about that person who is forever developing the congregation's website but never quite gets it done. And even if you know a lot about IT and can even design the congregation's website, odds are very slim that the congregation called you to be their IT expert. They want you to be their pastor. Depending on the size and complexity of your congregation, you may well decide to employ someone to manage the IT and website design and construction. For more ideas on websites and congregational communication, see Lynne Baab's *Reaching Out in a Networked World: Expressing Your Congregation's Heart and Soul.*[10]

C. Personnel

Personnel problems in congregations are among the most difficult issues pastors and boards have to deal with. When there are good relationships among staff members and between staff members and the congregation, the congregation usually does well. When relationships break down, there is heartache. Developing good personnel policies and procedures helps ensure that relationships are positive. Otherwise, staff members may be abused or taken advantage of or staff members (including pastors) may abuse their position.

Your responsibility as pastor is to clarify lines of authority. I think (as does Wimberly) that the pastor should be the head of staff. Wimberly observes, "As head of staff, one of my responsibilities is to communicate clearly and firmly to a few wannabe managers among our membership that I have the staff management responsibility under control."[11] Some of my clients have told me about administrative assistants who resigned because assertive board members insisted that she or he do immediately what they wanted done, dropping whatever they were doing. In congregations I served, I typically told the administrative assistant and other staff to work with lay leaders as practical, but that if there were competing requests, to ask me which took priority.

In chapter 5 I stressed how important it is that staff members be a cohesive team. Regular staff meetings, optimally weekly, are key components of building and maintaining a strong team. In these meetings, you can both review the details of the week and continually make sure staff members understand the priorities of the congregation. You can also adapt particular tasks based on immediate needs and the gifts of the individuals.

I recognize that getting everyone to these regular staff meetings depends somewhat on the size of congregation. Scheduling staff meetings is easier if everyone is full-time or at least able to come to a meeting at a common time every week. However, musicians in smaller congregations usually have regular daily jobs and so are not able to come to a daytime staff meeting. In those cases, I have arranged to meet with the musician at another time, sometimes including an associate pastor in our conversation. Whether you have full- or part-time staff, find times when everyone can get together to both work and have fun.

Next, each staff person should have a job description based on priorities expressed in the congregation's mission and vision statements that have been mutually set by you and the board. Specific expectations for staff members then flow from the priorities. These expectations and priorities should be clearly communicated to the congregation. Staff appraisals follow from these job descriptions and expectations. I encourage you to design your own appraisals, basing them on the congregation's priorities and what the staff person is to do. Don't simply adapt some instrument used in government, nonprofit, or private sector jobs. You will see one example in Tool 22 below.

Basing appraisals on priorities and expectations protects both staff and the congregation. Both pastors and aggressive lay leaders sometimes abuse their power. I have seen pastors and other staff victimized by powerful individuals who jerked around the pastor, staff, or board members according to his or her whims. These power brokers sometimes simply decide that it is time for the pastor, for example, to leave the congregation. They make sure the pastor is fired, leaving the pastor out of a job and many others enraged. However, abuses work the other way too. I have observed or heard of pastors who, rather than tending to and leading their congregation, seem to spend most of their time on whatever hobby they please—serving on myriad judicatory committees or local nonprofit boards, participating in community theater or musical groups, gardening or woodworking, or spending an inordinate amount of time studying for sermons or classes, or an advanced degree. They focus on *their* priorities, not those of the congregation. Clear job descriptions, priorities, and appraisals help the board, pastor, and other staff determine how all of them should spend their time. They protect everyone against unreasonable expectations.

Job descriptions and appraisals need to be administered by a personnel committee or team made up of respected members, at least some of whom are familiar with personnel matters. This committee should develop clear personnel policies that spell out considerations such as vacations and sick leave, sabbaticals, and health benefits. See Wimberly's book for more suggestions. [12]

In addition to a formal appraisal, you might use a less formal tool I describe below, Feedback and Feedforward. This process solicits suggestions from members and colleagues about how you might improve your performance. Drawing from those suggestions, you take the initiative, work on improving your preaching, your administration, or other area of competence.

SO WHAT? MAKE SURE THE CONGREGATION'S ORGANIZATION WORKS WELL

A few years ago my wife and I remodeled our kitchen and dining room area. The kitchen was cramped and very inefficient. There was hardly room for both of us to be in it at the same time. It worked against us. We replaced a wall with a peninsula counter, added a new door to the backyard, put in new cabinets and lighting, and created a delightful kitchen that was a center for entertaining family and friends. The new structure worked *for* us instead of *against* us.

Like the structure of a home, congregational structure should work for you instead of against you if you, other staff, and the congregation are to minister effectively. The building needs to be in good shape. Finances and infrastructure need to be in order. Personnel policies need to be well designed and based on the congregation's mission and vision. You may have a glimpse of God's wonderful vision for your congregation, but if you and other leaders don't manage well, then you and others will be in trouble.

COACHING ASSIGNMENT 27: ASSESS THE CONGREGATION'S BUSINESS ORGANIZATION

Based on the material in this chapter and in books such as Wimberly's *The Business of the Church*, assess how well you and congregational leaders are doing with the business of the congregation. You might use questions like these:

• Organization—Does the way the congregation is organized work for you or against you? What might be done to improve the organization? Who might lead such an effort?
• Policies—Are there clear, well-understood policies describing authority, responsibility, and accountability?
• Finances—To what extent do reports give you and board members the information they need to make good decisions? Are there adequate safeguards for handling money? Assess the investment policies and practices. Are staff members and committee chairs clear about how much money they are authorized to spend without securing additional authority?

- Property—To what extent is the property and infrastructure being properly managed? Assess the attractiveness of the property. To what extent does it enable the congregation to fulfill its mission and vision?
- Personnel—Assess the personnel policies. To what extent are there clear job descriptions and appraisals based on the congregation's priorities? How respected is the personnel committee? Are the roles and responsibilities regarding staff supervision clear?

TOOL 22: SAMPLE APPRAISAL FORM

Following is a sample appraisal form for a pastor who is fairly new to a congregation. It is based on some I have developed with personnel committees in congregations averaging around 150 average attendance with an associate pastor or educator. Note that it assigns an A, B, or C priority to each area, with A being top priority. You will see in this example that the board wants the pastor to give top priority to worship, preaching, and congregational community building, and lower priority to teaching and mission leadership. Your priorities would obviously be unique to your situation. Members of the personnel committee gave the form to and sought input from board members, staff, and selected congregational members and then compiled the results into a final appraisal. I completed the Pastor Evaluation Form and gave it to the personnel committee chair. We then met, discussed their findings and my insights and hopes, and planned for the next year.

PASTOR EVALUATION

Pastor being evaluated:
    Date:
    Please evaluate the pastor in the following categories, circling the appropriate level of performance. Indicate how high the priority is for this expectation by using an A, B, or C ranking, with A being highest. Based on the requirements of the job, the pastor:

- Exceeds expectations: Performs most duties in a superior manner. Takes on many assignments using his or her own initiative and contributes more than is expected of the position.
- Meets expectations: Performs assigned duties in an acceptable manner and meets requirements of the position.
- Needs improvement: Performs duties at a less than acceptable level, needs improvement.

The current congregational priorities are:

- Worship—God calls us to engage in joyful worship using both traditional and more contemporary music and forms.
- Trust building—God calls us to move beyond the conflict and tension that we have experienced the past few years.
- Numerical growth—God calls us to identify alternatives and strategies for growth
- Spiritual growth—God invites us to deeper commitment to grow spiritually.
- Missional service—God is leading us to serve the lonely and lost in our affluent suburb and wherever we are.

Provide comments concerning the pastor's performance the past year, and provide specifics wherever possible. Highlight areas of exceptional effort, those that need improvement, and any particular areas that need attention next year. Note that the priorities indicate what the board determined the pastor should emphasize this past year.

1. Worship Development and Leadership

Develops liturgy (order of worship, choice of hymns, prayers, and so forth) that is appropriate to the congregation and community. Conducts meaningful prayers of the people. Administers sacraments effectively. Leads worship committee and program staff to consider changes and innovations, such as a "contemporary" worship service and new formats.

Priority: A

    Exceeds expectation
    Meets expectation
    Needs improvement

Comments:

2. Preaching

Content is solid theologically and biblically, applies to issues and experiences people are concerned about, and gives worshipers guidance on how to live in God's way. Practices effective and interesting delivery and organization, varied approaches, well focused.

Priority: A

    Exceeds expectation

Meets expectation
Needs improvement

Comments:

3. Administrative Leadership

Demonstrates effective organizational skills (team building, communication, planning, etc.). Supervises and works with staff as appropriate. Helps lay leaders clarify the congregation's mission and vision, make plans, and implement them; strengthens policies and organizational procedures.

Priority: B

Exceeds expectation
Meets expectation
Needs improvement

Comments:

4. Pastoral Care

Provides prompt and compassionate pastoral care to members of the congregation, especially in crisis situations. Refers members to other professionals as necessary. Helps develop climate of lay pastoral care.

Priority: B

Exceeds expectation
Meets expectation
Needs improvement

Comments:

5. Education and Teaching

Teaches classes or leads groups as appropriate. Encourages all ages and groups to learn and grow spiritually. Helps strengthen the Church Education program.

Priority: C

Exceeds expectation
Meets expectation

Needs improvement

Comments:

6. Mission Leadership and Involvement

Gets personally involved and encourages others to get involved in mission activities. Interprets denominational mission. Helps leaders and members commit to our mission as a church and their own mission as Christians.

Priority: C

 Exceeds expectation
 Meets expectation
 Needs improvement

Comments:

7. Evangelism and New Member Outreach

Organizes and participates in effective outreach to newcomers. Works with leaders to publicize church activities. Helps newcomers explore their faith and leads them to renewed commitment to Christ. Oversees assimilation of new members. Develops ways to encourage members to grow spiritually (for example, through groups, newsletter articles, sermons, and the like).

Priority: B

 Exceeds expectation
 Meets expectation
 Needs improvement

Comments:

8. Professional and Spiritual Development

Attends to his or her own spiritual development. Participates in activities that promote professional effectiveness and knowledge.

Priority: B

 Exceeds expectation
 Meets expectation
 Needs improvement

Comments:

9. Congregational Community Building

Leads efforts to build trust among leaders, members, and staff. Is a healing, nonanxious presence. Promotes opportunities for friendship and mutual support among members. Participates as appropriate in ongoing group activities such as the women's association or the senior's club.

Priority: A

    Exceeds expectation
    Meets expectation
    Needs improvement

Comments:

10. Relationship to Judicatory and Ecumenical Groups

Is appropriately involved with the denomination, local ministerial associations, and the like. Takes leadership as needed. Promotes positive attitude toward the denomination.

Priority: C

    Exceeds expectation
    Meets expectation
    Needs improvement

Comments:

Additional comments:

PASTOR'S SELF-EVALUATION

Date: _____

    To be answered by pastor and discussed with personnel committee

1. What are some of your significant accomplishments since your last evaluation?
2. What concerns do you have about the congregation and your job expectations?

3. What are your most important objectives for next year?
4. Are you going to reorder your priorities for next year? If so, how?
5. What do you propose for your professional development for next year?
6. What additional resources (monetary, spiritual) or assistance do you feel is necessary to help make you more successful?
7. Other comments:

Signed,
    Pastor _____ Date
_____

    Personnel Chair _____ Date
_____

TOOL 23: FEEDBACK AND FEEDFORWARD

Most of us don't really like feedback; it feels too much like criticism—and often is. We'd like to think we're doing a wonderful job. However, each of us can improve a little—or even a lot. So instead of feedback, seek *feedforward*. Look ahead and determine what you might do to improve your competence and exceed expectations of parishioners. This approach is adapted from Marshall Goldsmith's book *What Got You Here Won't Get You There.* Goldsmith offers an amazing array of resources in his online library of resources. [13]

First, simply ask about 10 people who know your work and whom you respect, "How can I be a more effective pastor?" or "How can I do a better job?" Don't ask how they feel about you or some other vague question. You're after a few simple suggestions about how you can do a better job.

Take notes on what they say. Maybe ask some clarifying questions, but that's it. Don't argue, don't rationalize, don't give examples of how you have already done precisely what they wish and or why are they asking you to do this. Just say, "Thank you for your suggestions."

Then reflect on all these suggestions and identify the one or two most important things to work on. Here's where it gets really interesting. You might learn that you need to listen more attentively. What are people really telling you with both their words and their actions? What are the underlying messages? Be sure to express thanks and appreciation for their suggestions. Obviously, if you learn from this feedback that you need to apologize for something, then do it. Have you inadvertently ignored or hurt someone? Tell them you're sorry and you'll work on changing your behavior.

Next, select an area in which to improve.

1. Pick the behavior. For example, to be a better listener to be better organized.
2. Describe your objective in one-on-one dialogues with individuals from whom you got feedback and several others whom you trust (for example, your best friend). (I'll call these your "helpers.")
3. Ask each person for no more than two suggestions for the future that might help you achieve a positive change in your selected behavior. As the person responds, take notes and listen carefully. Again, do not interrupt; do not disagree. Listen, clarify, and say thank you.

Third, change your behavior:

1. Consider the suggestions you get, decide what specific actions you will take (usually two or three things), tell your helpers what you have decided to do and begin doing what you have committed yourself to do.
2. Solicit feedback. After a month or so, ask your helpers, "How am I doing?" Again, listen carefully and say, "Thanks for your input." Doing this both shows them you are trying to improve and tells them that you value their suggestions. And it tells you whether you're on track. You win all around.
3. Keep at it, perhaps selecting more things to work on as you get better at the first things.

Taking time to do this feedforward process accomplishes two important objectives. First, you will improve in the areas you have committed to improve. Second (and just as important), your stock will rise in the minds of those whose suggestions you took seriously. You will have demonstrated your respect for them and, in fact, have become more effective. A positive cycle is in place. One of my clients used this tool in order to improve his preaching. When he collected the suggestions, he found that the ideas could be summarized: (1) keep your sermon structure simpler and (2) tell more stories. Some weeks later he told me, "My sermons seem awfully simplistic to me, but people seem to be getting a lot more out of them."

COACHING ASSIGNMENT 28: DO THE FEEDFORWARD EXERCISE

Do this feedforward exercise with 10 to 15 people, including several board members whom you respect and you think are likely to give you helpful suggestions. Tell your board what you are doing. Communicate your findings and plans for action to the congregation. Review the results and keep learning!

Chapter Ten

How Do I Deal with Difficult Behavior?

Perspectives and Suggestions

"She's the Wicked Witch of the West with her flying monkeys! If people do not do what she wants them to, then she comes after them!"

"He was passed over for promotion to colonel, so now he has to control the congregation's property!"

"Every time I make a suggestion, the first words out of his mouth are, 'No, that won't work.' I never met anyone so negative."

"An elected leader from *another* congregation started a contemporary service with the previous associate pastor. When I began serving the congregation as interim pastor, he told me that I wasn't to come to that service!"

I hear stories like this and shake my head. What is going on? Where are the other leaders? How do people get away with this kind of behavior? Because we church folks have confused being loving with being nice. Mind you, I am not saying that we should be nasty, but we have a problem confronting those who are emotionally immature. Think of a toddler running amuck in a supermarket, grabbing candy bars and tearing them open, and the parent runs along, seemingly unwilling or unable to deal with this irresponsible behavior. Instead of firmly saying, "Stop!" or simply strapping the child in the shopping cart, the parent does nothing. Too often church leaders just paste on a smile and say nothing when someone is acting like a self-centered toddler.

One of my clients was a retired military officer dealing with a bully, and I asked him how he and other officers would have handled someone like this man if he were a peer or subordinate in the armed services. "He might not have been court-martialed, but he sure wouldn't have been promoted," he noted. "Then why are you and the others on the board tolerating such behavior?" I asked. "What can you say to him?" He realized he needed another approach.

How *do* we deal with difficult people? In this chapter I will reflect more on what I discussed in chapters 5 and 7 and give you some more specific suggestions about dealing with some characters you may have met.

SOME CHARACTERS YOU MAY KNOW

Here is a list of some characters Alice encountered, augmented by some others I have known.

Queen (or King) of Hearts, aka, the woman (or man) who runs the church. These are often the matriarchs or patriarchs of a family-size church. Sometimes she has a flock of flying monkeys like the Wicked Witch in the *Wizard of Oz*. The pastor is simply the hired servant du jour.

- *Snipers*—Snipers shoot from behind the bushes with a sarcastic comment or a dismissive laugh, or they might simply start reading email or a book during your sermon. Whatever their method, they find ways to discount you and other leaders.
- *Bulldozers*—Similar to the Queen of Hearts, they will roll right over you and others to get their way. Unlike the Queen, they don't have to run everything; they want their way on just the issues they are passionate about. They believe they are absolutely right in their particular belief.
- *IEDs (Improvised Explosive Devices)*—You tiptoe around IEDs, because you know that if you touch them the wrong way—*boom!* They can exert considerable control if people let them get away with temper tantrums.
- *Authorities on Everything* (AoE)—They know all the answers to any question, and if you do not believe it, just ask them! When AoEs start their soliloquies, people start leafing through papers, looking out the window, or holding side conversations.
- *Cheshire Cats*—These are the folks who are all smile and no substance. Maybe they express great enthusiasm about an idea but never show up. At the first whiff of conflict or disagreement, they disappear.
- *Tweedledee and Tweedledum*—Joined at the hip, they fuss at each other over almost anything and distract you and others from what's important.
- *Mad Hatters*—Mad Hatters put normally understandable English words together in riddles or phrases that are quite unintelligible. Some of them use technical terms (e.g., a computer geek, financial wizard, or theology wonk). Others aren't articulate. Politicians often use normal words to mislead or deliberately confuse. They are all hard to understand.

- *White Rabbits*—These folks, with their aimless dashing about, are confusing and amusing.
- *Always Agreeables*—They always say "yes" and rarely come through. They desperately want to please everyone and can't stand any disagreements.
- *Clams*—It is really hard to know their thoughts or opinions.
- *Liars*—Hard to believe, but sometimes church folks just tell lies!
- *Downers and Whiners*—These folks always see the glass as considerably less than half full. If possible, they will snatch defeat from the jaws of victory!
- *Ultra-carefuls*—They want every possible option considered, all potential pitfalls guarded against, T's crossed and I's dotted! Their philosophy, "Do not decide until you absolutely must!" Of course, by then it's probably too late.
- *Gossips and Backstabbers*—These difficult people gain power by cutting down other people (especially the pastor).
- *BFP's (beloved former pastors)*—Former pastors can be both incredibly helpful *and* difficult.

Do Not Be Difficult Yourself!

Do you recognize any of these characters? Do other characters come to mind? Even more important: are *you* at times one or more of these characters? In chapter 7 I asked you to be aware of your internal reactions and your external responses to difficult people and other stresses. What did you discover about yourself?

I am acutely aware that I am sometimes difficult (and if I am not aware of that at the moment, there are those who remind me that I am being a bulldozer, control freak, or am distracted). I am fascinated that some people who bug me do not bother others, and conversely, some who are not problematic to me bother others. That bossy parishioner may remind me (both consciously and unconsciously) of my mom or dad, and I react like a rebellious teenager. Or I may evoke a parishioner's memories of an abusive teacher or boss.

Recall that in chapter 7, I asked you to be aware of your default stress styles. Are you a blamer, placater, computer, or distracter? What inner narratives govern your reactions to difficult situations and people? If you are not aware of those negative reactions and do not adequately control your responses, then you will likely be a difficult person. I have heard of pastors who lose their tempers when people disagree with them and then swear at staff members or stomp out of a meeting. If you perceive anyone's questioning of your opinion as an attack, then you are likely a difficult person.

Remember that some people will bother you who simply are not a problem to others, and that you will trouble some people and not be aware of your impact on them. By recognizing the types of people who hook you, you can then be aware of those irrational reactions and control your responses more constructively. Similarly, if you recognize that you set off alarm bells with certain people, you can simply be alert to their discomfort and act to assuage anxiety you may have accidentally generated.

Management consultant and coach Marshall Goldsmith writes about behavior problems he sees in those with whom he works:

> I find that the 20 flaws that hold most people back are rarely flaws of skill, . . . intelligence, . . . or personality. [These flaws] are challenges in interpersonal behavior, often leadership behavior. They are the egregious everyday annoyances that make your workplace noxious. They are transactional flaws performed by one person against others. [1]

He flags behaviors such as the need to always win; responding with "no," "but," or "however" without really listening to the other; or making destructive comments. One of the twenty bad behaviors that stopped me cold was the need to add value. In a speech to a conference of coaches, he declared that when a boss takes an employee's suggestion and says something like, "Oh, that's great. Now, here's how you can improve it!" the boss takes away 50 percent of the employee's motivation. I have had to learn to watch myself, especially as an experienced pastor and coach. It is so difficult for me not to dispense my vast wisdom! I encourage you to visit the online Marshall Goldsmith Library and learn more about yourself and others. Be aware of how you might lapse into one of Goldsmith's bad behaviors.

Peter Steinke stresses the importance of managing one's own anxiety. Instead of being defensive and automatically reactive to difficult people, we need to work at being a nonanxious person. According to Steinke, "Nonanxious responses include

- being thoughtful before acting
- staying calm and poised
- using I statements
- maintaining awareness of self
- focusing on larger purposes rather than winning an argument
- asking questions." [2]

Note that Steinke suggests using "I statements" in your interactions. An "I statement" simply indicates what your perception is. It expresses your feelings and describes the impact of the other's behavior on you; it sometimes seeks to connect and work things out. "When you blow up at me, I am scared and do not want to talk with you." "I felt put-down when you derided my suggestion at the board meeting. I wanted you all to discuss my ideas. Can we talk about what happened?" An "I message" is different from a "you message," in which you blame someone. "You're a jerk for getting mad at me." "Why do you always put people down in meetings?" "I don't think I've ever known anyone as dumb as you." Such messages put people on the defensive and shut down communication.

Steinke also recommends asking questions. I previously suggested using the Curious Card as a newcomer to the congregation. Keep using it! Asking lots of questions helps calm anxieties and opens possibilities. More on this later in the chapter.

DON'T LABEL PEOPLE

Chances are you chuckled at the list with which I began this chapter. You likely identified some of these characters who are part of your congregation. But wait! I suggested that you, like me, are sometimes difficult yourself and that one or more of these labels might be pinned on you. I also suspect that you wouldn't relish being labeled one of these characters. Right?

I find that I have an inner cast of characters ready to take the stage, depending on the situation. So an angry person who is shouting at me might surface a feisty terrier or a sniveling coward. A seeker might draw forth a sage or another seeker. A grief-stricken widow might elicit a compassionate shepherd or someone confronting his own mortality. A confused crowd might see me as master organizer or someone who's over his head. I am each of these at times. Further, some of my negative behaviors depend on my power and status in the particular situation. If I feel threatened and weak, I might act like a sniper, but if I have plenty of power, then I may seek to control everything. You can identify a cast of your inner characters, can't you? Some are very positive; some not so positive. Simply to label people as bulldozers or snipers or one of these other characters does not respect their wonderful complexity.

In *Never Call Them Jerks: Healthy Responses to Difficult Behavior*, Arthur Paul Boers observes, "Labels are merely sophisticated put-downs: schoolyard immaturity translated into churchly vocabulary . . . destructive . . . self-fulfilling prophecy." [3] "The first rule, then, for dealing with difficult behavior in the congregation is this: Never call a parishioner a 'jerk'! Therefore we must focus not on 'difficult people' but on 'difficult relationships' and 'difficult behavior'—a subtle but crucial distinction." [4] If we pastors start labeling parishioners, we engage in stereotyping. So, rather than labeling, we must deal with specific behaviors.

COACHING ASSIGNMENT 29: IDENTIFY
HOW YOU CAN BE DIFFICULT

Try to become more aware of what you say with both words and actions. Are you being difficult? To what extent are you being anxious and reactive in your interactions with those whom you find difficult? Do you slide into some of Goldsmith's bad behaviors? What mistakes have you made, and how might you improve your responses to reactive and difficult people? What have been helpful approaches? Seek input from trusted parishioners about how you can be more effective in your relationships.

STRENGTHEN THE FOUNDATION

I have encountered any number of people who engaged in difficult behaviors and, with some notable exceptions, have managed to work well with almost all of them. What were some keys in getting along? A vital foundation stone was that the lay leaders with whom I worked were emotionally and spiritually solid.

Dealing with people who engage in difficult behavior requires that leaders work well together, trust and respect one another, and have a clearly stated and widely owned mission and vision. Elected leaders who let emotionally immature people control the agenda are like parents who throw up their hands in dismay but do nothing when their spoiled preschoolers tear up a room. Grown-ups intervene and stop the misbehavior. Thus, you need to ask who the grown-ups are and strengthen them.

In chapter 1, I recommended you make an initial assessment of how the congregational system works, and I hope you have continued to examine and reflect on it. Recall the Five Dysfunctions of a Team that I discussed in chapter 5. If the leadership team cannot deal effectively with their differences, then you cannot expect them to deal effectively with others in the congregation who engage in difficult behavior. Optimally, the board will be made up of emotionally and spiritually mature grown-ups who can deal effectively with those who behave badly.

In addition, when you, the board, and other leaders develop a clear, widely owned mission and vision statement, you have a standard by which you can ask questions: "Is this proposal consistent with our sense of God's call to us or not?" "Does this person's request or demand help us implement the top priorities that we set for the next few years?" Having a clear sense of God's call is immensely helpful to you and board members when you are confronted by an angry, anxious person. Being that nonanxious presence when attacked by such a person can be difficult. Asking questions about how their concerns relate to the congregation's sense of call helps you and other leaders avoid being emotionally reactive to the difficult behavior. Asking questions that clarify and relate the concern to the broader mission of the congregation lowers the emotional temperature, so that everyone can think more clearly.

Review what I wrote in chapter 8 about authority and responsibility, and clarify leaders' roles and responsibilities. When relationships are well-defined, leaders can more easily restrain those who want to dominate everything by simply saying something like, "Dorothy, we agreed that Sharon was in charge of developing the new small groups. What concerns do you have? It looks like you're trying to take charge."

Explore again board agreements about how people treat one another. In chapter 2, I encouraged you to write down the spoken and unspoken rules that you have identified for how people behave. When people engage in difficult behaviors, it's time to review the norms. Maybe you will discover rules that you hadn't been aware, such as, "So long as the pastor doesn't try to change anything significant, then we will all behave nicely with one another, but when the new pastor introduces change, we start fighting." If you discover a rule like that, it is important to describe it in a curious, nondefensive manner and start a conversation with board members about how you might develop more positive norms about dealing with differences. Take some time to review the norms you previously identified and refine your list. If you haven't developed a covenant of behavior, then do so.

I know that I'm repeating much of what I've written in previous chapters, but keep on strengthening the leadership team. Build trust, help them deal with differences, ensure ownership, clarify accountability, and be clear about what God yearns for you to focus on. These are foundation stones for dealing with difficult behavior.

DEALING WITH SPECIFIC BEHAVIORS

When I think of people who others label "difficult," I think of "Susie," a woman with whom I worked very well for several years. Both of us are very organized. As she took on more leadership, I taught her how to design good agendas for meetings. I respected her intelligence and creativity. I admired her attention to detail and determination to get things right. However, others found her very difficult. Some might have pinned a bulldozer—or perhaps a Queen of Hearts—label on her. They found her picky about details and intolerant of their sloppiness and thought she was persistently critical. Some perceived that she challenged their authority and status when she questioned their performance. Why did I get along with her and many others didn't? I'm not sure, but I think it was because I listened to her with respect and asked lots of questions when I didn't understand her. I also pushed back when I disagreed with her, offering clear rationale for my ideas and concerns. It also helped that I exceeded her particular expectations for what a pastor should do!

People whom others sometimes perceive as bulldozers are often passionate about doing things well and are intolerant of those who don't meet their expectations. When you encounter such people, it is essential to treat them with respect, curiosity, and openness. Don't write them off as jerks. Rather, take time to hear them out. If they are critical of some aspect of your performance, then take notes and paraphrase back what you hear. Make sure they know that you understand their concern. Ask questions to clarify what is important to them. Then you can have a conversation about what you are doing or not doing and why. When they have valid concerns, tell them you appreciate their suggestions and take steps to correct whatever they found troublesome. I have found that simply taking time to hear someone out and responding positively to appropriate concerns goes a long way to strengthening my relationship with them. They know I care enough about them to hear their concerns, even if the board and I don't ultimately agree with them and do what they say.

Being respectful often helps with those who you are tempted to label as snipers. Sometimes they feel like they aren't heard or appreciated. When they have an opportunity to voice their opinions openly, then they don't feel the need to blindside the pastor or others. However, if someone still behaves like a sniper in a meeting, insofar as possible, address them right away. You might say something like, "Sam, I didn't quite catch what you said when Jean proposed having a mission trip. You seem to have an opinion. What are you thinking?" Responding in such a manner both catches the disrespectful behavior and elicits the other person's perspective. Members of the board or group learn that they don't have to be snipers to be heard; they can freely state their opinions.

Being curious about difficult behaviors also means asking what is behind someone's need for control. Has there been a clergy betrayal? Is she generally insecure? Or perhaps he has recently become an empty nester or retired and needs someone to supervise? Matriarchs or patriarchs of family-sized congregations are used to running things, since pastors don't stay long. Perhaps you might suggest to such people that their behavior saps morale, though I realize such a comment might not help. They might just respond, "Well, someone has to do it, and nobody else will." That may indeed be the case in family-size congregations, but then you might ask, "What if you drop dead tonight? Who will do this? Who else could we get involved?" Get them to help clarify the issue and generate options to solve the problem.

Those who seem to be hard wired to be pessimistic often respond to respectful listening and deep questions. I have found that many who are especially careful to dot the "Is" and cross the "Ts" oversee financial or property matters. They may recall previous financial or property mismanagement and so want to avoid any potential problems. If the board is discussing anything controversial, some financial leaders may be terrified that any initiative that has a whiff of opposition will result in members giving less. Make sure that you and other leaders hear their concerns. You might explore what impact previous controversies had on giving. But also help them see what good things are happening now (assuming there are some positive results you can point to).

Respect and curiosity often help those who aren't able to clearly express their ideas or are afraid to talk. Take a deep breath and be patient. Listen. Stress to them that you cannot read their minds. Clarify. You will often learn important things.

Being curious and open also implies that you will consider options other than what you have planned. When our older son was about three, our family went camping at a friend's farm midway between both sets of grandparents. Though it was naptime, he refused to settle down. "Go back in the tent and take your nap!" we demanded. He resisted. Then, recalling a parenting course we had recently taken, we said, "Doug, we are afraid that if you don't take a nap, you're going to be all tired and cranky when your grandparents come out here for supper, and nobody will have fun. Do you have any ideas for how you might take a nap?" To our amazement he replied, "Well, I could put my sleeping bag under that big tree and sleep." We agreed. He slept! Sometimes those who are engaging in behavior we find difficult have a much better option than the one we had decided on. Encourage them to suggest other options to solve a problem.

Two colleagues have told me about how their congregations resolved problems with poor attendance in Sunday morning church school. Both encountered people who were critical of their leadership, saying they should simply insist that parents bring their children on Sunday mornings. Realizing that berating parents to get their kids into church school would hardly be effective, my colleagues encouraged both parents and those who were upset to come up with options. In one case, they started an education program beginning with a light supper on a weekday evening. In the other, they decided to run children's education time concurrently with worship. Teachers take turns teaching once a month. In both cases the attendance has more than tripled. They were respectful and curious, explored options, and came up with solutions that worked in their settings. I smile a bit when writing this example, because I strongly prefer having a Sunday education program either before or after worship, but these pastors faced situations where that schedule didn't work. They explored options and developed a new schedule that achieved the objective of involving children in Christian education.

Listening carefully and reframing the issue from the perspective of the mission and vision of the congregation is an effective strategy and often helps both board members and those who are upset see the issue in a different light. "Joe is telling us that if we do not hire a new youth worker, he is going to leave. How does his request fit with our priorities? What might the impact be on other dimensions of our mission if we do hire a youth worker? What might the benefits be? How might we pay for a youth worker?" "Sue is demanding that we stop singing contemporary music. Let's think about the 2,000 years of church tradition, the traditions we have followed here for 20 years, and how musical tastes are evolving. How do different genres of music help us praise God? What kind of music might reflect the tastes of teenagers and inspire them to invite their friends to our congregation?"

Polarity management (see Tool 24 below) is another helpful approach to reframing issues so that members, including those who are often labeled difficult, can discuss subjects that cannot be ever totally resolved.

To further allay anxieties of those who are sometimes too cautious, I have found that having a congregational town meeting to assess buy-in for proposed initiatives helps, provided that a substantial majority approve of the initiative. If you have 80 percent consensus on major decisions, move ahead. Remember, consensus is not unanimity. If you insist on unanimity, one or two people can stop everything. Those who are often ultracareful will likely be pleasantly surprised by how well things work out. Of course, if there is significant opposition to the initiative, then acknowledge that their cautions were immensely helpful and aided the congregation in avoiding a huge mistake.

In sharp contrast with those who are especially cautious are those who sometimes get so upset that they start ranting and raving (what I labeled the Improvised Explosive Device in the initial list). When someone is quite out of control, sometimes you have to break the cycle with strong emotion. Assert yourself vigorously, raising your voice if necessary so you'll be heard, and say, "George (be sure to use the person's name), you're so upset we can't understand you! Let's take a break and let everyone cool off. Then we can talk some more." If the explosion occurs in a board meeting when there is a motion before the group, you can table the motion till the next meeting. The key is to break the cycle of irrational behavior. Think of yourself as a parent picking up a two-year-old during a tantrum and removing him from the store or room. So, take a break. Encourage participants to get some refreshments and talk with one another, especially to those with whose opinions they differ. I have found that simply taking a 15-minute break and offering prayer for peace and clarity does wonders for dialogue.

Sometimes all you have to do to assuage people who are anxious is to put your arm around them (literally or figuratively) and say, "Hey, it's going to be ok. We'll work this out." Such assurance was an important part of my role as an interim pastor. Most congregations who have recently lost their pastor have a number of people who are anxious about what's next for the congregation. One of my first jobs is to calm their anxieties. I achieved this goal by spelling out the process that we would be following: getting to know them, building trust, clarifying God's call to the congregation, and then finding their new pastor, all in 18 months to two years. I also assured them that I would preach and lead worship, provide high-quality pastoral care, and lead them through this uncertain time. Simply demonstrating that you know what you're doing lowers the anxiety temperature.

Humor helps ease anxiety too. I recall a woman who was terrified of our congregation's sharing space with a Korean congregation. She was afraid that their children would be ill-behaved and damage things. I grinned and said something like, "I can see it now! A hoard of 10,000 little Korean kids trampling over everything!" Recognizing that she was stereotyping Asian children, she laughed and ultimately supported this outreach. The partnership led to some delightful joint worship services and congregational meals.

Another approach I have used with such negative people is to ask, "What is the worst that can happen?" This usually leads to a conversation about possible negative consequences of a decision. Then elicit the possible positive consequences of the decision. Such conversations often yield important insights that prevent problems.

Inevitably, you will encounter situations in which ordinarily reasonable people will suddenly engage in surprising behavior. Respect them, listen intently to their concerns, explore options to solve the problem, and also be curious about what they offer by expressing themselves in what might not be the most pleasant manner. Such people are usually operating from very positive motives. So when confronted with people exhibiting difficult behaviors, I keep asking myself and others, "What can we learn from this situation or person?" I think of one man who clearly had ADHD (attention-deficit/hyperactivity disorder). "Joe" was not only physically busy but mentally very active. He drove leaders crazy with his many ideas. I reminded leaders, "Joe has 10 new ideas a day, and probably 65 of his ideas in a given week are terrible, but five are really important to consider. Most of us are lucky to have one good idea a month! So let's listen to Joe!" Just about everyone, when treated with respect and curiosity, stops their difficult behavior. They know they are being heard and their ideas considered.

WHAT ABOUT REALLY DIFFICULT BEHAVIORS?

Despite urging you not to label people as bulldozers and the like, my clients make me very aware that some people will not play fair. Perhaps they lie or they stab you in the back. They are out to win, even if the battle destroys the congregation or the pastor's career. Emotionally immature people enjoy being big shots, especially in small congregations. Sometimes they contribute a great deal of time and money, so other leaders don't want to jeopardize their contributions by standing up to them. When you encounter those who engage in persistently difficult behavior, you should not take them on by yourself. Involve the board and respected leaders in resolving the issue.

Getting the grown-ups involved is especially important when dealing with those who are fighting to get the congregation on their side of a controversial issue. Hugh Halverstadt, retired McCormick Seminary professor of ministry, distinguishes between "stakeholders" and "stockholders." The stakeholders are those for whom their particular issue is the most important issue in the world, and their passion can make them difficult to deal with. The stockholders are those for whom the well-being of the congregation comes first. I think of them as the "grown-ups." Too often, when a conflict arises over some hot-button issue, the true believers (stakeholders) on each side go at each other, and the stockholders simply observe helplessly or allow themselves to be drawn in on one side or the other. Halverstadt asserts that mature leaders (stockholders) need to bring order to the conflict and set some behavioral expectations.[5] As pastor, you need to be one of the grown-ups. Part of a pastor's role is to bring some sense of calm and elicit mature behavior from the other grown-ups in the room. But you need the other grown-ups to help seek the well-being of the whole congregation and to manage the situation. Don't try to do it yourself.

I recognize that managing emotionally immature people who are determined to get their way might be difficult, especially, for example, if one of the upset individuals is the brother-in-law of a board member. This kind of behavior is fairly common in more rural, family-size congregations where, for generations, members of various families have intermarried. Nevertheless, the grown-ups need to assert themselves. In these small congregations, most extended families have learned how to handle that cranky cousin. Grown-ups on the board might even ask members of the difficult person's extended family how they handle him. A family member might advise, "Get Sam to talk with Joe. He'll calm him down."

Should you encounter someone who is genuinely destructive, then it is critical for the grown-ups to limit the offender's power. If possible, keep that person from getting on the board. Sometimes it may be necessary to bring in an authority from your denomination or consult with a psychologist if your sense is that the person is exhibiting serious pathology. Don't try to handle it by yourself.

I think of "Louis," a man in one congregation I served. He frightened people with his angry tirades. I realized that his problems were beyond what we could handle. At the suggestion of a denominational official, I consulted with a psychotherapist, who suggested that a lay leader and I tell Louis that our congregation would never do what he wanted us to do and that he would be more fulfilled elsewhere. An experienced elder and I did talk with Louis, and he decided to find another congregation. We wanted to encourage and support Louis but came to realize that his emotional illness was quite beyond our ability to manage, so we got help. Get expert help if you are dealing with someone who you deem dangerous.

As you try to empower leaders to sideline destructive people, recognize that there may be some risk in taking them on. They may get mad and leave, taking their contributions of time and money with them. While this is an initial loss, typically people who have wanted to lead step forward. You may lose that difficult person, but you will more than recoup their contributions as new members are drawn to the congregation's vitality and unity, rather than being turned off by the tension they experience. Further, you will get more sleep!

Sometimes, however, confronting people who engage in persistently difficult behavior is risky for you. If other leaders do not step up and restrain them, one or more of the difficult people may decide you are the villain and that you must leave. In a more congregational polity, leaders can fire a pastor immediately, but in more hierarchical systems, powerful people still find ways to remove a pastor. Even if they decide not to fire you, however, you will be forced to accept that you are simply a hired hand and you will not be respected as the key leader of the congregation. You then will have to decide whether you will accept this lower status for a time or leave the congregation sooner rather than later. Thus, you may simply decide to not tackle this very challenging behavior directly but to work around these people to the extent possible. If you are in such a situation, I urge you to work with denominational officials or a coach to figure out the best approach.

BELOVED FORMER PASTORS—BANES OR BLESSINGS?

Beloved former pastors (BFPs) present unique challenges and opportunities for their successors. Unlike members who have continued as part of the congregation, BFPs are no longer part of the congregation, unless they haven't quite left. Depending on their behavior, BFPs can be either destructive or supportive. I define a BFP as someone who has been in a congregation for seven or more years and has built many good relationships. Typically, when I have been new to a congregation, I have made a point to get to know the previous pastor and learn all I can from his or her experience. A former pastor of the first congregation of which I was the solo pastor was incredibly helpful to me as a mentor, but he was also careful to demonstrate that he was not the pastor anymore. After you are well established as the pastor, I recommend that if it seems wise and the former pastor still lives in your community, you involve the former pastor in support roles, such as teaching and providing some pastoral care, provided that they are very careful to remind people that they are not *the* pastor anymore. As appropriate, and with board approval, invite the former pastor to offer words of memory at a funeral or to have a support role in a wedding. This will demonstrate your self-confidence and generosity.

However, BFPs can be problematic if they undermine your ministry. A friend of mine was called as a new pastor of a church where the retired former pastor continued singing in the choir and maintained very close friendships with members. While his participation seemed innocent enough at first, he began undermining the new pastor. When someone was hospitalized, rather than calling the new pastor, the former pastor's close friends called him. Despite attempts by denominational officials to rein him in, the BFP still caused problems, and the new pastor's ministry lasted only two years. I have heard stories of lay leaders who call and get advice from former pastors now living in different parts of the country.

What might you do to counter such difficult behavior? First, follow some of my counsel in the preceding section: discuss the behavior with your board, framing it from the perspective of what is best for the congregation. Find some grown-ups who will talk with the BFP. Involve judicatory officials and urge them to emphasize to the BFP that this behavior is not constructive. If your local judicatory does not already have a policy regarding former pastors, suggest that they develop one. If none of this dissuades the BFP from being involved, you will need to work informally with the BFP to develop mutual expectations that affirm your authority as the pastor and the contributions that the BFP made and still makes to the congregation. As with other very difficult behavior, do not try to do this on your own. Get help from a judicatory official or a coach.

TOOL 24: POLARITY MANAGEMENT

When discussing boundaries in chapter 7, I asserted that pastors need to manage the polarities of intimacy and openness. Polarity management is an approach to dealing with differences that recognizes that almost all the really big issues are not matters of either/or but both/and. I have found that someone whom others identify as "difficult" is often holding too tightly to one side of a polarity.

Former Alban senior consultant Roy Oswald and management consultant Barry Johnson have identified eight polarities that thriving congregations manage well.

• Tradition AND Innovation
• Spiritual Health AND Institutional Health
• Management AND Leadership

- Strong Clergy Leadership AND Strong Lay Leadership
- Inreach AND Outreach
- Nurture AND Transformation
- Making Disciples—Easy Process AND Challenging Process
- Call AND Duty[6]

Most people would agree that it is important to do both sides of the polarities well. An organization that focuses exclusively on one side of the polarity (for example, on nurturing members with kindness and good pastoral care) will slide to negative behaviors such as codependence and failure to challenge people to grow spiritually. Oswald and Johnson assert that to counter the downside of one pole, the congregation needs to move to the upside of the other. So, in the case of nurture and transformation, leaders would challenge each other and members to grow spiritually, live the surrendered life, and celebrate conversion.

One congregation with which I worked was wrestling with doctrinal standards for selecting officers. Some wanted very rigid standards; others were more flexible. The pastor and I developed a polarity map, with one pole being unity and the other purity. Using the polarity management process helped leaders balance the tensions in the congregation, ultimately increasing the unity in the congregation and becoming clearer about what elements of doctrine were most important.

COACHING ASSIGNMENT 30: MAKE PLANS FOR HANDLING DIFFICULT BEHAVIORS

- List those people whose behavior you find difficult.
- Assess how they affect others. Do they bother others as much as they bother you?
- Assess how you react and respond. How might you respond more effectively? How might you be less anxious and more creative? To what extent might you be more curious, respectful, and open?
- Assess how courageous board members been when reactive members confront and criticize them? To what extent have they been non-anxious, demonstrating curiosity and openness to these members but not letting themselves be infected by the anxiety?
- Identify steps you, the board, and other leaders might take to handle these difficult behaviors. How might you reframe issues and explore other options to deal with concerns and anxieties presented by the people you identified?
- Develop a board covenant of behavior if you do not have one? (See appendix F.)

- Decide if there are some people who are especially destructive and explore how to handle them. From whom might you get support and guidance?

Tip 23: Love the hell out of 'em.

One summer while I was a seminarian, I helped lead an inner-city work camp. The key leader, a university chaplain, explained to the college students that they would likely encounter some very difficult children and that they needed to remember that the essence of the Gospel was "to love the hell out of 'em." We were to love them so intensely that the hell in them was vaporized by love! One of the students went to a local print shop and had t-shirts made, emblazoned with "Love the Hell Out of 'Em!" I have tried to keep that slogan in mind throughout my ministry. Loving the hell out of 'em is always a good place to begin when dealing with difficult behavior.

Chapter Eleven

What's Next?

Reviewing Your First Year and Looking Forward

As you complete this book (and your first year), it is time to reflect on what you've done. Depending on the size of the church, you have preached 40 or 50 sermons; have likely hatched, matched, and dispatched a number of folks; have probably rubbed some members the wrong way; have built terrific relationships with many members; and have a good sense of who the real leaders are. You have met and exceeded the expectations of some members and have not met those of others. In chapter 3, I offered a design for a board workshop to clarify expectations in your first year. I further discussed the importance of clear priorities, job descriptions, and appraisals in chapter 9. These offered ways to measure your performance. Following is another framework from which to review how you're doing.

The Gallup organization surveyed some 10,000 people around the world, asking them to identify a leader who has made or makes a positive contribution to their life and then, in their own words, to list three words that described what the leader contributed to their life. The results had remarkable consistency, with over 1,000 respondents listing the *same* words. I was immediately struck by how they echo foundational biblical themes.

Gallup pollsters found that people need a leader who

- Builds trust
- Shows compassion
- Provides stability
- Creates hope [1]

Do not these characteristics sound like they come straight from the Bible? Think of Moses encouraging the people of Israel to follow him through the sea to a promised land. What trust the people had to have (even though they often complained bitterly!). How about Jesus' disciples leaving their nets and following this new prophet?

Think of the many scripture passages extolling God's love and compassion and similar passages urging God's people to love one another. They are far too numerous to mention here, but I think of Psalm 23, Psalm 139, Luke 10:25-37, John 15:9-13, 1 Corinthians 13, and 1 John 4:7-21, among others.

We proclaim God's strength and stability. Psalm 62:2 declares that God is our rock and salvation. Jesus stills the sea (Luke 8:22-25). Paul assures the people that though the ship would be lost, nobody would drown (Acts 27:22).

We pastors do not so much create hope as we point to the God who gives ultimate hope. Think of the apostle declaring, "By his great mercy he has given us a new birth into a living hope through the resurrection of Jesus Christ from the dead, and into an inheritance that is imperishable, undefiled, and unfading kept in heaven for you" (1 Peter 1: 4-5).

Here are key foundation stones on which a pastor can build a strong relationship with a new congregation. You know by now that I think that the pastor is the *key* leader of a congregation. You set the tone. As I think about pastors who have had led vital congregations, I think of any number who *have* built trust, shown compassion, provided stability, and who thus created hope and real change.

As I conclude this book on entering wonderland, I would like you to review your leadership using the framework of the qualities the Gallup pollsters found people valued.

BUILD TRUST

When you came to this new church a year or so ago, what expectations did you encounter? Depending on the circumstances, members' expectations likely varied wildly. Some might have expected you to immediately draw in lots of new young families. Others simply wanted you to keep things as they had been. If the congregation had been dealing with conflict, members hoped you would calm the waters.

I focused on building trust in chapters 3 and 5 and suggested several tools for building trust. How is the current trust level in your congregation compared with how it was when you arrived? What have you observed in board meetings that indicates a high degree of trust? Do board members interact easily with one another, or are they reserved and suspicious? How do they handle differences? Are they able to laugh at inevitable differences and resolve them, or do they harbor grudges and engage in behavior that creates or exacerbates rifts?

I have already acknowledged that I am a "trust nut." Without trust, you will pay a mistrust tax that costs time and money. An atmosphere of mistrust will erode not only your effectiveness as a pastor, it will be apparent to newcomers and they will look elsewhere for a healthier congregation. Building an atmosphere of trust is vital if your congregation is to thrive.

COACHING ASSIGNMENT 31: KEEP BUILDING TRUST

You have likely taken steps to systematically build trust. Review what you have done, and think about how to maintain and expand the practices that have been especially effective in your congregation. Take particular care to build trust among members of the staff and board. Identify specific steps you will take, and determine when you will take them. For example, you might have had a leader retreat after you had been there six months. When will you have another retreat to further build trust among members of your board?

SHOW COMPASSION

How have you demonstrated compassion? Compassion literally means "feeling with," of course. Most of us want close friends and family to feel with us and understand us. However, I believe most people need more than compassion. In a society where people are simultaneously connected by and separated from each other by high tech gadgets, I think there is a deep hunger for the genuine agape described in scripture. As you think of Jesus' command to love God and neighbor as self, how well do you and members of the congregation demonstrate the self-giving love he calls for?

Think about how you and members of the congregation demonstrate compassion. If you are in a family- or pastoral-size congregation, do you keep track of the parishioners? Do you encourage members to care for one another, both one-on-one and in small groups? If you are pastor in a program-size or larger congregation, how have you helped strengthen norms that say, "We will care for each other"? To what extent have you taught people how to care for one another? How do you model caring in the various classes, meetings, and other groups? Put bluntly, do members of your congregation have a strong sense that fellow members care whether they are there or not?

Part of showing compassion is being grace-filled. How do you demonstrate grace? I recall "Jane," who was employed to be the secretary in the church of which I was pastor back in the mimeograph-machine era. We had commercially printed bulletin covers that correlated with the lectionary. On her first week on the job, she prepared the mimeograph stencil for the bulletin, inserted it into the machine, and printed the bulletin. With horror she realized that she had printed the bulletin upside down! She expected to be fired immediately. Assessing the situation, I said, "Jane, I think there is grace, even for you!"

How do you model the grace of Christ? How does that grace show up in your church? In the staff? In the board? Elsewhere? If someone makes a mistake, do they feel secure enough to suggest, "God has grace, even for me!"

COACHING ASSIGNMENT 32: BUILD AND STRENGTHEN A CLIMATE OF COMPASSION

Identify what concrete steps you will take to both show that you care for members and to develop a deeper climate of love in the congregation?

PROVIDE STABILITY

Remember Jesus' story about the man who built his house on the sand (Matthew 7)? As you deal with the craziness of leading a congregation, you must anchor yourself securely to the solid rock of faith. If you are not well anchored, the winds will blow you every which way! When you become dizzy with the hurricanes of life, what anchors you?

Practically every week there are news accounts of leaders who, because they were not anchored, made some really dumb decisions. I think of the corporate leaders, bankers, hedge fund managers, and speculators in real estate who paved the way to economic chaos. I think of pastors and politicians. You can easily make your list.

Pastors sometimes become so busy handling immediate concerns that they do not take time to engage in study, prayer, or meditation. We pastors can let ourselves be seduced by the idea that since we're doing God's work, we do not need to take time to nourish ourselves from the spring of living water. In order to provide stability and point parishioners to the rock of salvation, you must anchor yourself. Do you anchor yourself in solid relationships? Do you have a spouse or other family or good friends who will tell you when they think you are full of baloney? How do you make sure you hear other points of view?

I find that starting the day by singing some of the chants from the Taizé community really helps me. This sung prayer reminds me who I am and whom I serve. It gives me inner peace and helps me focus on what is important. Daily Bible readying using one of the online lectionaries also helps me. I read the passages and try to be open to which verse or phrase jumps out at me. Then I ask myself, "How is God speaking to me through this text? How is God making me more aware of myself, my congregation, or my community? How is God pushing me to be or act differently?"

Keeping a journal is another form of anchoring. Writing down challenges, possibilities, temptations, fears, and commitments helps over time. For example, after I completed my coach certification program, I listed possible clients in my journal, finally deciding that my real call was helping pastors lead more effectively. When I started wondering what was next after retirement, I did the alternative narrative exercise for myself. When I review what I wrote some months or even years before it reminds me of forgotten commitments, affirms accomplishments, and gives me perspective on current challenges.

Now consider your congregation and its leaders and organization. Perhaps it was quite stable when you arrived. Systems worked well. Leaders were responsible and effective. If so, have you maintained that stability? Or, if the congregation was in some organizational turmoil, what did you do to provide stability? How did you demonstrate being a non-anxious presence who trusted in God and helped people handle their differences effectively?

COACHING ASSIGNMENT 33: TAKE SOME TIME AND THINK ABOUT WHAT ANCHORS YOU

- How are you anchored in a deep relationship with the living God?
- What are some daily practices that help anchor you? What practices might you try?
- What are you doing to bring stability to your congregation? What next steps might you take?

CREATE HOPE

As a pastor, you understand that you do not create hope by yourself! You point to the Lord as the source of true hope. Nonetheless, you must nurture a climate of hope. If you are pessimistic, then members pick up that pessimism. As you help members identify signs of God's acting now in their lives and in their congregation, they will become more hopeful. "The Spirit is moving!" some may exclaim!

I think of a client who is pastor of an aging pastoral-size congregation. People were losing energy and hope. After significant work and prayer, they suddenly realized that they were already working with families from a nearby elementary school. They identified more actions they could take. Hope rose! And then something else happened. They began working with a fairly new seminary graduate who was developing a new kind of congregation with young adults through pub and coffee house ministries. My client's congregation signed on to help and discovered that this, too, was energizing them. They realized that they were already making a difference! Hope rose even more. This congregation is beginning to catch God's vision for them.

In chapter 8 I discussed the importance of discerning God's mission and vision for your congregation. Now that you have served this congregation and community for a year or so, you are beginning to have a better glimpse of God's vision for you. How do you share your sense of God's vision with your members without purporting to have some special revelation? Recall my tip to describe reality as you see it and start a conversation? Here's a similar tip: Describe the *possibility* you see and start a conversation! When you share the possibilities you see, you help leaders and members see even more possibilities and so create hope, and that gives them purpose and energy.

Author and leadership consultant Daniel Pink declares that what really motivates people is not more money or the fear of punishment. He believes motivation has three essential elements. In his words, they are

1. "*Autonomy*—the desire to direct our own lives.
2. *Mastery*—the urge to get better and better at something that matters.
3. *Purpose*—the yearning to do what we do in the service of something larger than ourselves."[2]

See how this research echoes basic themes of scripture and faith!

Paul declares, "For freedom Christ has set us free. Stand firm, therefore, and do not submit again to a yoke of slavery" (Galatians 5:1). Jesus assured his disciples, "Very truly, I tell you, the one who believes in me will also do the works that I do and, in fact, will do greater works than these, because I am going to the Father" (John 14:12). He charged them to go and make disciples of all nations (Matthew 28:19). When we who are faith leaders help our members catch God's call, we point them to the greatest motivator: *God's* transcendent purpose!

COACHING ASSIGNMENT 34: ASSESS AND BUILD HOPE

- How hopeful are you about yourself and your ministry in this congregation? What people, programs, and purposes give you hope?
- How have you led people to find the hope that is inherent in following Christ? How do they demonstrate that they have a sense of purpose and hope?
- What are some archetypal stories of the congregation that demonstrate how God has and will continue to move in them? How might you retell those stories to instill God's hope?

- What are some concrete steps you will take to build hope in the congregation?

COACHING ASSIGNMENT 35: REVIEW THE CONGREGATION'S NORMS AND VALUES

In chapter 2, I encouraged you to take some time and write the congregation's basic norms and values in simple declarative sentences. Please do it again. Compare your results with those you identified as you reflected on what you heard in interviews with leaders.

What new insights do you have? What do they tell you about the strengths of the congregation? Which of these build up the congregation? Which destroy faith and community? How might you affirm those that are positive? How might you address those that are negative? Are you still dealing with old baggage (for example, a pastoral betrayal)? With whom might you have a conversation about the negative norms? How might you affirm the positive norms and counter the negative ones in sermons? How might you bring a message of hope to the anxious?

Tip 24: Describe the possibilities you see, propose initiatives, and start a conversation.

Share your best ideas about how to improve things and invite people to improve the ideas. I have found that when I describe possibilities and propose initiatives and then invite people to improve them, they jump right in and come up with even better ideas.

COACHING ASSIGNMENT 36: IDENTIFY YOUR TOP PRIORITY FOR THE NEXT SIX MONTHS

Patrick Lencioni urges leaders to clarify their answer to the question: *What is most important, right now?*[3] Lencioni's insistence echoes Jesus' command to prune our vine. We cannot do everything at once. What does Christ want you to focus on to bring about his new reign of love, peace, justice, and joy? Work on becoming crystal clear about your top priorities.

"But I cannot set just one priority!" you may be saying. "I must make sure that we have dynamic worship, that my sermons are terrific, that we reach out into the community, that we get small groups going, that the roof gets repaired, and so on" All true—and all things I've said myself. Why is clarifying your top priority so critical? Because everything else flows from your setting this top priority. Having a top priority does not mean that you will not have another four very important priorities, though I urge you to have only about four to five important priorities. A top priority helps you focus your energy.

For example, if your leadership team is dysfunctional, caught up in little feuds and turf protection, then things are going to grind to a halt until you build trust and teach them to fight effectively. Your top priority should probably be to build a trusting leadership team. If people do not know how to care for each other, then perhaps your top priority will be building an atmosphere of care and compassion in the congregation. During the days following September 11, 2001, my top priority was to help people cope with these awful events.

As you set top priorities, do not let pastoral care and compassion slip through the cracks. Remember that showing compassion was a vital quality of respected leaders. Even if you are pastor of a large congregation and must administer a busy staff and program, you must show you care and develop an atmosphere of care.

Setting a top priority will help you decide how much time to spend on your various responsibilities, perhaps cutting down on some to focus on others. Most pastors give a very high, if not the highest priority to preparing excellent sermons. Obviously this is important, but if the congregation is in conflict or the roof is leaking, then perhaps you will not be able to spend as much time in the library! On the other hand, if most aspects of the congregation are going well but you are hearing complaints about your sermons being dull and predictable, then your top priority might well be to write and preach more effectively.

What might be your top priority for the next six months? What might be the next three or four most important emphases? I encourage you to clarify what you think and then discuss these priorities with the board. Perhaps lead the board on a half-day retreat to clarify mutual expectations for both your and their priorities. Then implement these priorities, especially the most important one. As you act on the priorities, seek feedback and guidance from trusted leaders.

Tip 25: Distinguish between what's urgent and what's important.

Having clear priorities helps you organize your time so that you are not sidetracked by distractions. Though this book has been one of my top priorities, I succumb to the temptation to read email or check Facebook and do not focus. When members step into your office and want to talk, you need to decide if they and their concern are really important or simply urgent to them at the moment. For example, if Sue wants to talk about how she just found out that her son is taking drugs, that is likely urgent and important. If, on the other hand, she wants to discuss the color of a new chair for the foyer, that might be urgent for her but not important when measured by your priorities. You would have to find a way to either postpone the conversation or direct her to someone who might be better to talk with. Clear priorities help distinguish between the urgent and the important.

COACHING ASSIGNMENT 37: REVIEW ALTERNATIVE NARRATIVES

Go back to chapter 7 and review the tool on alternative narratives. Recall I asked you to envision heroic, mediocre, and failure stories for yourself as you imagine the next 5 to 10 years.

- Did you use that tool then?
- Which narrative are you living into?
- Is your heroic narrative drawing you forward with energy and clarity? To what extent do you sense the Holy Spirit leading you and energizing you?
- How would you revise the heroic story now that you've been with the congregation longer?
- What commitments do you make to change your practices and behaviors in order to live up to your best intentions?
- With whom will you discuss these commitments? Who will hold you accountable to your best aspirations?

CONCLUSION

By the time you read this, I hope you have made a good entry into your new church. Like Alice in her Wonderland, you have encountered surprises, riddles, and puzzles. Chances are you met some very interesting people. You have probably learned a lot.

No doubt you are clearer about who you are and what gifts you have to offer to this new church. You are clearer about the strengths and weaknesses of many members, especially the leaders.

I hope you and other leaders have formed a well-functioning team. Or perhaps you're still building trust and just beginning to learn to handle differences.

I hope you are reasonably clear on where the Lord is leading you, that you have a sense of where the Holy Spirit is blowing, providing you and the congregation with direction and power. Members of your congregation are likely clearer about priorities and about what it means to be disciples of Christ.

You can bet, though, that God still has many surprises in store for you and the leaders. Remember the story of Peter and Cornelius related in Acts 10? Peter, a good Jew, followed not only Jesus but the Jewish Torah, so to the extent possible, he did not associate with gentiles. And then the Spirit intervened. Prodded by a dream and the Spirit, he went to Caesarea, baptized Cornelius and his family, and was astounded that God gave them the gift of the Holy Spirit. God offered the gospel to gentiles. Now think about how God's Spirit has surprised you—how when you thought you had things figured out, the Holy Spirit threw you a curve. The Spirit is still acting!

Walking a labyrinth is a great metaphor for the spiritual life: when I have walked a labyrinth, I felt like I was progressing very quickly and logically toward the center, and then suddenly I was out at the periphery! I have found that my relationship with God is like that. Sometimes when I have felt closest to God, I find myself drifting away and need to be blown back to the divine center by the Spirit. So, when you encounter surprises (note I said "when," not "if"), I urge you to take time, pray, and reflect both by yourself and with your congregation's leaders and others on what's going on. Get perspectives from several persons who have varying expertise and life experience. How is the Holy Spirit moving in this surprise?

Keep being curious. How is the Holy Spirit already present in new residents in your community or in that person whose behavior you find difficult or in a young person who asks that you sing more contemporary music? Be curious especially in the crises, seeking the opportunities inherent precisely in them. Never waste a good crisis!

I have personally found that Paul's counsel that "all things work together for good for those who love the Lord" is really true. Things maybe do not work out as I planned. I was fired. I did not get that call. My kids, wife, and grandkids do not see me as the font of wisdom or paragon of all that is right and good. Welcome to the real world—and the real me. But anchored in the Lord and led by the Spirit, I have learned to welcome and anticipate new challenges and, however unwelcome, adapt to meet them (fairly well). As you anchor yourself in faith, I am confident that the Holy Spirit will lead you and encourage you in this ever-evolving wonderland in which God calls you to lead.

Appendix A

Tips Arranged by Chapter

PREFACE

Tip 1: You don't know the situation, so keep asking questions. Be curious.

CHAPTER 2

Tip 2: Play the Curious Card.
Tip 3: Invite members of the congregation to tell you their name on seven different occasions.
Tip 4: Describe reality as you see it, and start a conversation.
Tip 5: Ask, "What is obvious?"

CHAPTER 3

Tip 6: Step up during a crisis.
Tip 7: Catch them in the act of doing something well!
Tip 8: Plan your sermons a season ahead.

CHAPTER 5

Tip 9: Ask, "Why is this important?"
Tip 10: Be aware of your internal reactions and your external responses to stress.

Tip 11: Learn how to have a good fight.

Tip 12: Develop ground rules with the board.

Tip 13: Don't take yourself too seriously.

Tip 14: Conclude the board or staff meeting by asking people to affirm any major decision.

Tip 15: Don't let the perfect become the enemy of the possible.

CHAPTER 8

Tip 16: Use Robert Schnase's book, *Five Practices of Fruitful Congregations*, as a framework for doing a mission vision discernment.

Tip 17: Be on the lookout for low-hanging fruit!

CHAPTER 9

Tip 18: Limit the size of the governing board to about 10 members.

Tip 19: Have an all-committee or ministry team night.

Tip 20: Base income statements and cash flow reports on prior years' experience

Tip 21: Follow the KISS principle.

Tip 22: Ask financial leaders to tell you about any who have stopped giving altogether or who have significantly increased or decreased their giving.

CHAPTER 10

Tip 23: Love the Hell Out of 'Em.

CHAPTER 11

Tip 24: Describe the possibilities you see, propose initiatives, and start a conversation.

Tip 25: Distinguish between what's urgent and what's important.

Appendix B

Tools Arranged by Chapter

CHAPTER 1

Tool 1: Checklist for a Facilities Scan
Tool 2: A Sample of Perceptions and Perspectives of People Outside the Congregation

CHAPTER 2

Tool 3: Eleven Curious Questions

CHAPTER 3

Tool 4: Meet Members in Small Groups
Tool 5: Clarifying Expectations and Top Priorities

CHAPTER 4

Tool 6: The Competence-Commitment Grid
Tool 7: The Myers-Briggs Type Indicator
Tool 8: The Gallup StrengthsFinder

CHAPTER 5

Tool 9: Sharing Bible Study
Tool 10: Sharing Formative Scripture Passages
Tool 11: Sharing a Life Challenge
Tool 12: Sharing Something about Your Childhood and Young Adulthood
Tool 13: Large Floor Exercises
Tool 14: Lead a Staff and/or Board Retreat
Tool 15: Grounding Yourself
Tool 16: Exploring Stress Communication Styles
Tool 17: Holding a Town Meeting
Tool 18: Preparing Reports for the Board

CHAPTER 8

Tool 19: A Percent Contribution Calculator
Tool 20: SWOT Analysis
Tool 21: Discernment Through Small Groups and One-Day Leader Retreat

CHAPTER 9

Tool 22: Sample Appraisal Form
Tool 23: Feedback and Feedforward

CHAPTER 10

Tool 24: Polarity Management

Appendix C

Coaching Assignments Arranged by Chapter

CHAPTER 1

Coaching Assignment 1: What Have You Learned So Far?

CHAPTER 2

Coaching Assignment 2: Learn Members' Names
Coaching Assignment 3: Interview Members of the Congregation
Coaching Assignment 4: Analyze What You Heard in the Interviews

CHAPTER 3

Coaching Assignment 5: Assess the Level of Trust among Members, Especially the Leaders.
Coaching Assignment 6: Assess the Level of Trust toward the Office of Pastor
Coaching Assignment 7: Decide What Steps You Will Take to Build Trust
Coaching Assignment 8: Deal with Major Breaches of Trust

CHAPTER 4

Coaching Assignment 9: Using the Competence-Commitment Grid
Coaching Assignment 10: Using the Myers-Briggs Type Indicator

CHAPTER 11

Coaching Assignment 31: Keep Building Trust
Coaching Assignment 32: Build and Strengthen a Climate of Compassion
Coaching Assignment 33: Take Some Time and Think about What Anchors You
Coaching Assignment 34: Assess and Build Hope
Coaching Assignment 35: Review the Congregation's Norms and Values
Coaching Assignment 36: Identify Your Top Priority for the Next Six Months
Coaching Assignment 37: Review Alternative Narratives

Appendix D

Information about Coaching

As I indicate in the preface, a coach asks lots of questions designed to lead the client into deeper analysis and strong commitments. The core competencies of coaching include, among others, building deep trust and intimacy, active listening, direct communication, creating awareness, and designing action. Every pastor will benefit from using these skills.

With some 20,000 members when this book was written, the International Coach Federation (ICF) oversees coach training and credentialing programs worldwide. It sets core competencies for coaching, performs research into best practices, and seeks to raise standards for coaching as a profession. See the ICF website for much more information: www.coachfederation.org.

Parish pastors can use coaching techniques. See *A Generous Presence: Spiritual Leadership and the Art of Coaching* by Rochelle Melander (Alban 2006), an Evangelical Lutheran Church in America pastor who has been coaching individuals since 2000. Another helpful book is *Anytime Coaching: Unleashing Employee Performance* by leadership consultants Teresa Wedding Kloster and Wendy Sherwin Swire (Management Concepts 2009). These authors offer a simple paradigm for using coaching skills in leading.

Appendix E

Word-Share-Prayer Bible Studies

E. Stanley Ott, president of the Vital Churches Institute, has designed a simple exercise that helps participants grow closer to each other and grow spiritually. Here are the instructions for Word-Share-Prayer and a sample exercise. Readers can get more information from the Vital Churches website (http://www.vitalchurchesinstitute.com/pages/word-share-prayer).

The website includes more detailed instructions and three sets of Word-Share-Prayer Bible studies—for general usage, about ministry to others, and about personal growth.

These Word-Share-Prayer (Read-Reflect-Respond-Request) sessions are for use with small groups, committees, ministry teams, and boards. The focus texts are short, so groups with limited time can still "be the people of God before doing the work of the people of God." Longer texts may be used, or groups may spend more time discussing each segment.

Ott recommends groups follow a seven-seven-seven format—seven minutes for individual Bible Study, seven minutes to share one insight per person, and seven minutes to pray for one another. If they use Ott's guide sheets for an hour-and-a-half-long Bible study, then the biblical passage could be a bit longer and the format expanded: the word (30 minutes); sharing of lives (blessings and prayer requests; 45 minutes) break into fours, at least for the sharing of prayer requests and prayers for one another.

1. Give every person five to seven minutes to reflect on the text in silence. (Do not ask people read the text as homework before the gathering, because many will fail to do so.)

2. For another seven minutes or so, invite people to briefly share one insight from their paper. If the group is larger than 14, you can have them break into groups of four to save time.
3. Ask for one-sentence prayer requests. Spend more time on this phase if someone in the group is in real distress about something. Otherwise, just a sentence or so per person allows time to lift one another up, unless the group is willing to take more time for prayer. Pray for one another aloud by name, giving everyone the complete freedom to pray in silence if they prefer. Groups that want to spend more time in this portion of the meeting might simply work to be more efficient in the rest of the meeting.

SAMPLE

Word-Share-Prayer

For personal and small group study
Name _____
Date _____

Read: Psalm 103:1-5, NIV (Blessings)

> 1 Praise the LORD, O my soul;
> all my inmost being, praise his holy name.
> 2 Praise the LORD, O my soul,
> and forget not all his benefits—
> 3 who forgives all your sins
> and heals all your diseases,
> 4 who redeems your life from the pit
> and crowns you with love and compassion,
> 5 who satisfies your desires with good things
> so that your youth is renewed like the eagle's.

Reflect: Enjoy this wonderful passage. Our God is the God who loves to bless his people.
Make a list of every blessing our Lord has blessed you with in the last week to ten days.
Respond: How will you respond to the God who blesses you?
Request Jot down prayer requests that you and others may have.

Appendix F

Sample Covenant of Behavior

The following is from Christ Presbyterian Church, Fairfax, Virginia. (The "session" is the board of a Presbyterian Congregation.)

A Covenant of Church Leadership
  Affirmed by the Session of Christ Presbyterian Church

Our Promise to God
  We promise to pray, alone and together, to thank God and to ask for God's help in our lives and in our work for our church and we promise to listen to God's answer to us.

Our Promise to Our Church Family
  We promise to try to discover what is best for our church and where and how God may be leading our church as a whole.
  We promise to discern and achieve God's calling for this congregation and to work toward the harmonious achievement of that vision.
  We promise to serve the church actively in both word and deed.
  We promise to demonstrate our leadership and commitment by example.
  We promise to use our authority and discretion for the benefit of the church family.
  We promise to support the pastor and staff so their efforts can be most productive.
  We promise to listen and prayerfully consider the ideas and concerns of those in our church family.

We promise to communicate openly and clearly with our church family regarding Session actions and how they support the church's vision and mission.

Our Promise to Each Other on the Session

We promise to treat our time on the Session as an opportunity to make an important offering to our church.

We promise to listen with an open, nonjudgmental mind to the words and ideas of others.

We promise to discuss, debate, and disagree openly and honestly so others on the Session understand our perspective.

We promise to support the final decision of the Session, regardless of whether it reflects our perspective.

We will be open and curious to feedback. We assume responsibility for providing constructive feedback.

We will communicate openly and give others the benefit of the doubt when we perceive a breach of trust.

We will grant each other grace.

Adopted May 12, 2010

Appendix G

Sample Mission and Vision Statements

Following are two sample mission and vision statements. One is in the form that I spelled out in the text. The other is slightly different, in that it isn't written in the first person plural. I encourage you to review the statements of a number of congregations, so you can develop one that works well for your own.

CHRIST MEMORIAL PRESBYTERIAN CHURCH (COLUMBIA, MD)

Mission Statement

Grateful to God for his constant loving presence and guided by his Word, we are called to be a people who—

- praise God in worship and in our daily lives
- grow Biblically and spiritually in our life together
- reach out as witnesses of Jesus Christ, serving those in need
- share Christ's love with one another and everyone we meet

Vision Statement

We believe that God is calling members of Christ Memorial Presbyterian Church to

- Live as brothers and sisters in Jesus Christ, strongly bound together in loving relationship and equipped for ministry to one another and to the wider community.
- Engage all ages in uplifting worship that offers a variety of ministry styles to connect with everyone.
- Grow biblically and spiritually by offering all children, youth, and adults a variety of educational opportunities on Sunday mornings and throughout the week.
- Reach out to the unchurched in our community—especially younger families and adults, empty nesters, and believers who have no active church home—and invite them to participate in ministry with us.
- Emphasize mission by focusing on thriving projects and seeking meaningful opportunities for all members and youth.
- Strengthen our church community through love for one another, providing a variety of fellowship activities and outreach events that extends beyond church walls.
- Update and beautify our building and grounds to create new possibilities for worship and service in Christ's name.

STATEMENTS FROM WESTERN PRESBYTERIAN CHURCH, WASHINGTON, D.C.

Mission

Western Presbyterian Church is a community of believers and seekers growing together in God's Spirit. Empowered by our faith in God's ability to transform lives, we are an active force and passionate voice for a just and compassionate society.

Vision

Western Presbyterian Church is a community that endeavors to encourage individual spiritual growth, strengthen and nurture an open and diverse congregation, maintain the long-term viability of the Church, and care for the local and world communities.

Bibliography

CHURCH LEADERSHIP, PLANNING, AND RENEWAL

Armstrong, Richard Stoll. *Help! I'm a Pastor: A Guide to Parish Ministry*. Louisville, KY: Westminister/John Know, 2005. Armstrong, an experienced pastor and former professor at Princeton Theological Seminary, has written a very helpful book that is aimed at pastors in their first church out of seminary. It is very practical, touching on such subjects as balance of personal life and ministry, finances, working with staff and other leaders, and so forth.

Bass, Diana Butler. *Christianity After Religion: The End of Church and the Birth of a New Spiritual Awakening*. San Francisco: HarperCollins, 2012. Bass is a prominent researcher who studies factors that create vital churches in the United States. In this time when many people declare that organized religion is in decline, she has identified many congregations that are flourishing. She asserts that the United States is in a new age of the Spirit, a new Great Awakening. Her work is foundational for many who seek to revitalize congregations.

———. *Christianity for the Rest of Us: How the Neighborhood Church Is Transforming the Faith*. San Francisco: Harper, 2006.

Gray, Joan. *Church Officers as Spiritual Leaders*. Louisville, KY: Geneva, 2009. Gray recalls a compelling image of the early church: a sailboat. She notes that many churches are rowboat churches, relying only on the waning strength of leaders and members to keep them going. She calls for churches to hoist their sails and catch the wind of the Holy Spirit.

Sailboat Church: Helping Your Church Rethink Its Mission and Practice, Louisville, KY: Westminster John Knox Press , 2014 - An expanded treatment of the sailboat imagery used in her previous book, she writes this especially for board study. It contains questions for reflection and assignments for growth.

Halverstadt, Hugh F. *Managing Church Conflict*. Louisville, KY: Westminster/John Knox, 1991. Halverstadt, formerly a professor at McCormick Seminary, gives a very helpful approach to managing conflict. He notes there are stakeholders and stockholders in a typical church fight. The key to managing the conflict is to engage the stockholders (i.e., the grown-ups whose primary concern is the unity and integrity of the congregation) and not the particular issue that is so dividing the congregation.

Hirsch, Alan. *The Forgotten Ways: Reactivating the Missional Church*. Grand Rapids, MI: Brazos, 2006. Hirsch addresses the decline of the institutional church by reminding readers what the early church was like. He notes that the early church had around 25,000 members in AD 100, and in AD 310, before Constantine came on the scene, there were up to 20 million Christians. In China, as Mao took power and began persecuting Christians, it is estimated that there were some 2 million adherents. When the Bamboo Curtain lifted,

209

Western observers were startled to find some 60 million Christians! What happened? What can we learn?

Hotchkiss, Dan. "Governance and Ministry: Rethinking Board Leadership." Hotchkiss, a former senior consultant for Alban Institute, presses readers to make a distinction between governance and ministry. He asserts that governance has to do with direction and broad policies and that ministry is hands-on. Both are necessary. Problems occur when a group of leaders unthinkingly confuse the two.

Mann, Alice. *The In-Between Church: Navigating Size Transitions in Congregations.* Herndon, VA: Alban, 1998. Mann, an Alban Institute senior consultant, addresses the difficult transition from a pastoral- to program-size church. She notes that this in-between size is often the trickiest size church to lead. Incorporated in her book is Roy Oswald's monograph on ministering effectively in various sizes of churches.

Morris, Danny, and Charles Olson. *Discerning God's Will Together: A Spiritual Practice for the Church.* Herndon, VA: Alban Institute, 2012. Morris and Olson draw from Quaker and Jesuit traditions to lead readers in a process of discernment.

Ott, E. Stanley. Transform Your Church With Ministry Teams. Grand Rapids, MI: Eerdmans, 2004. Explains how ministry teams can promote spiritual growth, community, and accomplish a ministry task. This includes a lot of detailed advice.

Ott, E. Stanley. *Twelve Dynamic Shifts for Transforming Your Church.* Grand Rapids, MI: Eerdmans, 2002. This book addresses the adaptive shifts needed to transform a congregation from one that worked in the twentieth century to one that meets the changed culture of the twenty-first century.

Osborne, Larry. *Sticky Teams: Keeping Your Leadership Team and Staff on the Same Page.* Grand Rapids, MI: Zondervan, 2010. Osborne, a megachurch pastor, describes how he has learned to build strong leadership teams. He has some very creative ways of dealing with differences between members of both congregational boards and staffs.

Oswald, Roy, and Barry Johnson. *Managing Polarities in Congregations: Eight Keys for Thriving Faith Communities.* Herndon, VA: Alban, 2010. The authors note that too often leaders get whipsawed into an either/or mind-set when dealing with issues. Most big issues facing both society and faith communities are matters of not either/or but both/and. They are polarities to be managed, not problems to be solved. The authors introduce a very helpful model for engaging such polarities as tradition and innovation.

Rendle, Gil, and Alice Mann. *Holy Conversations: Strategic Planning as a Spiritual Practice for Congregations.* Herndon, VA: Alban, 2003. This foundational book presents strategic planning as a conversation among leaders and members as they discern how God is leading their congregation. Noting that this is not a one-size-fits-all approach, they offer many helpful suggestions and resources. It is a book to refer to again and again.

Schnase, Robert. *Five Practices of Fruitful Congregations.* Nashville, TN: Abingdon, 2007. In this slim volume, Schnase synthesizes the results of research on characteristics of vital churches: They can be summed into five basic practices: radical hospitality, passionate worship, intentional faith development, risk-taking mission and service, and extravagant generosity. While one might debate this particular synthesis, most lay leaders intuitively understand these practices and can begin leading their congregations to practice them.

Schwarz, Christian. *Natural Church Development: A Guide to Eight Essential Qualities of Healthy Churches.* St. Charles, IL: ChurchSmart Resources, 1996/2006. Schwarz and his organization have done extensive research into vital churches. They identify eight essential qualities: empowering leadership, gift-based ministry, passionate spirituality, effective structures, inspiring worship service, holistic small groups, need-oriented evangelism, and loving relationships. Focusing on these factors leads to natural development of a congregation. They draw from God's power.

Steinke, Peter. *Congregational Leadership in Anxious Times: Being Calm and Courageous No Matter What.* Herndon, VA: Alban, 2006.

———. *Healthy Congregations: A Systems Approach.* Herndon, VA: Alban, 1996. Steinke is one of the most important thinkers regarding church systems. All his books help pastors understand anxiety in systems and how to lead congregations to greater health.

Thompson, George B. *How to Get Along with Your Pastor: Creating Partnership for Doing Ministry*. Cleveland, OH: Pilgrim Press, 2006. Thompson, a professor at the Interdenominational Theological Center in Atlanta, addresses lay leaders of congregations, helping them prepare for and welcome their new pastor. He has assignments designed to help them appraise their congregational culture over against their community. What are congregational norms and patterns? He helps them assess where their congregation is on a typical congregational life cycle.

Weems, Lovett. *Take the Next Step: Leading Lasting Change in the Church*. Nashville, TN: Abingdon Press, 2003. Weems, a professor at Wesley Theological Seminary, guides readers through a helpful process for assessing their congregation's reality, discerning God's new vision for it, and implementing that new sense of mission and vision.

Wimberly, John. *The Business of the Church: The Uncomfortable Truth that Faithful Ministry Requires Effective Management*. Herndon, VA: Alban 2010. Wimberly notes that too many pastors don't want to waste their time managing church life. Rather, they want to be visionary leaders. Declaring that both leadership and management are needed, he outlines essential knowledge for effective pastors to manage and oversee their congregations.

Woolever, Cynthia, and Deborah Bruce. *Beyond the Ordinary: 10 Strengths of U.S. Congregations*. Louisville, KY: Westminster/John Knox Press, 2004. Woolever and Bruce present the results of the U.S. Congregational Life Survey, a study of over 2,000 congregations. They identify the strengths that lead to really vital churches:

- Growing spiritually
- Meaningful worship
- Participating in the congregation
- Having a sense of belonging
- Caring for children and youth
- Focusing on the community
- Sharing faith
- Welcoming new people
- Empowering leadership
- Looking to the future

GENERAL BOOKS ON LEADERSHIP AND ORGANIZATIONAL SYSTEMS

Collins, Jim. *Good to Great: Why Some Companies Make the Leap . . . and Others Don't*. New York: HarperCollins, 2001. This book is a classic on leadership. Collins presses readers to clarify what it means to be a servant leader, to face reality, and to focus on what the organization can really do best.

Covey, Stephen M. R. *The Speed of Trust: The One Thing That Changes Everything*. New York: Free Press, 2006. Covey does a superb job of describing how lack of trust debilitates organizations, identifies elements of trust, and gives suggestions for specific behaviors to build and keep building trust.

Greenleaf, Robert. *Servant Leadership: A Journey into the Nature of Legitimate Power and Greatness*. Mahwah, NJ: Paulist Press, 1977/2002. This seminal work is aimed at business leaders, pressing them to become servant leaders who help those served become wiser, freer, healthier, and more autonomous. It's a great book for any leader, whether in a faith community or in the public or private sectors.

Heath, Chip, and Dan Heath. *Made to Stick: Why Some Ideas Survive and Others Die*. New York: Random House, 2008. This is a terrific book on communicating effectively. Drawing from the elements of urban myths, they use an acronym: S (simple), U (unexpected), C (credible), C (concrete), E (emotional), S (story). This SUCCES acronym is a great filter to review sermons, books, and other attempts to communicate.

Heifetz, Ronald A., and Marty Linsky. *Leadership on the Line: Staying Alive through the Dangers of Leading.* Boston: Harvard Press, 2002. Heifetz and Linsky, both professors at the Harvard Business School, offer an exciting and illuminating overview of leadership. They encourage leaders to "get on the balcony" (see the big picture), manage their hungers, and anchor themselves emotionally and spiritually.

Lencioni, Patrick. *The Advantage: Why Organizational Health Trumps Everything Else in Business.* San Francisco: Jossey-Bass, 2012.

———. *Overcoming the Five Dysfunctions of a Team.* San Francisco: Jossey-Bass, 2006.

———. *Death by Meeting: A Leadership Fable.* San Francisco: Jossey-Bass, 2004.

———. *The Five Dysfunctions of a Team.* San Francisco: Jossey-Bass, 2002. Lencioni is president of the Table Group, a San Francisco Bay–area management consulting firm. He has a gift for describing dysfunctional organizational practices and showing how to build a healthy, strong organization. While his work is directed more at the private sector, it is readily adaptable to congregational organization. There are videos available in which Lencioni presents the dysfunctions. If you can get one of them and show it, do so.

Rath, Tom, and Barrie Conchie. *Strengths Based Leadership: Great Leaders, Teams, and Why People Follow.* New York: Gallup, 2008. The Gallup organization has identified thirty-four leadership strengths. Rath and Conchie lead readers to discover their strengths, grow them, and learn how their strengths complement others in their organization.

Reina, Dennis S., and Michelle L. Reina. *Trust and Betrayal in the Workplace: Building Effective Relationships in Your Organization.* San Francisco: Berrett-Koehler, 2006. Building on their extensive work in helping people build and rebuild trust, the Reinas offer seven steps that sum up the process.

Satir, Virginia. *Peoplemaking.* Palo Alto, CA: Science and Behavior Books, 1972. Virginia Satir is the grandmother of family systems therapy. This a wonderful book that addresses parenting, building a family, and forming healthy relationships.

Zander, Rosamund Stone, and Benjamin Zander. *The Art of Possibility: Transforming Professional and Personal Life.* New York: Penguin, 2000. In this delightful book, Rosamund Zander, a family therapist, and Ben Zander, conductor of the Boston Philharmonic, combine to inspire their readers to possibilities they haven't imagined before. Combining grace and vision, they deal with mistakes and failures, and learn and grow.

DEALING WITH DIFFICULT PEOPLE

Bell, Arthur, and Dayle Smith. *Winning with Difficult People.* Hauppauge, NY: Barrons, 2004. The authors identify a number of "SOPs" (sources of pain), with suggestions for dealing with them. They press readers to recognize how some people bug them and others don't. They have particularly helpful suggestions for dealing with scary people.

Boers, Arthur Paul. *Never Call Them Jerks: Healthy Response to Difficult Behavior.* Herndon, VA: Alban, 1999. Boers, a Mennonite pastor, draws extensively from Edwin Friedman and Peter Steinke's work to press readers to ask why particular people seem like jerks to you and not to others. He suggests very helpful approaches to analyze why difficult people behave the way they do, their impact on the system, and how leaders might respond effectively.

Bramson, Robert. *Coping with Difficult People.* New York: Dell/Random House, 1981. In this classic book with imaginative characters such as the Sherman Tank, the Sniper, the Clam, and the Super-Agreeable, Bramson gives very specific suggestions of how to deal with each type.

Brown, David. *The Art and Science of Dealing with Difficult People.* New York: Skyhorse, 2011. Brown presses the reader to know oneself better and gives many examples and suggestions to handle difficult relationships in this concise book using insights from emotional intelligence research.

Carroll, Lewis. *Alice in Wonderland and Through the Looking Glass.* These classic children's books have deeper meanings for congregational leaders. Charles Dodgson (Carroll's real name) was a child of an Anglican rector. Think how many characters in his books show up in congregations!

Keirsey, David. *Please Understand Me II: Temperament, Character, Intelligence.* Del Mar, CA: Prometheus Nemesis Book Co., 1998. Kiersey explores the Myers-Briggs Temperament Inventory with a simplified type survey. The idea is that by understanding one another's basic temperaments and tendencies, then getting along is much easier. The extravert who blithely slams into an introvert's carefully crafted idea isn't deliberately obnoxious. He just doesn't understand.

Notes

PREFACE

1. I don't think it's a coincidence that Charles Dodgson (Lewis Carroll's real name) grew up in a rectory. He encountered such folks regularly.

2. HOW CAN I REALLY GET TO KNOW THEM?

1. Max DePree, *Leadership Is an Art* (New York: Currency, 2004), 11.

3. HOW SOLID IS THE FOUNDATION?

1. http://www.gallup.com/poll/1597/confidence-institutions.aspx#2
2. http://www.gallup.com/poll/124628/Clergy-Bankers-New-Lows-Honesty-Ethics-Ratings.aspx
3. Stephen M. R. Covey, *The Speed of Trust: The One Thing That Changes Everything* (New York: Free Press, 2006), 54–55.
4. Patrick M. Lencioni, *The Advantage: Why Organizational Health Trumps Everything Else In Business* (San Francisco: John Wiley & Sons, 2012), 27–28.
5. Beth Ann Gaede, Ed., *When a Congregation Is Betrayed: Responding to Clergy Misconduct* (Herndon, VA: Alban, 2006), xv.
6. Nancy Myers Hopkins, Ed., *Restoring the Soul of a Church: Healing Congregations Wounded by Clergy Sexual Misconduct* (Collegeville, MN: Liturgical Press, 1995).
7. Michelle and Dennis Reina, *Rebuilding Trust in the Workplace: Seven Steps* (San Francisco: Berrett-Koehler, 2010), 7.
8. Michelle Reina and Dennis Reina, *Trust and Betrayal in the Workplace: Building Effective Relationships in Your Organization* (San Francisco: Berrett-Koehler, 2006), 129.
9. Lewis B. Smedes, *Forgive and Forget: Healing the Hurts We Don't Deserve* (New York: HarperCollins, 1984/1996), 29.

4. WHO'S LEADING AROUND HERE?

1. Karen Vannoy and John Flowers, *Ten Temptations of Church: Why Churches Decline and What to do About It* (Nashville, TN: Abingdon Press, 2012), 207.
2. The grid is set up in the normal mathematical style, with up and right being positive and left and down being negative.
3. Marcus Buckingham and Donald O. Clifton. *Now, Discover Your Strengths* (New York: The Free Press, 2001), 29
4. Tom Rath and Barry Conchie. *Strengths Based Leadership* (New York: Gallup Press, 2008)

5. ASSESSING THE LEADERSHIP

1. Patrick Lencioni, *The Five Dysfunctions of a Team* (San Francisco: Jossey-Bass, 2002), 188.
2. Peter Steinke, *Congregational Leadership in Anxious Times: Being Calm and Courageous No Matter What* (Herndon, VA: Alban Institute, 2006), 51.
3. Jacques Berthier, *Songs and Prayers from Taizé* (Taizé Community: Ateliers et Presses de Taizé, 1991), number 28.
4. Virginia Satir, *Peoplemaking* (Palo Alto, CA: Science and Behavior Books, 1972), 53–73.
5. Patrick M. Lencioni, *The Advantage: Why Organizational Health Trumps Everything Else in Business* (San Francisco: Jossey Bass, 2012), 82–83.
6. See: http://www.pcusa.org/peacemaking/guidelines.pdf.
7. See the full covenant in appendix C.

6. WHAT SIZE IS YOUR CHURCH?

1. This document can be found in Mann 1998 (see note 2).
2. Alice Mann, *The In-Between Church: Navigating Size Transitions in Congregations* (Herndon, VA: Alban Institute, 1998); *Raising the Roof: The Pastoral to Program Size Church Transition* (Herndon, VA: Alban Institute, 2001).
3. Mann, *The In-Between Church,* 12.
4. Ibid., 79.
5. Ibid., 79.
6. Ibid., 82.
7. Ibid., 85.
8. Susan Beaumont, *Inside the Large Congregation* (Herndon, VA: Alban Institute 2011). See a summary at http://www.alban.org/conversation.aspx?id=9822.

8. WHERE ARE WE HEADED?

1. Lewis Carroll, *Alice's Adventures in Wonderland* (Alice in Wonderland) [Annotated] [Illustrated] (pp. 44–45). Doma Publishing House, 2011. Kindle Edition.
2. Patrick M. Lencioni, *The Advantage: Why Organizational Health Trumps Everything Else in Business* (San Francisco: Jossey Bass, 2012), 82–83.

3. Gil Rendle and Alice Mann, *Holy Conversations: Strategic Planning as a Spiritual Practice for Congregations* (Herndon, VA: Alban Institute 2003), 84.

4. Ibid., 84.

5. Lovett H. Weems Jr., *Take the Next Step: Leading Lasting Change in the Church* (Nashville, TN: Abingdon Press, 2003), 92.

6. Gil Rendle and Alice Mann, *Holy Conversations: Strategic Planning as a Spiritual Practice for Congregations* (Herndon, VA: Alban Institute 2003), 85.

7. Ibid., xiv.

8. Danny E. Morris and Charles M. Olsen, *Discerning God's Will Together,* Revised and Updated Edition (Herndon, VA: The Alban Institute, Kindle Edition, 2012), Kindle Locations 260–63.

9. Joan Gray, *Spiritual Leadership of Church Officers* (Louisville, KY: Geneva Press, 2009), 18.

10. Scott Adams, Dilbert comic strip, June 10, 2007.

11. Rendle and Mann, *Holy Conversations*, 217–27.

12. Ibid., 37.

13. Ibid., xxi.

14. Darden, Robert, *What Business Are You In?* http://blogs.darden.virginia.edu/deansblog/2013/06/what-business-are-you-in/.

15. Robert Schnase, *Five Practices of Fruitful Congregations* (Nashville, TN: Abingdon, 2007), 7.

16. Ibid., 8.

17. Ibid., 20.

18. Ibid., 37.

19. For more information about Taizé, see their website: http://www.taize.fr/en.

20. Schnase, *Five Practices*, p. 87.

21. Ibid., 106.

22. Ibid., 112.

9. HOW'S BUSINESS?

1. John Wimberly, *The Business of the Church: The Uncomfortable Truth That Faithful Ministry Requires Effective Management* (Herndon, VA: Alban Institute, 2010), 21.

2. Dan Hotchkiss, *Governance and Ministry: Rethinking Board Leadership* (Herndon, VA: Alban Institute, 2009), 65–66.

3. Larry Osborne, *Sticky Teams: Keeping Your Leadership Team and Staff on the Same Page* (Grand Rapids, MI: Zondervan, 2010), 139–47.

4. E. Stanley Ott, *Transform Your Church with Ministry Teams* (Grand Rapids, MI: Eerdmans, 2004), 8.

5. Ibid., 112–13.

6. Dan Hotchkisss, *Governance and Ministry: Rethinking Board Leadership* (Herndon, VA: Alban Institute, 2009), 106.

7. Ibid., 105.

8. Wimberly, 7–8.

9. Ibid., 110.

10. Lynne Baab, *Reaching Out in a Networked World: Expressing Your Congregation's Heart and Soul* (Herndon, VA: Alban Institute, 2008).

11. Wimberly, 44.

12. Wimberly, 69.

13. Marshall Goldsmith, http://www.marshallgoldsmithlibrary.com/html/marshall/resources.html.

10. HOW DO I DEAL WITH DIFFICULT BEHAVIOR?

1. Marshall Goldsmith, *What Got You Here Won't Get You There* (New York: Hyperion, 2007), 39-40. See also http://www.marshallgoldsmithlibrary.com/cim/articles_print.php?aid=363.

2. Peter Steinke, *Congregational Leadership in Anxious Times: Being Calm and Courageous No Matter What* (Herndon, VA: Alban 2006), 43.

3. Arthur Paul Boers, *Never Call Them Jerks: Healthy Responses to Difficult Behavior* (Herndon, VA: Alban, 1999), 12–13.

4. Ibid., 14.

5. Hugh F. Halverstadt, *Managing Church Conflict* (Louisville, KY: Westminster-John Knox, 1991), 74. Halverstadt uses the terms "principals and bystanders" in his book but had changed the terms to "stakeholders and stockholders" in a week-long workshop on conflict management I attended at McCormick Seminary in Chicago in July 1998. I find these terms more understandable.

6. Roy M. Oswald and Barry Johnson, *Managing Polarities in Congregations: Eight Keys for Thriving Faith Communities* (Herndon, VA: Alban 2010), 4–5.

11. WHAT'S NEXT?

1. Tom Rath and Barrie Conchie, *Strengths Based Leadership: Great Leaders, Teams, and Why People Follow* (New York: Gallup, 2008), 79-91.

2. Daniel Pink, http://www.danpink.com/drive-the-summaries/.

3. Patrick Lencioni, *The Advantage: Why Organizational Health Trumps Everything* (San Francisco: Jossey Bass, 2012), 119.

About the Author

Robert (Bob) A. Harris has been coaching pastors and other leaders since 2004, helping them assess their church systems, strengthen leadership teams, and clarify personal and church goals. He completed the Georgetown University Leadership Coaching certification program and has attained the professional certified coach accreditation of the International Coach Federation. Having seen the difficulties that their blunders cause, he is especially interested in working with pastors who are new to a church.

He has a BS in physics from the Missouri School of Mines and Metallurgy and an MDiv from Pittsburgh Theological Seminary. A semiretired Presbyterian (PCUSA) pastor, he served some 30 years as a called pastor and another 8 as an interim pastor. He and his wife, Mary Helen, have two married sons and four grandchildren.